The Fiction of Tim Winton

SYDNEY STUDIES IN AUSTRALIAN LITERATURE

Robert Dixon, Series Editor

Alex Miller: The Ruin of Time
Robert Dixon

Contemporary Australian Literature: A World Not Yet Dead
Nicholas Birns

Shirley Hazzard: New Critical Essays
Ed. Brigitta Olubas

The Fiction of Tim Winton: Earthed and Sacred
Lyn McCredden

Coming in 2017 – *Colonial Australian Fiction: Character Types, Social Formation and the Colonial Economy*
Ken Gelder and Rachel Weaver

The Fiction of Tim Winton

Earthed and Sacred

Lyn McCredden

SYDNEY UNIVERSITY PRESS

First published by Sydney University Press
© Lyn McCredden 2016
© Sydney University Press 2016

Reproduction and Communication for other purposes

Except as permitted under the Act, no part of this edition may be reproduced, stored in a retrieval system, or communicated in any form or by any means without prior written permission. All requests for reproduction or communication should be made to Sydney University Press at the address below:

Sydney University Press
Fisher Library F03
University of Sydney NSW 2006
AUSTRALIA
sup.info@sydney.edu.au
sydney.edu.au/sup

National Library of Australia Cataloguing-in-Publication Data

Creator:	McCredden, Lyn, 1953– author.
Title:	The fiction of Tim Winton : earthed and sacred / Lyn McCredden.
ISBN:	9781743325032 (paperback)
	9781743325049 (ebook: epub)
	9781743325056 (ebook: mobi)
	9781743325063 (ebook: PDF)
Series:	Sydney studies in Australian literature.
Notes:	Includes bibliographical references and index.
Subjects:	Winton, Tim, 1960—Criticism and interpretation.

Cover image: Tim Winton in Denmark, south-west WA. Photograph by Erin Jonasson, courtesy Fairfax Media.
Cover design by Miguel Yamin

Contents

Acknowledgements		vii
Introduction: A Writing Life		1
1	Words and Worlds	19
2	"To Solicit a Becoming": Masculine and Feminine in the Fiction of Winton	35
3	Falling	49
4	Narrative Redemptions	67
5	"Liquid Elites and Bonded Shame": Winton and Class Identity	81
6	High and Popular: Straddling the Fiction Market	97
7	Becoming, Belonging	107
8	Winton's Narratives: Market, Reading, Impact	123
Afterword		143
Works Cited		145
Index		151

Acknowledgements

Nothing is sweeter in this world than the unconditional and ongoing love of a good person – a person able to ride the waves of change with panache, able to remember deeply. Such love is transforming. Thank you to those good people who have loved me, nourished me, and allowed me to love in return. Now *that* is sacred.

Thank you to the Australian Research Council who provided me with funds and therefore time to write this work. Many thanks to my tireless Research Assistant, Chloe Chandler.

Introduction: A Writing Life

Literary critics across the last fifty years have sonorously declared the death of the author. This idea – playful, metaphoric or literal – is hard to credit, however, if you are a reader who is made constantly, visually aware of a robust, pony-tailed figure, a surfie, fisherman and ordinary bloke who also happens to be multi-award-winning author Tim Winton. Those portraits of Winton as Aussie Puck by the beach, looking anything but a member of the literati, are widely recognisable. They are portraits of one of Australia's favourite writers, a local hero in his native Fremantle, Western Australia. For many readers this author is, first of all, *Cloudstreet* (1991), and very much alive.

Tim Winton does not simply equate to this over-familiar image, of course. Nor is he universally loved. Rather, he is a shape-shifter: a working-class child who became a class traveller with an adult vocation. Winton is not from the "civilised centres" over east, but from the western fringes of the continent. He is one of Australia's most popular writers, and also one of its finest literary authors; a children's writer and a complex wordsmith, a lyrical poet in prose with an ear for quotidian, vernacular speech. He chooses to live away from urban centres, in places where most of his readers do not live, and he maintains a firm and intriguing distance between author and critic. He is a self-identifying Christian in a largely secular nation; an outspoken and idealistic environmentalist with a prophetic streak of pessimism informing his fiction. Tim Winton: well-documented family man and somewhat of a loner; a masculine figure who creates complex, wounded characters, both male and female; an earthy regionalist who also offers glimpses of the sacred to readers in Australia, and globally.

Winton's fiction is both loved and derided; his religious and political views a little embarrassing or annoying, for some. For example, when Winton's novel *Breath* (2008) won the top Australian literary prize, the Miles Franklin Literary Award, a thread posted to the blog *Still Life with Cat* claimed:

> What with first the longlist and then the shortlist, I'm not really all that surprised that the 2009 Miles Franklin Literary Award has been won by what was by far the safer choice of the two front runners, a novel in which a bitter, twisted woman called Eva (geddit?

Small sections of this chapter have been adapted from Lyn McCredden, "Tim Winton's Poetics of Resurrection", *Literature and Theology* 29, no. 3 (2015).

geddit?) corrupts the young hero, takes away his innocence and warps his psyche for life with her nasty dangerous bent sick non-missionary sexing-on ways. She robs our hero of Paradise, that's what she does; she pushes him into his fall from grace. Because, as we all know, that's what women do. The Bible tells us so . . .[1]

A different way to read these characters in *Breath* is to see all the characters – Eva, along with Sando and the narrator, Pikelet/Bruce – as wounded, falling, and in need of compassion. Eva, injured and unable to pursue her high level of extreme sport; Eva, lonely and often abandoned by Sando; Eva, dying years later in an autoerotic act; Eva, full of longing and loss. Surely it is simplistic merely to see the depiction of this character as "bitter, twisted" and corrupting. The world of *Breath* is not black and white. It is not about heroes, villains, paradise and evil, at least not in the way that this blog's fundamentalist, moralising rendition of good men and ruinous women represents it. The novel is about an earthly, earthy, breathing, broken world in which all humans yearn and strive and fall. There is melancholy, falling short, pain and loss; but there is also great beauty, wonder and grace intertwined in this fractured world.

As the older narrator remembers his young self becoming a man, we read a page which is delicate and nuanced in the way it explores relationships between boy and man, man and woman:

> I basked in Sando's attention and treasured these brief moments of esteem . . . We were in the kitchen one day, as Sando ground the spices for his special fish curry, when I saw a photo that I'd never noticed before . . . The image was a figure in a red snowsuit, a skier more or less upside down against the whiteness of the mountain . . .
>
> Hey, I said. What's this?
>
> Sando paused a moment with the mortar and pestle. The smells of coriander and cumin and turmeric were not the sort of thing that ever came from my mother's kitchen . . .
>
> That, Pikelet, is my wife.
>
> You're shitting me . . .
>
> Mate, she's pretty well known. It's freestyle. It's a whole other scene. They're the bad boys and girls of skiing. That's Utah in '71. She's there now.
>
> Skiing?
>
> Jesus, no – not with that knee. Nah, they're trying another operation . . .
>
> There's no snow here, I murmured. How can she stand it?
>
> Sando rammed the pestle against the grist of spices. I rested my chin on the benchtop and I could feel the force of his arms pulsing in the wood.
>
> I think she prefers it here. I mean, if you couldn't surf anymore, would you want to live by the sea?
>
> The ocean's beautiful. That'd be enough for me . . .
>
> It seems odd to have remembered it but in later life I had cause to recall the moment. I was in my thirties before I learnt that I too would prefer not to see what I could no longer have.[2]

---

1 Kerryn Goldsworthy, "Biblical World View Legitimised: Australian Feminist Icon Turns in Grave", *Still Life with Cat Blog*, 18 June 2009. tinyurl.com/Goldsworthy2009.

Introduction: A Writing Life

In this moving tableau – representation of an alternative family, a hero-worshipping boy and a fallible hero – Eva is the absent, desired, wounded female. She is also deeply *present* to the man and the boy, a (literally) breathtaking heroine caught in a moment of great beauty, skill and daring in the photograph that Pikelet puzzles over. And for the boy a deep learning is taking place. He is learning firstly about coriander and cumin and turmeric, and about Sando's special fish curry; about the thrilling risks humans can take; about affection; and about place and time, two earthly mediums in which the child will have to learn about loving, and beauty, and loss. Do such moments lose their power – for the child, for the reader – when decisions and actions in the future issue the child into a world of alternative, disturbing sexuality and pain? Are we asked primarily in this novel to *judge*, or even condemn, these fallible characters?

The first sexual encounter between the fifteen-year-old Pikelet and Eva is narrated obliquely. There is no explicitness. The characters are in a haze of hash and lust and loneliness. Pikelet – "a great force rising behind me, pressing me on" – follows Eva to her bed, and we read simply that "[s]he did not wait for me to figure things out for myself" (198–99). This representation is indeed of a seductress and a young boy, but there is also the context of deep loneliness, guilt and mutual longing to consider. The dialogue goes on to focalise the fraught nature of their encounter from Eva's point of view:

> Jesus, she said. Maybe you shouldn't come out again.
> What?
> It's not right. It's not fair on you.
> What if I want to? I asked petulantly.
> Listen, Sando will be back soon.
> I stared at her. How soon?
> The rain's stopped, she said. Go home. (201)

Of course "the fall" continues, providing both the narrative arc and the moral drama of the novel: the boy tumbling into manhood and a stinging acquaintance with desire and grief; the woman into guilt and futility, as well as pregnancy. But the novel continues to offer shifting, unresolved perspectives on the relationship of boy and woman. One comes from the older Pikelet:

> For a long and ruinous period of my later life I raged against Eva Sanderson, even as I grieved for her. In the spirit of the times I held her morally accountable for all my grown-up troubles. Yet . . . (208–9)

There is a tremendous weight – an ethics – in that "Yet". It is an ethics that is deeply characteristic of Winton's fiction. The human drive to judge and seek revenge, to blame others and grieve over what they have done to you, is measured by Winton and found to be understandable but inadequate. For all his confusion, as boy and man, Pikelet learns that "[t]his was a woman not in the least bit ordinary" (209).

What is it that Pikelet learns, and that *Breath*, along with many other Winton novels, narrates with such moral complexity? In part, what the adult narrator in *Breath* grows to

---

2 Tim Winton, *Breath* (Melbourne: Penguin, 2008), 154–55. All subsequent references are to this edition and appear in parentheses in the text.

understand is that humans – men *and* women – act badly, vainly, selfishly; and that they can and do regret their actions so often. But he also learns that

> [p]eople talk such a storm of crap about the things they've done, had done to them. The deluded bullshit I've endured in circled chairs on lino floors. She had no business doing what she did, but I'm through hating and blaming. People are fools, not monsters. (211)

The theology of Winton's fiction – for this is what it is, a moral and ethical theology – reaches out well beyond this wry, forgiving, but also partly weary insight of the older narrator. Pikelet remains embroiled in the fallenness and pain of which he has been both the victim and the agent, but the novel offers us more: a vision of the depth of human need and degradation, *together with* glimpses of grace and refreshment, even resurrection. Further, it offers an understanding of these two aspects of humanness as twinned. The act of love and sexuality that turns to obsessive, autoerotic acts of strangulation is *Breath*'s most powerful image of this doubleness:

> It was intense, consuming and it could be beautiful. That far out at the edge of things you get to a point where all that stands between you and oblivion is the roulette of body-memory . . . You feel exalted, invincible, angelic because you're totally fucking poisoned. Inside it's great, feels brilliant. But on the outside it's squalid beyond imagining. (234)

Readers are, along with Pikelet, prompted to confront what such abject acts might *mean*, for the protagonists, and in fuller moral or psychological or spiritual frameworks. In Eva's desperate desire to assuage her loneliness and failure, in part through near-death sex acts, we surely also register her longing to come back, to be well, to experience some kind of redemption from the poison of her life. Pikelet, in the increasingly terrifying acts he is being drawn into, makes some form of decision, as he "hovered, palms down, like some kind of boy-shaman, willing life into her, holding off the shivering darkness" (235). It is not difficult to see that this role as rescuer and shaman becomes the older man's vocation. Bruce's work as a paramedic brings him constantly face to face with the abject – death and injury caused by accident, choice, stupidity and desire. He becomes, in his own wounded way, the indifferent angel of hope and rescue, or of consolation.

The novel begins in the present tense, as the older Bruce, a paramedic, attends the death by autoerotic asphyxiation of a young man in the presence of the victim's mother:

> I slip in beside her and do the business but the kid's been gone a while. He looks about seventeen. There are ligature marks on his neck and older bruises around them. Even while I'm going through the motions she strokes the boy's dark, curly hair. A nice-looking kid. She's washed him. He smells of Pears soap and freshly laundered clothes. I ask for her name and for her son's, and she tells me that she's June and the boy's name is Aaron. (3)

This is, of course, a representation of family tragedy, as well as a glimpse into the psychic state of the paramedic. There is the layer of professional observation and ministration, and there is the quiet, controlled registering of sympathy held in check, as the paramedic notices the achingly personal details of a young life ended, and of a mother's grief. There is a refusal to condemn in this scene, too:

June, I'm not the police ... So what do I tell them? the mother asks ... That's really for you to decide, I say. But there's no shame in the truth. It's fairer on everybody. (4)

Bruce's insight here, seasoned by years doing this job, and by his own acquaintance with grief, is informed by a half-conscious, deep-seated knowledge about shame and its human, abject root.

Breath is an important novel in Winton's oeuvre, unfolding as it does a theology that can confront the abject in the human condition, as well as the human potential for forgiveness and a refusal to condemn. These are deeply Christian values, which also characterise many other spiritual traditions. For Winton, such values have developed through his Christian experience, and in his writing life, and in this book's critical account they will be explored as central to his fiction.

Glittering Prizes

Whatever "Tim Winton" might be, he is the disciplined writer of twelve books of fiction for adults and six volumes for children and young adults – works that speak intimately to many Australians, and about Australia to the world. This book will seek to assess critically Winton's writing and his career, asking about his vision of Australia and Australians, and of the world beyond. Does his writing make this place – the many places that are Australia – come alive, confront itself, in new ways? How integral to Winton's writing is the theology of forgiveness, of longing for redemption and healing in the face of human fallenness? How are such terms – whether understood in sacred or secular frameworks – developed in Winton's oeuvre? In what ways does Tim Winton present us with sacredness, the quest for meaning in human, material, abject life?

As a young man of twenty-one, while still a creative writing student at Curtin University, Winton was awarded the 1981 *Australian*/Vogel National Literary Award for his novel *An Open Swimmer* (1982). The prize is awarded to writers aged thirty-five or younger. Winton's often-reported words in accepting this, his earliest prize, were: "It must be hard to have a son who wants to be a writer. This award will show that their faith in me was justified".[3] Further, Winton's written statement on winning the prize is characteristically wry and a little self-deprecating, but only to a point:

> The Vogel prize came along at the perfect time for me. I was writing fiction in earnest as a very young person and trying to publish it while living on the wrong side of the country and without literary connections. Winning the prize gave me a huge morale boost and the impetus that only affirmation can produce. It somehow, mysteriously, made it easier for editors to publish my stories. It set me on my way, and I lived on the $5000 for a year. Without the Vogel I suspect things might have gone differently.[4]

Twenty-eight years later, in 2009, Winton told a journalist, "I haven't been to an awards night since then [the Vogel], once I realised you don't actually have to go ... I'm not good

---

[3] Tim Winton cited in Rosemary Neill, "Fully Formed: 30 Years of the *Australian*/Vogel Literary Award," *Australian*, 23 April 2011. http://tinyurl.com/Neill2011.
[4] Winton cited in Neill, "Fully Formed".

in a crowd".⁵ Since those heady days of the early 1980s, Winton's books have garnered over thirty national awards, including the nation's top literary prize, the Miles Franklin Literary Award, four times (in 1991 for *Cloudstreet*, 1994 for *Shallows*, 2002 for *Dirt Music* and 2009 for *Breath*). Judges Dagmar Schmidmaier, Hilary McPhee, Elizabeth Webby, David Marr and Father Edmund Campion, who awarded Winton the 2002 Miles Franklin Award for *Dirt Music*, wrote of the novel in a statement on the award's official website:

> *Dirt Music* is a huge, powerful novel about love, guilt, pain, fear – and the visceral, transforming power of music. Beginning in a redneck fishing town, it takes to the road as Luther Fox, abalone poacher, on the run from himself, heads into the trackless country to the north. With his extraordinary powers of physical description and his readiness to take risks with his writing, Winton conjures a primordial land and seascape and unforgettable characters who live on the edge of the continent on the edge of their nerves. Contemporary Australia, on the surface so money-grubbing and self-absorbed, at its heart so deep and unfathomable, has rarely been laid as bare.⁶

This fascinating blend of myth and marketing, concocted by an exclusively eastern seaboard judging panel, arguably cries out for an extended postcolonial reading. Western Australia is depicted in the judges' account as "on the edge of the continent", which factually it is, but then so is the eastern seaboard. It is also "trackless country" (a surprise to Aboriginal Australians), "primordial", populated by rednecks, and, by extension, "deep and unfathomable": the heart of darkness (or light), it doesn't seem to matter. But this blend of myth-making and realist response by the judges is of course a projection, describing a "Winton effect". Winton's narratives, so loved by many and dismissed by others looking for less, or different, "Australianist" self-representation, do themselves oscillate between realism and myth-making.

Winton's Everyday Stories

It is not myths of heroic dimension, however, that we read in Winton's novels, but narratives of the everyday, stories about what it means to be an "ordinary" Australian, a West Australian from outside urban cultural elites. Winton's work takes us into working-class, regional, vernacular places. It casts a light and it holds up a mirror; it employs a writer's eye and ear for the "dirt music" of Australian life. It is hardly *everyone's* life, but it resonates widely. Is this myth-making or meaning-making? What *That Eye, the Sky* (1986), *Cloudstreet*, the *Lockie Leonard*⁷ books for children, *The Turning* (2004), *Breath* and *Eyrie* (2013) all do is create white settler myths/narratives of belonging, but also of un-belonging, of the struggle to belong, of finding ways to approach the land's and the oceans' magnificent

---

5   Winton cited in Neill, "Fully Formed".
6   "Miles Franklin Literary Award 2002,"
https://www.perpetual.com.au/MilesFranklinAward-and-Recipients.
7   Tim Winton, *Lockie Leonard, Human Torpedo* (Melbourne: McPhee Gribble, 1990), Tim Winton, *Lockie Leonard, Scum Buster* (Sydney: Piper, 1993) and Tim Winton, *Lockie Leonard, Legend* (Sydney: Pan Macmillan, 1997).

beauty and ontological challenge. These stories probe gently but insistently the ways in which characters – Australians mostly – attempt, and fail, and try again to make meaning.

For British reviewer Stephen Abell, vernacular language, landscape and characterisation in Winton are all in the service of a kind of meaning-making, partly informed by common myths of Australianness, partly an attempt to make sense of a place where white Australians do not belong. Abell aptly describes the characters' and Winton's need for storytelling in *Breath*:

> At one point, they swim down to touch the sea floor "to make solid the idea of the place and the stories we fed on". Winton does something similar in his prose, using solid metaphors for the natural world: "manes of spray hung above the rivermouth"; "sun blazed down in rods through the big old gums". Or else the country is compared to animals: the "shaggy and animal contours" of the shore; "the estuary was like a wide, shining gut that was fed by the river as it coiled back and back". As with many Australian novels, the characteristics of the land and sea form a central character in the text.
>
> If Winton metaphorically represents the natural world, he is keen to naturalistically represent the people who inhabit it. Winton doesn't use quotation marks for dialogue, which emphasises the fact that the narrator and characters often speak in the same easygoing manner, as if confiding to the reader over a beer: "water's as cold as a witch's bits", "black as a dog's guts" and so on. This makes the novel feel like an oral history: "she slapped me so hard that I rode home and lay on my narrow bed and shouted at my mother to please turn the bloody vacuum off and get a life".
>
> Hemingway once said that "there was always one true sentence that I knew or had seen or had heard someone say"; Tim Winton writes true sentences that reflect precisely the known, the seen and the spoken.[8]

Abell may well be running rough shod over the careful, critical distinctions between art and reality, "true sentences" and "truth", but he is getting at something of the processes in Winton's prose, processes which constantly seek to draw together written language and orality, lived life and the human need to construct meaning. The land and the ocean are, as indeed they are for many Australian writers, huge canvases on which Winton seeks to probe such meaning-making in response to place.

The reviewer here deals well with the languaged materiality of Winton's prose, its solid, worlded metaphors, but he makes no mention of what constantly informs the work, beyond "the known, the seen and the spoken". It is something Winton referred to as "soul" in his 2015 Palm Sunday public speech, which was widely disseminated in the media. It is "soul", conceived of as both individual and collective: "by which we recognise the Divine spark in each other, the presence of God".[9] These are challenging or embarrassing words, depending on where you stand in relation to questions of "the sacred". But recurrent in Winton's work is a struggle to comprehend "the presence of God", or "the sacred", often in the most recalcitrant and obdurate materiality of the world, but also in its magnificence.

---

8 Stephen Abell, "Australian Small-Town Life," review of *Breath* by Tim Winton, *Telegraph*, 23 May 2008. http://tinyurl.com/Abell2008.
9 Tim Winton, "Tim Winton's Palm Sunday Plea: Start the Soul-Searching Australia," *Age*, 29 March 2015, transcript of a speech delivered at a rally for refugee rights in Perth. http://tinyurl.com/Winton2015.

Significantly, Winton has never won the prestigious UK-based Man Booker Prize, although *The Riders* (1994) was shortlisted in 1995, and *Dirt Music* in 2002. He has a strong international readership (especially in China and the UK, with a smaller following in the US), but international prizes have been few: one Commonwealth Writers' Prize, South East Asia and South Pacific Region (in 1995 for *The Riders*), and some others including the UK-based *Deo Gloria* prize for *Cloudstreet* in 1992, for "[p]romoting the Good News about Jesus Christ and encouraging Christians to share it with others".[10]

Why is it that the Australian colonial boy with the ponytail and a whiff of the sea about him doesn't succeed in the glittering courts of Europe? Perhaps Winton's regionality, his vernacular vision, has kept his work largely out of the Booker race? Winton's strangely disturbing 1994 novel, *The Riders*, is the only one of his works with settings not largely Australian, and more specifically Western Australian, although the novel does carry "Australia" right up to the chin of Europe. *The Riders*' demotic language, emanating from the mouth of Scully and placed in complex juxtaposition with "European sophistication", constructs a European outrider, a wounded Aussie bloke, a semi-tragic buffoon. But for critic Andrew Taylor:

> There is nothing of easy romance, no predictable plotting and characterisation, no comforting ideological conformism in his fiction, and certainly not in *The Riders* . . . his fiction has been Aussie in a very non-bourgeois way: snotty-nosed, scratchy around the crotch, sweaty under the armpits. Adults are often viewed from below, from the perspective of children such as Ort in *That Eye, The Sky* or Fish Lamb in *Cloudstreet*. The names of the children in Winton's fiction – Ort, Fish, Quick, for example – signify their demotic, non-canonical status. They signify their lack of an accepted place in sophisticated adult discourse.[11]

In seeking to interpret the ongoing, evolving accomplishments of this regional writer with global reach, critics and readers inevitably confront the locatedness of Winton. For some, this locatedness equates with parochialism, a restricted representation of the world – beach, sand, desert – with splashes of Aussie slang: "Aussie in a very non-bourgeois way: snotty-nosed, scratchy around the crotch, sweaty under the armpits". See for example the funny, often scathing "Wintoning Project" posts on the website *The Worst of Perth*,[12] which satirises and thus inadvertently pays tribute to Winton's work, in its detailed mockery and imitation of Winton's style and preoccupations. The question of regionalism and of identity constructed in relationship to a particular place – a landscape, a region, a nation – also receives poor press from modernists and globalists, who often dismiss any supposedly monolithic or single-stranded characteristic of a writer, a reader, or a character as passé in a contemporary, mobile and multiple world. It's difficult to determine exactly what irritates most of the contributors to "The Wintoning Project", but it is clear that they find Winton's vision of Western Australia to be parochial.

---

10   "Project Archive," Deo Gloria Trust. http://deo-gloria.co.uk/projects_archive.php.
11   Andrew Taylor, "Tim Winton's *The Riders*: A Construction of Difference," *Westerly* 59, no. 3 (Spring 1998): 111.
12   "The Wintoning Project," *The Worst of Perth*, 30 April 2011. http://tinyurl.com/Wintoning.

"The World Itself": Local and Global

On the other hand, in broader literary debates about the local and the global, regionalists have written back to complaints about the parochial. Some of this writing back can sound defensive or rearguard. In 2008, a group of North American academics published the critical volume *Regionalism and the Humanities*, seeking to interrogate the "simultaneous decline and revival of regionalism":

> Once viewed as a reaction against the forces of modernism, [regionalism] has emerged in a globalized world as a repackaged, more-aggressive endeavour to make a claim for the role of place and space – as opposed to gender, race, ethnicity, class, demography, or other cultural or physical distinctions – in the effort to understand ourselves and what it means to be human. What distinguishes regionalism from these other efforts at self-understanding is its focus on locating oneself in the space lived in, inhabited, made home, or travelled through. This emphasis is itself rooted in man's [sic] fundamental interaction with nature: the land, climate, flora and fauna, and the physical environment.[13]

This critical discourse has a number of worrying features which need noting in relation to Winton's writing: the assertion of "regionalism" as a framework, "as opposed to gender, race, ethnicity, class, demography"; the universalising of "ourselves", "what it means to be human", but also "man's [sic] fundamental interaction with nature"; and the potency (or otherwise) of regionalism as "a repackaged, more aggressive endeavor". The apprehension by these critics that regionalism may be dismissed for producing static or monolithic notions of identity can be felt, even in this discourse which seeks to emphasise the opposite, with the addition of the phrase "travelled through" completing a list of more "rooted" and "fundamental" understandings of place and nature. Winton's "regionalism", if this is what it is, surely raises many questions about the local and beyond, in response to such defensive regionalist discourse.

Twenty years earlier, and in mildly structuralist mode, Australian critic Graham Turner wrote of regionalism:

> Australian texts employ a particular language in that they draw on those myths, connotations and symbols, which have currency in the Australian culture; and they also reveal what formal preferences – the encouragement of certain genres, conventions, and modes of production – are exercised in that culture. The nation's narratives are defined not so much by factors such as the birthplace of the author or whether a text was written in Sydney or London, but rather by the bank of ideologically framed myths, symbols, connotations . . .[14]

This account sees writing as purely material in nature (forms, genres, modes of production), only in reference to the writing produced, and not in terms of the ontologically and existentially material effects of land and place – effects on the body and

---

13 Wendy Katz and Timothy Mahoney, *Regionalism and the Humanities* (Lincoln: University of Nebraska Press, 2008), ix.
14 Graeme Turner, *National Fictions: Literature, Film and the Construction of Australian Narrative*, 2nd ed. (1986; St Leonards: Allen & Unwin, 1993), 19.

the psyche – of weather, water, heat, dryness, desert and cave. Place must be read for its real material, anthropological and somatic effects, but also for its psychic and ontological effects. The peoples of the so-called deep south of America, for example, a place known by Winton in part through his love of the works of Mark Twain and Flannery O'Connor, have different accents and manners, but also different belief systems and values to those people who grew up in Western Australian desert, or bush, or beside the ocean, in a colonised country with an Indigenous presence.

Critic Salhia Ben-Messahel, writing in 2006, helpfully combines the writerly and mythological emphasis of Turner with an understanding of the ontology of place, arguing of Winton's locatedness:

> The geo-economic division of Western Australia [from the rest of the country] articulates unity and fragmentation; landscape and its influence on the individual are an effect of the shifting, mysterious, unpredictable nature of the Australian continent.[15]

Arguing for the isolation of Western Australia as a major shaping force in Winton's writing, Ben-Messahel's account buys into myths of frontier, colonial isolation, eastern versus western Australia and desert loneliness, and into something "mysterious". Arguably, however, it finally fails to give content to the weave of writerly *and* ontological, to unpack other internal (psychological, spiritual, childhood) factors influencing Winton's writing about place. It thus produces a kind of reified regionalism that remains mythologising, and vague.

As a child Winton was a reader of regional, vernacular children's books: *Treasure Island*, *Tom Sawyer* and *Huckleberry Finn*. Perhaps this partly explains his creation of many small boys and young men as central characters – Jerra and Sean, Ort, Pikelet, Quick and Fish, the narrator of "Aquifer" in *The Turning*, and many others – representations of ordinary boys who are defined by the local, by home and family and place, but who find themselves in overwhelming, life-defining situations. The limits or limitations of "rootedness" and family often create the narrative tension in the novels, as they did in Twain's and O'Connor's work. Hence, nature in Winton is rarely given or known, and is not merely "regional". It is more often volatile and anarchic for the child growing into manhood. Confronting the wild and non-human in the ocean, and in surfing particularly, offers the perfect metaphoric space for such challenges. One US critic reviewing *Breath* reads Winton as being all about

> moving out of your depth, getting in over your head, having your soul damaged beyond repair . . . But against all this pointless sorrow, there remains the evanescent beauty of the world, and Winton matches that with limitlessly beautiful prose.[16]

Further, Winton's novels do not simply oppose place to "gender, race, ethnicity, class, demography", as Katz and Mahoney argue. Place gathers up and compounds these many aspects in the novels' creating of meaning and value, and the questioning of it. In fact,

---

15   Salhia Ben-Messahel, *Mind the Country: Tim Winton's Fiction* (Crawley: University of Western Australia Press, 2006), 231.
16   Carolyn See, "Young Men and the Sea," review of *Breath* by Tim Winton, *Washington Post*, 27 June 2008. http://tinyurl.com/See2008.

questioning becomes the ontological atmosphere of all of Winton's novels, as the supposed stabilities of place are pummelled beyond individual control: by events, accidents, chance, family, gender, class, temporality, rules, falls in status, purpose and economics, loss of relationship, and death.

Childhood: Innocence and Experience

In *The Turning*, the narrator of "Aquifer" looks back on his suburban childhood:

> I grew up in a boxy double brick house with roses and a letterbox, like anyone else. My parents were always struggling to get me inside something, into shirts and shoes, inside the fence, the neighbourhood, the house, out of the sun or the rain, out of the world itself it often seemed to me.[17]

The Twain-inflected tensions between prescribed place, family, law and order, and an imagined freedom to immerse oneself in "the world itself" are shared by many of the child characters in Winton's fiction: in *That Eye, the Sky*, Ort communes with the stars and bush as the enormity of his family tragedy unwinds; *Cloudstreet*'s Fish and Quick, before the accident, and in a different way afterwards, are enveloped by the natural world, "Fish standing up in the middle of the boat with arms out like he's gliding, like he's a bird sitting in an updraught. The sky, packed with stars" (*Cloudstreet*, 114); and Queenie in *Shallows* remembers her childhood dreams:

> I was a little girl. I heard the voice of God calling from down in the bay... this thunderous splash and the whole farm shook and in the moonlight I saw this glistening black... whale inching up towards the house...[18]

These located scenes of childhood and the way they shape the imaginations and the material, as well as psychic, existence of Winton's characters into the future are often precise and earthed. It is important that Fish and Quick live on the river. It is important that Luther Fox's drama in *Dirt Music* takes place in specific locales: a small fishing town, the ocean and desert. At one point the narrative places Luther Fox in the cave-pocked escarpments overlooking Aboriginal middens on the tropical, coastal wilderness of northern Western Australia:

> [A] wide-mouthed cave shrouded with rock figs. On the ledges outside the overhang are tiny dancing figures the colour of dried blood upon the yellow rock... Inside the cave he sees other paintings in a different style. He stoops to look, but hesitates...[19]

This is a detailed, located moment in Luther Fox's journey, as he seeks peace after the death of his family, a moment of intense observation; but it is simultaneously a moment

---

17 Tim Winton, *The Turning* (Sydney: Picador, 2004), 39. All subsequent references are to this edition and appear in parentheses in the text.
18 Tim Winton, *The Shallows* (Sydney: Allen & Unwin, 1984), 1.
19 Tim Winton, *Dirt Music* (Sydney: Picador, 2001), 364

of otherness, a registering of Indigenous place, and of white negotiation with Indigenous country. Luther doesn't feel alienation, but he does register presence and difference: "Halfway out into the light Fox catches himself making the sign of the cross and he stifles a laugh. Hasn't done that for a while" (365). What Winton achieves here is a doubleness of place – locatedness and otherness – a representing of place from radically different perspectives. This moves Winton's narratives well beyond a simple, representational "regionalism". It introduces the ontological dramas of belonging and non-belonging into his narratives of place.

Numinous Zones

In details of location, of humans discovering or making meaning in the non-human world of ocean, cave, desert, birds, sun, rain and stars, "this black glistening whale" (365), Winton's are indeed recognisable places. But they are also numinous zones, places that become larger than one place, defined by what happens there, unexpected, in the flash of a moment, or a tail, alone or in relationship, in response to place as presence. Such moments and places can be seen as glimpses of the sacred, beyond the known or expected or humanly planned for. They challenge and extend the humans who find themselves there, and they can be dangerous, or ecstatic, or funny or nourishing. But they present characters that are formed by both the earthiness of place and the possibilities of sacredness and meaning. In this way, Winton's novels share intimately what Edmund Burke in his 1757 treatise on the beautiful and the sublime saw as the compound effects of nature:

> The passion caused by the great and sublime in nature, when those causes operate most powerfully, is astonishment: and astonishment is that state of the soul in which all its motions are suspended, with some degree of horror. In this case the mind is so entirely filled with its object, that it cannot entertain any other, nor by consequence reason on that object which employs it. Hence arises the great power of the sublime, that, far from being produced by them, it anticipates our reasonings, and hurries us on by an irresistible force. Astonishment, as I have said, is the effect of the sublime in its highest degree; the inferior effects are admiration, reverence, and respect.[20]

Burke's meditation on the horror, as well as the "admiration, reverence and respect" shaping human responses to the sublime in nature, can be read historically, as well as poetically. His attitude is in many ways Eurocentric, unsurprisingly, and written in the shadow of the surrounding decades when, in Winton's words:

> Dutch mariners began making landfall [in Terra Australis] in the early 17th century ... confounded by what they saw. Almost two centuries later the French and English viewed the enigmatic southland through the lens of their own hemisphere. And they were appalled. It wasn't simply that they were baffled by Terra Australis and its indigenes – what they saw offended them. It seemed deranged, perverse.[21]

---

20 Edmund Burke, "Of the Passion Caused by the Sublime," in *The Works of the Right Honourable Edmund Burke, Vol. 1 (of 12)* (1757; Project Gutenberg, 2005), part 2, sect. 1. http://tinyurl.com/Burke2005.

Winton's sense here of a Eurocentric inability to read the Australian landscape is an additional overlay to Burke's "horror", but it is an extension rather than a break with the double nature of Burke's perception. To be dwarfed by the huge wildness of nature is one thing, but not to be able even to read the forms you see before you, to have no context through which to understand those forms, adds a further layer of "horror" and offence. However, Burke's major thesis still resonates closely with the ontological perspectives of Winton's fiction. From the beginning of Winton's career, in early works such as *Shallows* and *In the Winter Dark*,[22] in the mythopoesis of *The Riders*, through to the short story collection *The Turning*, we see non-human forces – coincidence, accident, serendipity, nature, time – figured in his work as beautiful, but also threatening and overwhelming. Winton, after all, is a white European Australian learning, as many white Australians still are, to read the country and to live in it.

The two epigraphs to *Shallows* are from Dryden's "Annus Mirabilis" and Canadian singer Bruce Cockburn's 1980 song "Grim Travellers". Dryden's 1667 iambics prefigure Burke's sense of horror, akin to the *Moby Dick* imprint on *Shallows*: "So, close behind some promontory lie / the huge leviathans to attend their prey"; while Cockburn's contemporary lyrics combine human and non-human agents: "Those grim travellers in dawn skies / See the beauty – makes them cry inside / Makes them angry and they don't know why / Grim travellers in dawn skies", perhaps a presaging of those otherworldly figures in *The Riders*.

These forces – metaphysical but permeating this world, non-human but penetrating the human – decimate the Flack family through the father, Sam Flack's, horrendous accident in *That Eye, the Sky*. They rip Fish away from ordinary adult life in *Cloudstreet*; introduce us to the nameless adult narrator of the short story "Aquifer", witness as a ten-year-old to the drowning of a class bully. In "Aquifer", the adult slowly comes to recall the details of a childhood drowning, a memory sunk below consciousness, as he contemplates the invisible forces which still impose themselves on his imagination:

> The brown land, I figured, wasn't just wide but deep too. All that dust on the surface, the powder of ash and bones, bark and skin . . . the air sometimes turns pink with the flying dirt of the deserts, pink and corporeal. And beneath the crust, rising and falling with the tide, the soup, the juice of things filters down strong and pure and mobile as time itself finding its own level . . . All the dead alive in the land, all the lost who bank up, mounting in layers of silt and humus, all the creatures and plants making thermoclynes in seas and rivers and estuaries . . . I have, boy and man, felt the dead in my very water . . . (49–50)

These are the idiosyncratic – often abject – ponderings of an adult narrator speaking partly through his innocent childhood self, contemplating the forces of time and death, the impersonal processes of nature, "the juice of things", "all the dead alive in the land". In childlike enthralment, the man registers the child's awareness of human and non-human forces, the tidal ebb and flow that pays no special regard to human existence. This sense of astonishment and even horror is apprehended by the adult who respects his childhood vision. It emanates from the fervid considerations of the child and the more poised, but enthralled, recollections of the adult: "I have, boy and man, felt the dead in my very water".

---

21 Tim Winton, *Island Home: A Landscape Memoir* (Melbourne: Penguin, 2015), 14.
22 Tim Winton, *In the Winter Dark* (Melbourne: McPhee Gribble, 1988).

"Horror", Burke's description of the passion invoked by the sublime in nature, is likewise one of Winton's characters' responses. But there is also, in Winton's oeuvre, a hungry, sometimes ecstatic, sometimes simply celebratory desire, a highwire connection between the abjection and horror in so many of his narratives, and a redemptive impulse. Both point towards sacred possibilities. This double set of impulses is most often created through a juxtaposing of the local, regional, earthed, material world *and* a never merely rationalistic vision of forces beyond the human. What is created throughout Winton's works, in this way, might be seen as a poetry of the sublime or the sacred; a dialogue between the known and the unknown forces intuited by characters in the natural world, in place. These forces are larger than the human or rational; sometimes abject, imagined and remembered, they surface in language again and again, as the writing seeks, or lies itself open to, meaning. Such intimations of sacredness are at the core of Tim Winton's fiction.

At the climax of *Cloudstreet*, as the Lambs and the Pickles conduct their ramshackle, joyous picnic by the river, Winton's prose reaches for a style which forges realist and magical heights, a bringing together of the ontological hope of the novel, even as its most abject notes are sounded. Fish, the child-man, is let go, into the element that is both ecstatic and deadly, beautiful and horrific:

> Fish leans out and the water is beautiful. All that country below, the soft winy country with its shifts of colour, its dark, marvellous call. Ah, yes . . .
>
> Fish goes out sighing, slow, slow to the water that smacks him kisses when he hits. Down he slopes into the long spiral, drinking, drinking his way into the tumble past the dim panic of muscle and nerve into a queer and bursting fullness . . . and I'm Fish Lamb for those seconds it takes to die . . . I burst into the moon, sun and stars of who I really am. Being Fish Lamb. Perfectly. Always. Everyplace. Me. (557–8)

What is the novel reaching for here, in its stream of consciousness prose, and in its overarching question about where and how human hopes for justice might be founded? What seems central in this sprawling, much-loved novel is a theology of reconciliation: between place and human; between the materiality of now and the transcendence of "Perfectly. Always. Everyplace". Fish is reaching across the bars of human abjection and death, becoming the first person, "I". It's as if Winton is challenging his readers, in the third-person narrative, to be not merely secular, earth-bound, untransformable. This is indeed a "queer" vision, queer in its reading against the merely somatic grain of physical "bursting", the "panic of muscle", the reality of death, towards the narrative's insistence on its dream of ecstatic freedom, a vision of what can be called sacred. Critics such as Michael Griffiths question *Cloudstreet*'s exclusively "white" narratives of belonging and place, in regard to Indigenous displacement and the novel's putatively inadequate treatment of Aboriginal characters.[23] Griffiths' stance helpfully opens up the relationship between politics and the sacred and their status in Winton's works – a relationship that receives attention in later chapters of this volume.

However, at this point it is important to recognise that the theology of this scene from *Cloudstreet* meshes powerfully with Winton's later Palm Sunday declaration. It is a

---

23   Michael R. Griffiths, "Winton's Spectralities, or What Haunts *Cloudstreet*?" in *Tim Winton: Critical Essays*, edited by Lyn McCredden and Nathanael O'Reilly (Perth: UWA Publishing, 2014), 75–95.

theology that is both political and sacred in scope. The speech was delivered at a rally in solidarity with refugees against their treatment by the Australian nation. Winton declared the need for Australia to rediscover its "soul", saying:

> For those of us of religious faith, [the soul is] the means by which we recognise the Divine spark in each other, the presence of God. To those who aren't religious, it's the way we apprehend the sacred dignity of the individual.[24]

The terminology of the sacred, and participation in it, are off-putting to many Australians. However, sacredness and its languages are still – and perhaps always will be – under dynamic construction; refused by many Australians, but embraced by religious and non-religious in different ways. However, this book will argue that to ignore the potency of the sacred as a category in Winton's fiction – subterranean, palpable in many characters' passion for the natural world, part of the moral and ethical fibre of his novels, informing Winton's choices of style – would be seriously to under-read his work.

John Frow's provocative 1998 essay "Is Elvis a God? Cult, Culture, Questions of Method" stands as a helpful provocation for this book on Tim Winton, as Frow argues for a response to the phenomenon of religion in the contemporary world and, specifically, in the discipline of cultural studies:

> [W]e need to take religion seriously in all of its dimensions because of its cultural centrality in the modern world; and we need to do so without ourselves participating in those religious myths of origin and presence ... Finally, let me make the observation that for many Australians these lessons have come from our increased awareness of Aboriginal spirituality, and our sense both of the need to respect and honour traditional belief systems, and of the tensions between a religious cosmology and the Enlightenment ethos which governs, and which rightly governs, our work.[25]

While arguing for a methodology which respects and honours "traditional belief systems", Frow characterises his own methodological (and philosophical) preference as an "Enlightenment ethos", a form of objectivity that takes religion seriously but "without ourselves participating in those religious myths of origin and presence". This is an intriguing position, representative of views that in more recent years have come under scrutiny in relation to different critical practices. Such practices include those which have been re-evaluated as anthropological "participant observer" roles, and the approaches of contemporary "participating" religious literary critics such as David Jasper, Heather Walton and Kevin Hart. Hart writes from a knowledgeable *participant* position about the tradition to which he belongs and in which he participates, nuanced in the ways he outlines the potential of current contemporary religious methodologies. Leaning on Husserl's account of "reduction" ("reduction" not in the general sense of abbreviation or oversimplification, but of "leading back to"), Hart offers us a theological *and* phenomenological method of being in the world, and of critical thinking as a religious person:

---

24 Winton, "Palm Sunday Plea".
25 John Frow, "Is Elvis a God? Cult, Culture, Questions of Method", *International Journal of Cultural Studies* 1, no. 2 (1998): 208.

When Husserl introduced his version of the reduction, he made a point of saying that it allows us to step back from the "natural attitude", that set of unexamined assumptions and habits of perception that characterize our existence when we think on automatic pilot (usually as uncritical empiricists or dogmatic physicalists). The reduction is not an act that one performs once and for all, no more so than cleaning the house is something one does once and for all. One's consciousness is altered by repeated acts of reduction performed from various positions and angles. Having made the reduction, Husserl says, we can see the ways in which our intentional acts are embedded in hidden or neglected horizons: we can discern how our perceptions, desires, memories, and so on are intimately involved with what they aim at.[26]

Hart is fully aware of living in a multiple world, and of reading and critiquing texts from positions of faith and non-faith. He does not process that multiplicity dismissively or defensively, but in creative and constitutive ways, as he examines the phenomenology of being religious and of being in the world. This examination involves, for Hart himself, an understanding of the tension between dogma and intelligent imagination (the institutional believer, and the poet); between human habit and rigorous self-examination; of the need to participate fully in questioning our intentional acts which are, contra Frow's proposed Enlightenment objectivity, inextricably bound up in the sublime's "hidden or neglected horizons". Hart is seeking rigorous, informed *and* participatory ways of writing about religion, or the sacred, in relation to literary and other kinds of texts. One of the major focuses of this present volume is an examination of such methodologies – ways of reading, writing, thinking – in relation to the sacred in Winton's oeuvre.

The Critical Debates

This book is structured around thematic and theoretical literary debates that are larger than "Winton", but which Winton's work attracts in highly significant ways. These critical debates are not recounted here in a chronological or "book by book" approach, but are addressed and readdressed under the different chapter foci: the relationship of literary representation and a writing life to the "life worlds" of Winton's imagination and experiences; relations between men and women; notions of falling and redemption that recur in Winton's work, both in sacred and secular frames; the ways in which class operates and forms lives in Australian society; how Winton's work moves between, and challenges, popular and literary categories; what it means to belong, to be in place, and how this forms the ontological substrata of Winton's characters; and finally, asking who is reading Winton, and what impact does his work have?

But it's fair to declare, from the outset, that this critical volume has designs on its readers, and even on "Tim Winton". It seeks to argue that throughout all of the following chapters a sustained critical inquiry into the sacred and secular aspects of life in Australia, and beyond, is being conducted. It is the role of the novelist to present for readers a rich feast of forms and characters and imagined places in which to revel, or to be disturbed from complacency. Equally, it is the role of the critic to seek engagement with readers

---

26   Kevin Hart, "Reading Theologically: Reduction and Reductio", in *Intersection in Christianity and Critical Theory*, ed. Cassandra Falke (London and New York: Palgrave Macmillan, 2010), 18.

around what she or he sees as the core critical questions – and even the paradoxes – that arise from the literary work. These questions are about the nature of being, about how human agents choose and act and be. It will be argued that in Winton's writings, the deeply sacred aspect of being is constantly addressed. This address is sometimes made in fleshy, earthed, sexual, material, embodied forms, and sometimes it is about more intangible, sublime, awestruck, even epiphanic ways, about human desire for transcendence even as we feel the sand between our toes, or the loss of everything we hold dear.

Winton's writing is not static. This critical volume also seeks to trace what it sees as the development of Winton into his mature writing years, from the earliest works. There is, this book argues, a deepening sense of reverence towards the earth even as there is a returning, again and again, to the ways in which belonging, being in place, respecting of the earth and its material realities are inevitably bound together with an understanding of human vulnerability, of the human not as the limit marker of being but as the place in which both earthed and sacred potential are unfolded. A large part of this intuiting of the sacredness of human meaning is to be found in Winton's approach to Indigenous Australia, and to places where meaning has been sought and made on this continent for hundreds of thousands of years. Throughout Winton's creation of *Australian* places and peoples, which are also human places and people, there is always a deep, pulsing exploration of the power of writing, of signs and their claim to make and sustain meaning and being. And undergirding all Winton's writing is an awareness of the fragility of men and women and children, of families and individuals, and of the earth; and a need to create, and to offer narratives of redemption, earthed and sacred.

1
Words and Worlds

> She loved books, even to hold them and turn them over in her hands and smell the cool, murky breeze they made when you birred the pages fast through your fingers. A house with a library!
> —*Cloudstreet*[1]

A preoccupation with words – written, spoken, storytelling, vernacular, lyrical, humorous, abject, ideological – is central to many of Tim Winton's characters, from the early novel *Shallows* (1984), through to *Eyrie* (2013). To some critics (and not always admiringly), Winton uses words like a literary prophet offering a "vision of the whole...whole community, whole being and whole masculinity...the desire for both demotic and sacred unities".[2] It is crucial in the context of this claim to examine just how Tim Winton's fiction negotiates what theorist Jacques Derrida, as early as 1969, described as *logocentrism*, "the exigent, powerful, systematic, and irrepressible desire for such a [transcendental] signified".[3] In this chapter I will argue that language is a key conundrum, a question of agency but also of exigency and the world beyond the individual, for both Winton and his characters.

In a recent critical essay, Fiona Morrison builds a persuasive argument about Winton's "vernacular presence" in *Cloudstreet*. It is a novel, she argues, in which "the speaking community is...everywhere to be found, and this is the powerful and ambiguous point of collision between speech, writing and a mediating consciousness".[4] Morrison argues for the ways in which Winton's *Cloudstreet* admirably constructs, technically and thematically, working-class, regional, vernacular speech patterns, in quite experimental and humorous ways; but also in ways that can marginalise other voices, particularly Indigenous and

---

1 Tim Winton, *Cloudstreet* (Melbourne: McPhee Gribble, 1991), 40. All subsequent references are to this edition and appear in parentheses in the text.
2 Fiona Morrison, "'Bursting with Voice and Doubleness': Vernacular Presence and Visions of Inclusiveness in Tim Winton's *Cloudstreet*", in *Tim Winton: Critical Essays*, ed. Lyn McCredden and Nathanael O'Reilly (Perth: UWA Publishing, 2014), 51.
3 Jacques Derrida, "Structure, Sign, and Play in the Discourse of the Human Sciences", in *The Languages of Criticism and the Sciences of Man: The Structuralism Controversy*, ed. R. Macksey and E. Donato (Baltimore: Johns Hopkins University Press, 1972), 147.
4 Morrison, "Bursting with Voice", 52.

female voices. In Morrison's essay, and in what follows in this chapter, words are investigated as profoundly ideological in their relationship to the worlds of the characters. I will argue further that Winton's recurrent inquiry into the scope and power of words is driven primarily by an ontological questioning. For Winton, it will be argued, words promise to build all kinds of communities and identities, but they are also apprehended, at some level of the text, as able to smash and dissipate meaning. His fiction, in other words, is alive to the riven nature of language. As Jon Stratton has succinctly put it: in the classical episteme "there was once, before the linguistic fall, a world of perfect representation, a totalizing of identity", but for the contemporary world "[l]anguage is articulated as both the site of fracture, the spacing of representation, and the site of the possibility of the closing of the spacing".[5] Hence, in response to what seems to be a widespread, popular understanding of Winton's works as fictions of wholeness, of "demotic and sacred unities",[6] I will argue that in many different ways across his career Winton is teasing out this question of the double effect of words, as both fractured and plenitudinous.

While literary critics are sometimes prone to unify an author and his works – Winton is this, Winton stands for that – across Winton's oeuvre there is arguably no single attitude to language, both technically and in what its impact and value might be. In a coruscating set of literary endeavours, language is tested out by Winton for its offer of plenitude, presence or authenticity; but also questioned for its limits. Do words have power to transform, or authenticate or establish meaning? How can words promise to be deeply constructive of identity, time, place and belonging, but equally to be excluding and inadequate?

Shallows: Reading the Wide World

In *Shallows*, we read about Nathaniel Coupar – the ancestor whose journal of his youth as a colonial whaler in the 1830s so compels the contemporary character, Cleve Cookson. Coupar had scrawled in his journal:

> How strange to write this all into a journal to keep in an old sea-trunk; as a youth and an old man, the most constructive and the most useless labour of my life.[7]

And for Queenie, Coupar's great-granddaughter, waiting impatiently for her fellow activists to begin enacting their intention of saving the threatened whales, her seedy boarding house in 1978 offers only "hardbound novels . . . mostly about the writing of more novels, and the poetry concerned itself with itself, and between them they posed no threat to sleep" (127). In these different ways, the purposes and effects of words and texts are questioned. The gaps between words and the world, between language and action, between construction and uselessness, are a compelling and motivating problem for Winton.

---

5   Jon Stratton, *Writing Sites: A Genealogy of the Postmodern World* (London: Harvester Wheatsheaf, 1990), 92.
6   Morrison, "Bursting with Voice", 3.
7   Tim Winton, *Shallows* (Sydney: Allen & Unwin, 1984), 174. All subsequent references are to this edition and appear in parentheses in the text.

Journals, newspaper cuttings, novels, family lore, and brick-like volumes of history are what Cleve Cookson devours eagerly, in secret midnight readings. Queenie, whose family is the source of the whaling journals he is reading, flips back and forward between words on the page and messages uttered by the phenomenal world:

> When she was a child Queenie climbed the windmill to see the whales surfacing in the bay, spouting vapour like gunsmoke. Up there among the winter green of the farm, she had thought about the story of Jonah, how the whale was God's messenger, and she had hooked her limbs about the salt-stained legs of the mill and watched the big backs idling, and waited for a message from God, the one she was certain would come. She waited for the whales to belly up at the foot of the mill to attend to her queries. Each winter she climbed and waited, each year the questions were modified; one year the whales did not appear at all . . . They'll be talking about those bloody journals, she thought. God knows, I thought Poppa'd have more sense – he knows what Cleve's like. (16–17)

What *is* Cleve like? He is an avid reader of others' stories, someone who finds in the historical journals a place where he might "cast off his unremarkable heritage" (18). The journals of a past era of whaling become a substitute narrative for all that Cleve feels he lacks in identity and purpose; and this constant process of reading, fuelled by lack, is a deep disappointment to his wife. Queenie, in contrast to her husband, opens herself from childhood onwards to reading not just books, but the signs of the world, expecting in such signs a fullness not yet apparent, but coming. The promise of plenitude and meaning is felt by Queenie not as fairy-story, but as violence and "gunsmoke", terrifying messages from God partly known to Queenie through her identificatory childhood readings of the biblical stories of Jonah, the reluctant prophet; Jonah, who had to learn through physical suffering to read and respond to God's messages in the world.

A startling scene occurs in *Shallows* shortly after the just-married Queenie has somewhat accidentally joined the anti-whaling activists. Queenie is depicted "settled into the pink slush" (38), lying prone and bloodied in protest on the flenching floor of the Angelus whaling station. Going afterwards to visit her young husband at his night watchman's station, in order to explain to him what has happened, she finds him reading the journals yet again. Queenie angrily knocks to the floor the hefty historical journal Cleve is reading admiringly. She is frustrated that he devours *Moby-Dick* and the whaling journals with such relish, as stories of heroism, but fails to read the present moment's political realities, its pointless, barbarous killing of whales. In the hut on the pier, perched above the deep water, Queenie

> was suddenly on all fours with the book tight in the space between floorboards with all her weight pushing down on it and him screaming at the thought of years falling away unread, sinking into the Sound . . . and his fist came down on her back and she went flat. (65)

The scene is a turning point. As Queenie lies prostrate for a second time that day, "[h]er cheek rested against the upright spine of the bitter-smelling book" (65), Cleve is immediately repentant: "his testicles shrivel at the memory of those other hundreds of moments, years, he would dearly love to be stripped of" (65). Queenie departs, the word "unforgivable" echoing between them, and "the journal stuck up out of the floor, wedged between the planks, like a tombstone" (65–6). This is a scene reeling towards abjection.

Words – writing and reading and speaking – clamour in the space between the two characters. The abject processes of flenching, stripping the whales of life and flesh – "do you know how big a whale's brain cavity is?" (64) – have become increasingly horrific to Queenie; for Cleve, "[t]hey're just animals you know" (64). Both characters are depicted as still coming, lurchingly, into their adult identity, not yet knowing what that might mean. Both are confronting the anxiety of not being fully formed. They are, in their search for meaning and identity, starting from the place of the abject, the very place that threatens to obliterate meaning.

Writing a Self: Abjection and Meaning-making

As Kristeva theorises the abject:

> Here ... consciousness has not assumed its rights and transformed into signifiers those fluid demarcations of yet unstable territories where an "I" that is taking shape is ceaselessly ... at the limit of primal repression that, nevertheless, has discovered an intrinsically corporeal and already signifying brand, symptom, and sign: repugnance, disgust, abjection. There is an effervescence of object and sign – not of desire but of intolerable significance; they tumble over into non-sense or the impossible real, but they appear even so in spite of "myself" (which is not) as abjection.[8]

Kristeva's famous essay of 1982, *Powers of Horror*, traces the constitutive nature of abjection, the way it stands in intimate relation to its other, the place of stable meaning, identity, sense or purpose. Abjection is constitutive of stable meaning in the same way that the conscious and the unconscious are mutually defining. The border between "I" and all that threatens to dissolve or undo selfhood and stability – the abject place where death and dissolution are preeminent, the place of the pre-linguistic, the place where words do not stand up – amplifies "repugnance, disgust, abjection" in the human subject. Language (signifiers, the desire to make meaning, to take shape, the "already signifying brand, symptom and sign") is crucial in Kristeva's theoretical narrative, a site from which the intolerability of significance is brandished – a taunt, a reminder. Why "intolerable"? Perhaps because language, particularly in Kristeva's argument about *poetic language*, papers over our double knowledge: that humans seek meaning and identity, power, and corporeal shape; and that we know we die, that "repugnance, disgust, abjection" constitute human reality just as much as reality demands "significance". From the side of abjection (death, violence, bodily decomposition, loss or impossibility of identity and agency, the horror of this loss, the failure of language to ever adequately signify), the hope of significance seems laughable, an intolerable taunting. From the other side of the border, the side of clean, proper, meaning-making humanness, the abject so often causes horror and the denial of radical instability.

How does this drama of abjection, this awareness of "intolerable significance", inform Winton's own language – written, poetic, vernacular, ambivalent, as weapon and as reconciler – in the multiple ways the author approaches language? So far we have identified

---

8 Julia Kristeva, *Powers of Horror: An Essay on Abjection*, trans. Leon S. Roudiez (New York: Columbia University Press, 1982), 11.

thematically the centrality of written words for Cleve in *Shallows*, his seeking to paper over his own sense of insignificance by burrowing into the narratives of others.

Daniel Coupar, Queenie's grandfather, seems more like his granddaughter. A lonely farm boy who grows into a lonely old man, Coupar turns backwards and forwards between written words and the signs of the world:

> [H]e let the world inform his senses. Sometimes when he lay on the granite breast of the hill above the pastures and the beaches, looking up into the mesmeric blue of the sky, he felt the world swallow him, enfold and engulf him; he felt its milk-warm breath and its sap-sweetness. He learnt to name the things about him with the aid of some water-stained cyclopaedias. His mother read to him from the Bible and he lived and re-lived the magical stories of Moses and Ruth and Jonah . . . (88)

Winton here is trying out the possibility of unity between written words and the things of the world. From both the "breast of the hill", "its milk-warm breath", as well as from cyclopaedias and his mother's reading to him, signs of meaning proliferate for Daniel Coupar as a child. His experiences are of being swallowed, taken into a semiotic place of fullness that is deeply unified. But the possibility of engulfment, of being swallowed as Jonah was for his failure to hear the words of God, had not yet come to Daniel Coupar as a child. As the novel progresses, drowning in the world, and through the failure of words, are recurrent tropes. In his last moments, an old man, Coupar lies prostrate on the hill above his drought-devastated farm. What comes to him is a long awaited breaking of drought, "the thickest mass of rain coming, hissing on the water" as "he felt heavy drops hit the back of his throat and roll into him" (289). What comes also are words, a text from childhood: "Deep calleth unto deep at the noise of thy waterspouts: all thy waves and thy billows are gone over me" (289). In their context, Psalm 42, these words are fitting for an old man who has been, throughout the novel, alive to both the promise of words and the signs of the world, but also deeply questioning of their relationship to each other. The psalm Winton has chosen for his novel closes with the words:

> Why art thou cast down, O my soul? And why art thou disquieted within me? Hope thou in God, for I shall yet praise Him, who is the health of my countenance and my God.[9]

This is both a hymn of hope and "health", and the dying song of Daniel Coupar. It sings, as David the psalmist did, of hope and praise, *and* it sings from the side of abjection, of being "cast down" and "disquieted", recognising the double inheritance of words as harbingers of plenitude and of fracture.

Queenie and Cleve are not yet reunited at the close of the novel, but are moving in that direction. They witness the coming of the whales along the coast as they travel away from Angelus, the scene of their disunity. The cries of the whales are a speech, calling to them just as they did when Queenie was a child, waiting, and watching "this glistening, black . . . whale inching up towards the house . . . It was God . . ." (4). But as the novel closes, as Daniel Coupar succumbs to the "deep", "Queenie and Cleve wake up to the sound of the whales and are paralysed by joy and disbelief, hearing the sounds come closer every

---

9 *Psalms* 42:5 (King James Version).

moment as though nearly with them" (289). It is, however, a coming that must include the abject reality of the whales:

> [H]uge, stricken bodies lurching in the shallows... Masses of flesh and barnacles covered the sand, creeping up, floundering, suffocating under their own weight. A pink vapour from spiracles descended upon Cleve and Queenie Cookson as they moved between the heaving monuments. (290)

How are readers to understand Winton's vision of what human language and whale speech are subjected to at the closing of *Shallows*? In the form of an abject baptism, a sprinkling with the "pink vapour from spiracles", Queenie and Cleve are reading signs – those "heaving monuments" – as both full and empty. At the moment of reunion between the characters, the whales' song seems to offer a sign of reconciliation, a union of human and nature. They turn, instead, into dying monuments, but of what? Signs of hope and change have been occurring for Queenie and Cleve – she is pregnant, he is beginning to see himself, and the world beyond himself, as worthy of love – but at the last moment, as the novel ends, signs are emptied, joy and disbelief turned to a suffocating sorrow. Readers of *Shallows* are left with this deep ambivalence towards the power of signs and their claim to make and sustain meaning.

That Eye, the Sky: Beyond Language?

The status of signs and the linguistic processes of meaning-making are also central to another early Winton novel, *That Eye, the Sky* (1986), published two years after *Shallows*. There are many affiliations too, between *That Eye, the Sky*, told by twelve-year-old Ort Flack, and *Cloudstreet*, on the one hand, and *Eyrie* on the other. *That Eye, the Sky* and *Cloudstreet* both employ – and indeed construct – strongly vernacular language, with the centre of wisdom being a young boy touched by suffering and near-death injury. Both these novels seek to write almost "beyond language", pushing at their climax into writerly visions that exceed or stretch the material limits of words, straining to comprehend sacred meanings in the midst of abject experience. The literal, twenty-seven-year distance and differences between *That Eye, the Sky* and *Eyrie* are indicative of the metaphoric path Winton has been treading, linguistically and ontologically, in regard to the efficacy of words.

Ort Flack, knocking on the door of adolescence, is the consciousness through which *That Eye, the Sky* is focalised. Ort is a brain-injured, intuitive and feeling child who muses on the night sky, on falling stars, the possible existence of a knowing and caring God, even as all the signs seem to point elsewhere. There is a stubborn, beautiful capacity for hope and recuperation in Ort's hurt skull, demonstrated in his practical tenderness towards his suffering father Sam, and his grief-struck mother Alice. Ort, I would argue, is also pre-eminently a reader, a would-be decipherer of signs, a willing collaborator with the fullness of signs. This is what defines Ort: as voyeur, momentary Christian convert, reader of the natural world and reader of sacred texts. As voyeur, he is impelled – akin to the reader and the novelist – to read the intimate lives of others. So, he becomes the eye in the peephole:

> Fat calls it perving, but it's really just checking on them. I like to see them. To see they're alright, that they're still the same. This old house is full of holes... I just sit and watch

for a while . . . Fat reckons it's wrong. Checking on people I mean. Mostly I reckon it's the best way of making sure you know how your family is getting on. You get looked at all day and all night anyway. That eye of the sky sees you – why worry about your kids or your brother looking? It's honest enough.[10]

Like Fish in *Cloudstreet*, Ort is something of a holy fool. He lacks a stable, fixed centre, having survived coma as a baby, and endures the near-death of his father. Or rather, Ort lacks *fixity* of self, as he reaches for fullness and meaning in the midst of an abject and terrifying reality. In *That Eye, the Sky*, as in *Shallows*, there is no simple opposition between abjection and joy, but an emphasis on human choice and meaning-making in the heart of suffering:

The forest moves quiet tonight. Jarrahs move a long way up and out of sight. Now and then I hear little animal noises . . . My back hurts and my bum stings and the back of my legs too. I've got no clothes on out here in the forest. Prickles and burrs and twigs stick in me all over. I rub them in, squirm and shake around. It hurts a lot. I'm hurting myself. I want to . . . There is something over the house. Like a cloud. *Like* a cloud. It glows, just sitting over the roof. Hell! It's bright as the moon . . .
  Moorr-toon! Mum is yelling.
  Oh. Not murder. Please.
  Morton! Morton!
  She sees me coming . . .
  "It's your father," Mum says, looking at me like she's not sure of anything in the world any more. "Ort, he's awake. He's awake". (42–3)

Ort often goes out into the bush, sensing an eye looking down on him, neither malevolent nor knowable. In this scene from early in the novel, Ort reads the night's signs – the language of moving tree tops, its animal noises – and he reads the pain in his own body, propelling himself into further pain, rubbing himself into the prickles and burrs like an ancient martyr as he mourns for his father. He is looking for a way to make his inner and outer worlds, his feelings and his body, cohere: "I'm hurting myself. I want to". It is the first of many episodes in the novel where Ort seeks sense out of nonsense, healing from injury, and a story that will suffice.

Ort is a subtle, responsive reader. He never forces coherence or plenitude. As he writhes in the night bush, seeking to feel, to share his father's pain, to understand the trajectory of meaning in this pain, the house is illuminated by something "[l]ike a cloud. *Like* a cloud". Even as he runs for the house at his mother's cry, twice falling down – "in the nick, raw as a prawn, me shorts back in the bush" – Ort takes in "something over the house", "bright as the moon", seeing it is *not* a cloud, but "like" (43). This scene is of course a precursor to the final pages of the novel: as the boy who has done his reading of the sacred texts, shared in the family's makeshift sacraments, runs for the safflower oil and the big black bible, to anoint his father. And "that beautiful cloud creeps in. This house is filling with light" (150).

---

10   Tim Winton, *That Eye, the Sky* (Melbourne: McPhee Gribble, 1986), 23–4. All subsequent references are to this edition and appear in parentheses in the text.

Out of grievous need, but also out of hope, a choice to side with meaning, Ort is a particular kind of reader. Poised between childhood and the inadequacies of adulthood embodied in his father and mother, Henry Warburton and Mr and Mrs Cherry, Ort chooses to construct meaning from what seems like hopelessness. At the end of the novel Sam Flack may be awake, and he may have tears streaming down his face, but readers are left with a potential resurrection only, moved perhaps, but not necessarily, *with* Ort as he claims meaning and new life for his father. In his role as anointer, Ort is a small, vernacular priest ordaining the king, handing on the mantle of hope to his struggling father. Or readers may choose to remain with the ambiguity and unfinished nature of the scene, the moment before miracle.

It is Henry Warburton, the unlikely, abject prophet who has the most effect on the boy, slowly revealing himself as an evangelist to the family that is greedy for comfort and something to hang on to. Henry does this first of all silently, through actions, coming as a stranger out of nowhere to help with the most menial of jobs in support of the family. But he also comes to his mission, eventually, through words and stories, and Ort is the perfect, hungry listener:

> Henry Warburton keeps talking and we listen. He talks and talks about this bloke Adam and this bloke Eve who had no clothes on . . . And you can see God but you can't. And all these stories about God in burning bushes and piles of fire and tornadoes and little clouds. Stories! Piles of 'em. He tells stories like you've never heard boy. (88–9)

Ort listens, withdraws, muses, watches, hopes, reads, attempts to decipher the signs. The charismatic story-teller Henry finds his ideal listener in the boy who has been deprived of his father's stories, and who is open to the possibilities of words as plenitudinous signs pointing to a different dimension. But for Ort, and for the novel as a whole, this other dimension is grounded in the earthed, observable world:

> "So God's up there?" I say, pointing to all those wonderful stars. "A someone?"
> "Everywhere, Ort. He's in everything. The trees, the ground, the water. Everything stinks of God, reeks of him." (89)

This possibility of an all-seeing God is already known to Ort, communer with the sublimity of the bush and the night sky around his home. But the power of words – their fullness or emptiness – is tested when Alice and Ort attend the local bush church. Driven by sorrow and seeking solace, they arrive at the Watkins' drapery store church – "a kind of storeroom where the rows of chairs are" (124) – and are greeted by an avalanche of words from up front:

> "We praise and thank Thee our Father that Thou has given unto us plenty . . ." He goes on in this funny talk, like he comes from another planet and talks a little bit like us, but not enough to let us understand right. Thee and Thou. Dunno where they fit in, but the bloke up there in the blue suit and oily hair knows 'em pretty well.
> "The text for today, brethren and sisters, is taken from the book of Revelation, chapter sixteen. Ahem. Hurumph." (124)

Focalising through Ort the child narrator enables Winton to ponder with humour this strange little gathering in all its clubbiness and eccentricity. Words divorced from actions and spoken by figures in blue suits with oily hair, who remain anonymous, become small hammers of control, "funny talk" that fails to embrace the two most needy members of the congregation. It's the same man with blue suit and oily hair that amplifies this alienation for Ort and Alice, as he "gets up and shouts at us" (126). Through the eyes and ears of Ort, the church service turns into a bizarre circus:

> It's like algebra and arithmetic and geography and story time all wrapped into one. There's 666 and dragons and beast and seven heads and four angels and 144,000 and Babylon and Russia and China and a thousand years and seven seals and Sodom and Gog and Magog and Mt Arafat and Com-munism and Blasphemy and Lambs and more blood drinking.
> "Read the signs! Read-the-signs! The Antichrist himself comes. We have no doubt of it. The prophecies are fulfilled daily . . ." (126)

After the equally eccentric stories of Henry Warburton – but whose stories were accompanied by profound deeds of compassion – this litany's arrogant declarations seem both laughable and empty to Ort.

> "[W]e have no doubt of it" cries the oily-haired man, using the same texts, the same stories as Henry Warburton, but declaimed self-righteously, words turning into warnings, condescension, god-like certainties. Ort and the reader are shocked when Alice stands up in protest; but they cannot be surprised when she drags Ort behind her to the door, Alice's words resounding: "You don't have to shout. We're not animals, you know. And not even God's animals should be shouted at like they're made of mud" (126).

This is Alice's understandable response, complemented, however, by Ort's still hopeful actions on their return home. Instead of brushing the dust from their thonged feet and dismissing their church experience, Ort immediately takes his pyjama-clad father in his wheelchair down the drive for a walk:

> "Do it, the mundanity of kitchen safflower oil, the mundanity of kitchen safflower oil," I say. "Make him get up and walk." I sit back on the warm brown dirt and wait. And Dad sits there waiting too." (126)

Despite his religious experience, Ort acts *with* belief, *with* an expectation that texts and signs and reality will come together. But it's in silence, beyond words, that Ort "waits" for the fulfilment of signs.

The last chapter of *That Eye, the Sky* begins with Ort's marvellously pragmatic line: "In the morning I know. Mum is crying. I get up and do a check" (149). But Ort's is a very different kind of "knowing" to that of the oily-haired churchman. It's difficult for the boy – the reader and recorder of his family drama, the consoler, the perve – to do his checking, because "[t]here's this mist, like me eyes've got something in them. Cloudy" (149). The stream of consciousness prose here telescopes abjection and miracle, death and resurrection. Grammar dies and Sam shows signs of waking from his coma; the mist is both cloud, blocking clear sight and meaning, and it is light, it is "warm and it tastes good" (149). While the moral universe teeters around him – Henry Warburton and Tegwyn have eloped overnight along "big skid marks all over the drive", and the sole trace of Henry is "only his Bible on the sofa" (149) – Ort acts out the messages from the sacred text he is only just coming to know, and "it's like the whole flaming world's suddenly making sense" (150). Ort takes on the role of high priest, ready to anoint his father who threatens to resurrect: "[A]nd there's my Dad with these tears coming down his cheeks, pinpoints of light that hurt me eyes, tears like diamonds, I tell you" (150). It is through experience and affect – Dad's tears, Mum's laughter – that Ort knows. But it is also a moment deeply informed by text, a bringing to life of the sacred texts Henry and Alice and Ort have been stumbling through, half knowingly, throughout the novel. The anointing draws together Old Testament rituals and Christian hope of resurrection, becoming a tale told by Winton in which text and world are, momentarily, precariously, united: "[A]ll I can see is his eyes burning white and I know that something, something here in this world is gonna break" (150).

It is an ecstatic moment, prepared for from the opening pages, and it treats the spiritual texts as plenitudinous, bearing down on and connecting with human life. But of course the reader is left in mid-air, for it hasn't quite happened yet. That final word "break" carries with it a double sense of damage and vulnerability, but also of news being heralded, something just about to be announced to human eyes. Or at least to Ort's eyes. And there he is, shouting his prayer, or obscenities, acting out what the sacred texts have foretold, his single word meaning everything, or nothing: "'God! God! God!'" (150). In *That Eye, the Sky*, readers are asked to read along with Ort's hope, but also to recognise along with Stratton's critical insight

> That the text may contain a plenitude of meaning but that plenitude was always determined by the relation of the written language to the material world from which the language drew its meaning ... realism as a convention rather than as a representation inevitably guaranteed by the material world – marks the postmodern privileging of representation over presence.[11]

Winton's realism is always seeking ways beyond straight or realistic method, feeling towards ways of representing the world but also of drawing us into the unrepresentable, the unseen, towards the possibility of transformation.

Eyrie: Shifty Signs

Eyrie, with its title echoing *That Eye, the Sky*, opens with an introduction to the central character, Keely – deeply hung over, suffering loss of memory from the night before – trying to read the stain on his carpet. Oddly recalling Henry James' short story "The Figure in the Carpet", with a vernacular, modern twist, Keely tries to read the stain and to remember:

---

11 Stratton, *Writing Sites*, 93–4.

> So.
> Here was this stain on the carpet, a wet patch big as a coffee table. He had no idea what it was or how it got there. But the sight of it put the wind right up him . . . the strange sensation under foot. The carpet. It was wet. And not just wet, it was sodden. [12] . . .
> The stain was a metre long. It squelched as he stepped out of it. He noted, for what it was worth, that there were two distinct wet patches – one large, the other small – like elements of an exclamation mark. Like two blasts of a horn, which at least had the courtesy of signifying something. (9)

Suffering one of his recurrent hangovers, and in the middle of the ruins of his life, Keely seeks to read the signs around him, to make some sense of his present life as a deject. He is preoccupied with whether he'll be able to read the stain, know what has happened, and work out whether he is a moral man or whether he has, perhaps, perpetrated some violence. *Eyrie* is a book about whether it's possible to decipher the significance of signs, and that most intimate of signifying fields, one's life. From all the structures of meaning in his life – his role as son, his career, marriage and status as public spokesperson for the environment – Keely has fallen dramatically; blear-eyed, squinting at the stain on his carpet, staring out for glimpses of meaning in the world from the silent height of the seedy Mirador hotel. The stain is "like an exclamation mark", but it stubbornly refuses to signify.

The world of words and word-spinning had, after all, been the proving ground on which Keely had built his public relations career and identity:

> [B]elching out soundbites like a PR flak. All the while trying to hold to the long view, the greater hopes he'd begun with . . . the toxic adrenaline, the ceaseless performance . . . Finding yourself in the office at midnight, after the final, five-way phone hook-up, shaking with rage, caffeine and fatigue. (7)

Keely is indeed one of Kristeva's dejects, caught in a vortex of suffering in which he tries to steady himself, memories and accidental meetings from his past crowding him with the possibility of meaning, and its erasure. As Kristeva describes the dynamics of the deject:

> It is not the white expanse or slack boredom of repression, not the translations and transformations of desire that wrench bodies, nights, and discourse; rather it is a brutish suffering that "I" puts up with, sublime and devastated . . . A massive and sudden emergence of uncanniness, which, familiar as it might have been in an opaque and forgotten life, now harries me as radically separate, loathsome. Not me. Not that. But not nothing, either. A "something" that I do not recognize as a thing. A weight of meaninglessness, about which there is nothing insignificant, and which crushes me. On the edge of nonexistence and hallucination, of a reality that, if I acknowledge it, annihilates me. There, abject and abjection are my safeguards . . .[13]

Kristeva's description of the deject is an identikit of Keely, crushed by the "weight of meaninglessness", driven to the borderland between abjection – drunken, ill, hung over,

---

12 Tim Winton, *Eyrie* (Melbourne: Penguin, 2013), 3. All subsequent references are to this edition and appear in parentheses in the text.
13 Kristeva, *Powers of Horror*, 2.

guilt-ridden, haunted by duty and a messy relationship – and the taunting possibility of selfhood. The narrative is fuelled by this tension between abjection and the power to make meaning. Into this liminal zone there enters a shard of his former life in the shape of Gemma, his childhood neighbour, and her strange young grandson Kai. They seemingly offer connection, family history, the shape of a life. In Keely's slow-forming relationship with Kai we see a mirroring between man and child, built in large part around words and reading:

> On the tiny kitchen table Kai had a book on raptors open, a picture and description of the brahminy kite.
> He haunts that library, said Gemma, setting some chops into a pan.
> I was the same, said Keely, taking in the third chair pulled up to the table.
> Don't worry, I remember. Always had your face in a book.
> No wonder I never noticed anything, eh? (133)

In another of Winton's strange, alternative or fractured family tableaux, doubt is raised as to the nature of words and what they can and can't signify, how they might connect to the world. Kai and Keely reflect each other, obsessive in their always having their "face in a book". For Winton, who might be described as a non-literati kind of literary author, this characterisation opens up a multitude of questions about the efficacy of books, reading and literature. While readers are holding *Eyrie*, a piece of literature, in their hands, two wounded characters are depicted as ineffectual and impractical in their bookishness. Keely buys Kai a second-hand Scrabble set and the two sit opposite each other, absorbed in words:

> [F]rom the outset Kai seemed less interested in scores than in the words themselves. Games might begin in a spirit of boyish competition, but Kai seemed to fall into a trance, rousing now and then in a momentary shiver of recognition. Keely imagined the syllables emerging from chaos. He recalled his own childhood, how words hid as if aching to be found, transformed by his gaze, reaching out to meet him. He was fascinated by the way the boy handled the tiles, how he turned them over in his hands, running the tips of his thumbs across their faces as if tempted to slip them into his mouth like milky chocolates. His fingers twitched, tantalised, over the board, as he breathed upon his row of letters on their little pine plinth. (232)

In the developing relationship between man and boy, books and words – playing Scrabble in particular – become their connection. The materiality of words, their separate existence, haunt child and man. Words taunt and goad, threatening to define the user's identity, and therefore needing to be resisted. In this scene they are part of a semiotic relationship, tactile and sensuous, "like milky chocolates", intimate in their proximity and physicality. But words also emerge "from chaos". They make the child Kai ache; they "reach out to meet him". There is both comfort and threat experienced by both players, as words offer their meaning-making power, but also remain uncanny, on the edge of threat.

Words – signs, messages, stories, reading – play a central role in *Eyrie*, both thematically and as slippery tools of Winton's craft. Winton chooses the generic framework of detective fiction, with Keely as the farcical, stumbling detective. The novel can be read as a spoof of the genre, in fact, as Keely the detective views his life playing out before him, from childhood through early family life, defunct marriage and crumpled career. He becomes the hapless sleuth who must solve the riddle of his own disappearing meaning. Who to blame? Who are the bad guys? Who must be made to pay? Against Stewie the thug, it is the threat of words that Keely seeks to utilise in his increasingly desperate and farcical attempts to protect Gemma and Kai, as well as himself. As the rigours of the detective fiction genre move into overdrive, Keely writes his absurd letter of warning against those who threaten Gemma and Kai:

> Jesus loves you, Stewie.
> Which is just as well.
> Because we are watching you.
> All day. All night.
> All eyes. (328)

The materiality of words is emphasised here, the novel replicating Keely's would-be expressiveness. Drawing on his religious childhood and family beliefs, even Keely to some extent registers the ludicrousness of his plan. He leaves the note with its message of threatening justice – "trembling as he was, suppressing the spasms of laughter that welled up in his neck" (329) – embellishing his twisted little message with a further sign: two threatening eyes. He delivers "Jesus on the doorstep" (329) for Stewie, with signs that shudder and warp, carrying too much meaning, and not enough. Can Keely's words stand in for legal or manly actions? Does his twisted religious message suffice? What *is* his message, this shambling prophet who posts his cards at Stewie's front door, stabbing himself on a stray veranda post nail, impaling the sign of a gun and another of the cross, "shoved bloodied into the letterbox", and then runs away "like a maniac" (330)? The message reduces to something like: please don't hurt us, or we'll hurt you back. A child's frightened utterance: "[A]n effervescence of object and sign", an "intolerable significance",[14] a language that teeters on the edge of power and giving up.

But just as Keely's world threatens to implode into utter abjection, a moral pivot is tentatively established in the shape of Keely's attempt to act on behalf of others, caring about the injustices tumbling down on Kai and Gemma. Keely is (however farcically) taking on the moral agency he has for so long been trying to deny in himself. So, teetering between abjection (non-identity, consumed by farce and terror, unable to make meaning) and a desire to fix things, to mean something morally and manfully, Keely is attempting to stand up, an "I" who can overcome threat. Keely is thus depicted in the ambiguous drama of abjection, where "I" and "You" merge and separate:

> We may call it a border; abjection is above all ambiguity. Because, while releasing a hold, it does not radically cut off the subject from what threatens it – on the contrary, abjection acknowledges it to be in perpetual danger. But also because abjection itself is a composite of judgment and affect, of condemnation and yearning, of signs and drives. Abjection preserves what existed in the archaism of pre-objectal relationship, in the immemorial violence with which a body becomes separated from another body in order to be . . .[15]

---

14 Kristeva, *Powers of Horror*, 11.
15 Kristeva, *Powers of Horror*, 9–10.

From Keely's childhood, and his intimate, fraught relations with his mother and father, Gemma has appeared through coincidence back into his life. Drawing with her an abandoned, traumatised grandchild and the memory of violence that she suffered in her family and in the neighbourhood, Gemma amplifies in the man Keely an earlier time of vulnerability and instability, of "perpetual danger", when the children's identities were still being formed; as Kristeva describes it, under the heading of the abject, a time of "immemorial violence with which a body becomes separated from another body in order to be". It's as if the novelist is asking his readers to consider the story of a life *as written, and then constantly rewritten* across a lifetime, and beyond: "From the broad vaults and spaces you can see it all again because it never ceases to be" (3). But in *Eyrie*, arguably, the telling and re-telling seems to harvest only ambiguity as the one constant. Signs – in novels, for novelists, for readers – shift and coalesce across the border between stability and abjection, a contest of "judgment and affect, of condemnation and yearning, of signs and drives", oscillating between language as meaning-making and language riddled with symptoms of abjection, ceaselessly taunting us with the possibility of meaning.

There are great gaps and differences between *Shallows*, *That Eye, the Sky* and *Eyrie*, between the concept of words and any world they seek to represent or unite with. The latter two titles might echo each other aurally, but there are fascinating differences between them. Cleve Cookson, in *Shallows*, seeks to replace the significance he lacks in his life with the stories of others, while Queenie, when "only a little girl" (3–4), heard the voice of God calling from down in the bay. Like Ort, Queenie is inundated with meaning, always waiting and expecting even when the signs disappear. Ort, the child narrator through whom we experience *That Eye, the Sky*, never stops seeking meaning (there *ought* to be meaning). Alive with hope, he keeps urging himself and his family towards a redemptive reading of their lives, bringing into being what the suffering world seems intent on deconstructing: a transformative coalescence of signs and reality. He has not yet accepted language in terms of "the letter ... evoked *en souffrance*, in the wings, in suffering, leaving a trace of the fundamental discordance between knowledge and being";[16] even if the novelist, early in his career, has an inkling of such discordance. Rather, Ort runs ecstatically towards meaning, the bottle of oil and the big black bible in hand. He will act, bringing meaning to life.

But twenty-seven years later, *Eyrie* more bleakly poses questions about language – its efficacy, its edging towards abjection, its ambiguous role in making meaning. The later novel is far more stripped back, arguably less hopeful. Does *Eyrie* – and Winton as author – stand closer in his later work to Kristeva's claim that "all literature is probably a version of the apocalypse ... on the fragile border ... where identities ... do not exist or only barely so – double, fuzzy, heterogeneous, animal, metamorphosed, altered, abject"?[17] Literary reviewer Michael McGirr reads *Eyrie* in *political* terms, seeing the novel as exploring the loss of idealism in Western Australia's frenzied capitalism. However, he does not agree that *Eyrie* lacks hope, nor that it dissolves into the abject: "The lexicon of the book embraces words and phrases such as shriven, redeemed, salvation, mercy, prayer, deliverance, fierce saviour, Great Defender and so on".[18] But readers might ask if *referencing* such a lexicon is the same as sharing the idealism of such a vocabulary. For McGirr,

---

16   Dominique Hecq, "Writing the Unconscious: Psychoanalysis for the Creative Writer", *Text* 12, no. 2 (October 2008). http://www.textjournal.com.au/oct08/hecq.htm.
17   Kristeva, *Powers of Horror*, 207.

> [I]t is enthralling to see a writer blunting the sharp edge of contemporary culture with such a hard stone as intelligent theology, which is a very different beast from the self-righteous mush that generally gets passed off as the religious contribution to public debate.[19]

The reviewer (like Ort) maintains his sense of the content-ful nature of theological debates, as distinguished by intelligence, by firmness of purpose, as opposed to "self-righteous mush". Meaning-making as still possible.

However, the ending of *Eyrie* has left many readers gasping with frustration at its apparent refusal to resolve any kind of meaning. How do we read the ambiguity of that final image? Keely, sprawled on the pavement after his thwarted pursuit of the thug:

> So many people. Coming. Surging in, a gathering flock of heads and legs. Whatever it was out there on the road, whatever had happened at the kerb, it was waiting for him, just within reach. He swam the hot air, reaching, clawing the breeze towards the flare of turning faces, open mouths, buffeting against the empty space of morning, puzzled, happy, still reaching. (423)

Meaning – "[w]hatever it was . . . whatever had happened" – is either just within reach, or just out of reach. "Reaching" for it is what is emphasised, but we are left not able to ascertain whether such falling, and such reaching, is ridiculous or heroic, abject or salvific. Chapter 3 of this volume explores further these tropes of falling, with particular emphasis on the notion of "fallenness". But here, at the end of *Eyrie*, the reader is teased by the possibility of meaning-making, asking whether Keely's pursuit of the thug, his risking himself for others, throws him further into abjection, or whether it buoys him, filling "the empty space of morning" with some significance beyond his own solitary dejection. Perhaps what is most perplexing, for this reader at least, is trying to decide whether the double potential of words – of making meaning, or recognition of the vertiginous ambiguity of human endeavours – is somehow held together by Winton, as Keely lies sprawled but well at the close of *Eyrie*, "puzzled, happy, still reaching". And if so, what does such a double vision of words, and their relationship to the worlds of the characters, suggest?

---

18   Michael McGirr, "Great Leap of Faith," review of *Eyrie* by Tim Winton, *Sydney Morning Herald*, 2 November 2013. http://tinyurl.com/McGirr2013.
19   McGirr, "Great Leap of Faith".

2
"To Solicit a Becoming": Masculine and Feminine in the Fiction of Winton

> Desire is therefore neither the appetite for satisfaction, nor the demand for love, but the difference that results from the subtraction of the first from the second.—Jacques Lacan, *Ecrits*[1]

What happens when myths of identity – of what it means to be feminine and masculine, human and other than human – and their varying understandings of desire confront contemporary social changes? One set of answers might be found in Tim Winton's *The Riders* (1994), *Breath* (2008), or his short-story collection *The Turning* (2004). But already, in Winton's two earliest novels, *An Open Swimmer* (1982) and *Shallows* (1984), desire, the difference between individual satisfaction and love, prickles through Winton's writing and motivates his characters. This difference is represented in the first pages of *An Open Swimmer* as "a long fight between Jerra Nilsam and the fish" comes to an end.[2] The boy has captured the turrum, which lies grunting, "clenching and unclenching" (1) on the bottom of the boat, its mate the black diamond cruising beside the vessel. Jerra's dad is satisfied, proud of the boy and his manly conquest, but Jerra is torn:

> Bashing. It was bashing the gunwhale. The fish buckled up, almost out of the boat. He fell on it, hugging, feeling the fin spikes in his chest. With a spastic twitch it deflated, mumbling.
> "It's dead," his father said.
> He let it go and sat up with glistening scales on his chest and glistenings on his cheeks.
> He looked over the side. The diamond had gone.
> "Want to open it up for the pearl?"
> "No."
> "It might have one."
> "I don't want to cut him up, Dad."
> He wished they had a bigger engine and that the fish would be alive again. (1–2)

---

1 Jacques Lacan, *Ecrits: A Selection* (Hoboken, London: Taylor & Francis, 2001), 287.
2 Tim Winton, *An Open Swimmer* (Sydney: Allen & Unwin, 1982), 1. All subsequent references are to this edition and appear in parentheses in the text.

With childlike short sentences and sensual observation, the passage is told partly from the boy's perspective, as he becomes part fish, "glistening scales on his chest and glistenings on his cheeks". Jerra, "hugging, feeling the fin spikes", is both captor and fellow victim. The passage offers an understanding of the "manliness" of the boy's feat, but also his anguish: "'I don't want to cut him up, Dad'". Given the opportunity to verify the myth of the pearl inside the fish, the boy pulls back. He wishes that the fish "be alive again", and for himself to be elsewhere.

The jagged, unsatisfactory journey towards manhood, and the myths that hover around a boy becoming a man, are explored throughout Winton's oeuvre. Across the 1970s, 1980s and 1990s, the same period in which Winton was building his writing career, feminists were seeking to expose and deconstruct prevalent patriarchal myths of gender: woman as castrating *vagina dentata*; or contradictorily, as submissive and domestic angel of the house; or woman as the sexual corruptor (harlot or seductress); or as mystery, other, the unspeakable. Sometimes, more dangerous because more subtle, woman is represented as the shadow of man, a warped copy, or "not quite right" version, derived from Adam's rib. There is no single ideological thread to these long myths of gender, except that they stand twinned to the equally mythical constructions of male status – as sovereign, self-sufficient, physically and intellectually supreme, and as ruler over their dominions. Jerra, holding the glistening fish, not wishing to see its body cut, daubed by its glistenings, is a palpable figure complicating and questioning such claims to domination and dominion.

But myths remain, influencing even the best of alternative intentions, working as they do at unconscious levels. Polarised, binary approaches to gender identity continue to emerge in essentialist criticism: "Women aren't like that!" "Boys will be boys." "Men are from Mars, women from Venus." Feminist myth-making (patriarchal monsters, Amazons, superwomen) had its politically strategic uses in the early days of second-wave feminism, but these static notions of identity do not any longer acknowledge the multifariousness of current gender struggles and debates.

The Riders and the Terror of Identity

Contemporary discourses about identity seek ways to resist fixed or essentialist boundaries of self and other, with many points along the spectrum: male, female, animal, human, more than human. Judith Butler, for example, argues in her 2004 essay for a place beyond such static boundaries, where self and other lose their hard lines. She writes of self and other in the context of grief and loss:

> [W]e cannot represent ourselves as merely bounded beings, for the primary others who are past for me not only live on in the fiber of the boundary that contains me (one meaning of "incorporation"), but they also haunt the way I am, as it were, periodically undone and open to becoming unbounded.[3]

We might fruitfully read Winton's *The Riders* in relation to this ontological approach, seeing the traumatising disappearance of Jennifer, the female other, as the very space

---

3   Judith Butler, *Precarious Life: The Powers of Mourning and Violence* (New York and London: Verso, 2004), 17.

through which Scully must pass, as he struggles to salvage and re-form his identity; and reading Jennifer's absenting of herself as part of the same unfixing. As the terror of what is happening to Scully first begins to dawn on him, that his wife has disappeared, and probably through choice, Winton writes the early sections of the novel, Scully's unmanning, in a series of objective correlatives that powerfully mimic the frozenness of the man, his incomprehension of the situation by any of his known parameters. The narrative deftly builds the sense of terror and haunting that is creeping over him:

> The sun was gone before four o'clock. Scully found himself out behind the barn in a strange cold stillness looking at the great pile of refuse he'd hauled out there on his first day . . . a slag heap, a formless blotch here at his feet. In the spring, he decided, he'd dig up this bit of ground and plant leeks and cabbage, and make something of it. Oh, there were things to be done, alright. He just had to get through tonight and the rest of his life would proceed.[4]

What does such an externalised description of inner turmoil elicit from readers? We might empathise with Scully's need to mend, build and control, in the face of the powerlessness and vulnerability that come, surely, at such a moment. As Scully seeks to mend the brokenness of his life, to reassert his known boundaries, to do what he has always done, what is also evident is that Scully is an ingénue, inadequate, or uncomprehending in the face of the grief that is pouring over him like the "strange, cold stillness". The need to build, grow, provide, "make something of it", "to get through tonight", might be identified as masculine qualities of control and order; or they could equally be seen as feminine, domestic traits: Scully, the father and stay-at-home dad, nurturing, helping, soothing, providing safety for his child. Or, might they not be read at the very border of self-containment described by Butler, where loss undoes human borders, producing an openness to becoming? In this latter frame, Scully's is the same kind of quest on which Jennifer, presumably, has started out. This is Butler's notion of the unfixing of identity, akin to Julia Kristeva's state of abjection, examined in the introduction to this volume.

However, critics of *The Riders* were sometimes perplexed. Seemingly uninterested in complex ontology, Nicolle Flint, in a 2013 essay entitled "Misogyny Lurks in Winton's World of Fiction", writes, in the first instance, in relation to *Dirt Music* (2001) and then to a range of other Winton novels:

> [T]he moment I became bothered by Winton's portrayal of female characters was when the Miles Franklin Award-winning *Dirt Music*'s tough and capable Georgie Jutland inherited a sailing boat from her father, and, instead of setting sail to find her missing lover Lu, sold the boat, returned to Lu's house, and cleaned it. I did not expect Georgie, the talented nurse and lifelong sailor, to sit around cooking and cleaning. I expected her to get on that boat, to find the hapless Lu, save him from himself and live happily ever after. But, of course, that would have meant Jim, Georgie's partner on whom she is cheating with Lu, could not forcibly deliver her to Lu so that he and Lu could deliver absolution to one another. As his men do . . . [just as] *Cloudstreet*, another Miles Franklin

---

4 Tim Winton, *The Riders* (Sydney: Macmillan, 1994), 98. All subsequent references are to this edition and appear in parentheses in the text.

Award-winner and the novel that made Winton's career, presents the classic Madonna-whore, saintly-mother-versus-fallen-woman stereotype.[5]

When a critic describes the characterisations in a novel as "stereotyping", it is always good to ask whose stereotyping we are dealing with. How critics see characterisation in a novel – as realistic, shaped by the cultural context to which the characters belong; as stereotyping, archetypical, hyperreal – may well be influenced heavily by the methodological questions that inevitably circle around ontology: do we think first (and perhaps *only*) in polarities of male and female, in regard to ontology? Or do we look at and along the spectrum of gendered and human being? Do we employ "the human"? For understandable, political reasons we might well bring strong poles of male and female, masculine and feminine to bear in our readings, especially if we decide that the author is consciously or unconsciously reflecting such polarised representations. However, with Butler we might ask how fixed such terms are in a novel, and also in our own ontology. What happens if we open up to Butler's less bounded, less fixed notions of identity, and go on to read *for* such mobility of representation?

A worried critic of *The Riders*, Pilar Baines Alarcos, summarises her argument in the following way:

> Although the ending promotes the integration of the culturally constructed masculine and feminine qualities as personified in the character of Billie, this does not serve to erase the negative images that have been ascribed to Jennifer and Irma from the very beginning. Therefore, it can be said that *The Riders* contributes to spreading deep-rooted conceptions of women that go against the pluralism of contemporary female roles.[6]

Alarcos' essay has taken the novel's representations of women to be negative forms of myth-making, describing the figures of Jennifer and Irma as stereotypes of the castrating and the needy woman, respectively. Jennifer's absence and silence in the novel are read by Alarcos through a general feminist approach that sees women's silences as patriarchally ordained:

> Another stereotypical way of presenting Jennifer is by not allowing her to speak. She does not really appear in the novel. We only know her through the focalization and the memories of other characters, mainly Scully.[7]

Such an approach carries a number of assumptions that remain vague in this critical essay, but which nevertheless shape the argument. For Baines Alarcos these assumptions circle around who, in relation to the novel, is to be held accountable for such putatively negative mythologising: Scully? Winton? The novel? Winton ventriloquising through Scully? Patriarchy? The critic gestures to all of these possibilities, softening her argument only at

---

5   Nicolle Flint, "Misogyny Lurks in Winton's World of Fiction", *Age*, 1 August 2013, http://tinyurl.com/Flint2013.
6   M. Pilar Baines Alarcos, "She Lures, She Guides, She Quits: Female Characters in Tim Winton's *The Riders*", *Journal of English Studies*, 8 (2010): 20–1.
7   Baines Alarcos, "She Lures, She Guides", 15.

the end when she argues that the child Billie is something of a redemptive presence, an "integration of the culturally constructed masculine and feminine qualities".[8]

The critical question of who is accountable for such mythologising is, arguably, not really answerable, although a number of critics of *The Riders* are quite clear that it is "Winton" who is culpable. For Flint, again:

> What remains most remarkable about Tim Winton's writing, in the context of ongoing allegations of sexism and misogyny, is that the literary left leaves the handiwork of one of our most revered cultural icons unexamined. "Sometimes," as Bob Dylan once sang, "the silence can be like thunder".[9]

Readers' love and embrace of Winton is one response to Flint's accusation of unexamined silence, unless of course "readers" and "the literary left" are considered mutually exclusive categories (as Flint seems to think). It is important, however, to press a bit harder in our reading of *The Riders*, asking whose myths and stereotypes – if this is what they are – we (readers, left-leaning types, and others) are dealing with. With *The Riders*, is it sufficient merely to conflate Scully's musings, and his responses to his wife's desertion, with Winton's conscious or unconscious position, even conceding that "Winton" could be distilled to a single, homogenous entity? Surely we need to ask how the focalisation through Scully operates, and what kinds of masculinity are represented in his character. How trustworthy a narrator is Scully in his approaches to the feminine, embodied for him by Jennifer? How do the interventions of Billie in the novel temper readers' responses to her father, and to the driven nature of Scully's impossible journey to recapture his wife?

Beyond questions of narrative voice, stereotyping and representation, what can be said about *The Riders* and its social and historical contexts of production, and future readership? What were the major aspects of feminism, and the emerging roles of men and women in Australian and global cultures, in 1994 when *The Riders* was published? What were the new possibilities being generated for gender relations, and for the manifestations of desire, across this period? How does this novel reflect and/or intervene in the debates around such relations? The broadest questions of all, reflecting on feminist methodologies and future-oriented ontologies of gender, might be something like: how do we as readers weigh up the literary evaluations of individual voice and characterisation in the novel, in relation to broader, changing gender debates, including new, emerging mythologies of gender?

In some feminist approaches, the distinction between stereotyping mythologies on the one hand, and the historical depiction of the characters' struggles to emerge and rise towards something new, to move into the future, is not engaged with adequately. If in the early 1990s new formations of gender, in relation to heterosexuality, gay sexuality, marriage, monogamy, parenting, and multiple versions of all these, were being negotiated in often highly volatile debates, why is it that some critics seem to require not a representation of such struggles but an already *solved* version of gender relations? That is, why is an already idealised set of demands and judgements made, rather than an analysis of representations of the ongoing struggles?

---

8 Baines Alarcos, "She Lures, She Guides", 15.
9 Flint, "Misogyny Lurks".

The pain of seeking to emerge into mobile, less fixed gendered identity, and human identity more broadly, however fixed or unbounded in concept we see them to be, is a central concern in many of Winton's novels and short stories. The sometimes brutal physical consequences of such emergence can be seen in *The Riders*, but also, for example, in a number of stories in *The Turning*, as failed sexual relations are represented through characters who experience violence and deep trauma.

Melancholy Men: *The Turning* and *The Riders*

South African critic Bridget Grogan, in her discussion of *The Turning*, argues that the struggle to emerge into identity often involves the reoccurrence of past pain, and experiences of loss and mourning. Grogan's is very different to Flint's approach, in its response to Winton's representations of gender and the ways in which both men and women struggle to move beyond the stereotypes and myths which can be seen to have shaped them. She writes:

> Like the narrator of "Big World" [in *The Turning*], at their most complete and tender Winton's men embrace transience and the inevitable loss this entails; simultaneously, they acknowledge the wide beauty of the temporal world and the love of and for others that is both impermanent and yet eternal . . .[10]

The recognition of beauty and transience and love of the other might, in older, polarising discourses, be equated with femininity, but they are certainly characteristics shared by many of Winton's male characters, as Grogan argues.

Similarly, Butler writes about the recognition, in love, of the other. Often, individual *and* corporate loss in the struggle for self-identity is seen as the key to such love of the other. Such ethics are informed by a psychoanalytic approach to relations between lovers, between selves and others, be they male to female, female to female, or moving across a changing spectrum. Butler writes:

> When we lose some of these ties by which we are constituted, we do not know who we are or what to do. On one level, I think I have lost "you" only to discover that "I" have gone missing as well. At another level, perhaps what I have lost "in" you, that for which I have no ready vocabulary, is a relationality that is neither merely myself nor you, but the tie by which those terms are differentiated and related.[11]

This description of loss of other and accompanying loss of self powerfully illuminates the core understandings of gender in *The Riders*. It does this by unfastening the over-simple critical hierarchy of patriarchal male/silenced female. Instead, the experience of pain in loss is seen to undo the identity of the one left behind, to plunge him into a grief in which both the one who is gone and the one who is in mourning are understood to lose selfhood,

---

10 Bridget Grogan, "The Cycle of Love and Loss: Melancholic Masculinity in *The Turning*", in *Tim Winton: Critical Essays*, eds. Lyn McCredden and Nathanael O'Reilly (Perth: UWA Publishing, 2014), 217.
11 Butler, *Precarious Life*, 12.

to "go missing". If we think about Butler's main contention, placing it in relation to *The Riders*, we might want to pursue a more nuanced, more troubling thread of the struggle between self and other, and about the nature of desire and gendered identity. Both Jennifer and Scully are travelling away from any fixed or safe understanding of self, whether they want to or not. Jennifer is portrayed through silence, but she has taken powerful steps in liberating herself from the known in her life, from motherhood, marriage, intimacy with Scully. Rather than simply judging her as immoral or irresponsible, the novel's fictive proposal is to read her, and Scully, through the power dynamics of the relationship they once had, understood through Scully's grief and his half-demented journey across Europe, as well as his growing self-knowledge that he has been dependent on Jennifer for his own identity. As Scully reels from the events unfolding for him, he is both grieving his past and speaking into the void of the future. As Butler puts it, the story we tell in the midst of grief is wild, abandoned, inchoate; and this seems an accurate description of Scully's narration. Butler writes further:

> I might try to tell a story here, about what I am feeling, but it would have to be a story in which the very "I" who seeks to tell the story is stopped in the midst of the telling; the very "I" is called into question by its relation to the Other, a relation that does not precisely reduce me to speechlessness, but does nevertheless clutter my speech with signs of its undoing. I tell a story about the relations I choose, only to expose, somewhere along the way, the way I am gripped and undone by these very relations. My narrative falters, as it must.
> Let's face it. We're undone by each other. And if we're not, we're missing something.
> This seems so clearly the case with grief, but it can be so only because it was already the case with desire.[12]

The faltering narratives of desire have formed Scully and Jennifer from the beginning of their relationship, unmanning and re-manning him, shaping her narrative in ways the novel only hints at. At the opening of the novel, before Scully knows what is about to descend on him, Pete and Scully work companionably, repairing the derelict Irish cottage in readiness for the longed-for arrival of Jennifer and Billie. Pete asks about how the couple met, and how they came to leave Australia for Ireland:

> "Whose idea was it?"
> "Hers, I spose."
> "And you followed."
> "I was game for a change, yeah. I didn't exactly follow."
> "Used to be the women who followed."
> Scully laughed but it stung somehow. Admit it, Scully, he thought. You followed, you'd follow her anywhere. A few weeks ago you couldn't sleep for dreams of home, of hot white beaches . . . you turned on a penny for her sake. On a queer feeling, a thing she couldn't explain, just to see her happy.
> "Well, maybe it's our turn to follow anyway," he said.
> "Mebbe so. I don't know about women . . ." (40–1)

---

12 Butler, *Precarious Life*, 13.

Scully thinks often of how he is "in thrall" to his wife, how she draws him and rewrites the story of their life together, causing him to turn "on a penny" for her. Until now, he has been willing to turn, follow, work for her. But there is loss in his desire already, a giving up of those "hot white beaches" of home, in adopting a migratory life, working slavishly to prepare the new place. Winton writes a narrative of desire that involves both sheer commitment and being "stung", unmanned, directed by another. Away from his native home, and from the slowly forming comforts of the old cottage, Scully is drawn into Europe as his fate hovers, still unknown.

A first step occurs on his walk one day into the Irish landscape and through the Norman castle ruins and the "rubble-strewn pit of the great hall", where "[e]verything had fallen through onto everything else. Great oak beams lay like fallen masts and rigging across cattle bones and tons of cellar bricks" (49–50). The novel here is presaging the abject, nightmarish journey of desire into Europe that Scully is about to undertake, that he is already impelled towards. Hence, Scully's first, mysterious encounter with the unknown riders comes at a moment of rising anxiety and desire, the night before he is hoping to reunite with Jennifer and Billie:

> Scully moved between the riders, all but touching the heaving, rancid flanks of their mounts. Some of the horses had black, congealed wounds on their chests, and they looked as tired and cold and dazed as their riders. Some were boys, their scrawny legs bare and stippled with gooseflesh. And how they craned their necks, these riders. It was as though any moment some great and terrible event would explode upon them, as if something, someone up there could set them in motion ... He felt himself craning, waiting, almost failing to breathe ... His feet took root in the ground as they continued to wait and he waited with them. It was true, he knew it, something was about to happen.
>
> But the awful stillness went on. (81)

Little has been written about the symbolic identity of the riders, these eponymous figures who appear in the night, in Scully's moments of wildest anxiety. They are, obviously, figures of the ancient past, warriors coming from savage scenes of battle, wounded boys and men, prophetic presences, but signifying what? As so often with *The Riders*, the figures act as objective correlatives of Scully's terror. They are European, warrior figures from a world and time that Scully doesn't know. They are both threatened themselves, and terrifying to Scully. This ambiguity in what they signify is partly because of their wild, unknown identity, seemingly from a world beyond the known, civilised, Christian safety of Scully's acquaintance, rearing up in a landscape which is not his own. They also embody, psychologically, the terrible, rushing, oncoming events of Scully's life beyond his control. And they are men, and boys, savaged by the violence of their initiation into the masculine traumas of war.

Anthropologist Susan Greenwood has written of the prolific, pan-European myth of "the Wild Hunt", to which the riders in this novel seem affiliated. Amongst the related myths and heroes of the Wild Hunt, led sometimes by men and sometimes by women in different narratives, are the Germanic god of the wind and the dead, Woden, the goddess Freya, and the Irish mythical hunter Fionn mac Cumhaill, or Finn MacCool, whose son was Oisín. Greenwood writes:

> As far as practitioners of nature spiritualities are concerned, the Wild Hunt offers an initiation into the wild and an opening up of the senses; a sense of dissolution of self in confrontation with fear and death, an exposure to a "whirlwind pulse that runs through life". In short, engagement with the Hunt is a bid to restore a reciprocity and harmony between humans and nature.[13]

A wild hunt is exactly what Scully is about to embark on, though he doesn't rationally know it yet. However, *The Riders* both broadens and intensifies the significance of the wild hunt motif, embracing psychological, material and ontological concerns. The novel's deployment of a long series of sensual, objective correlatives for Scully's inner turmoil brings into focus the material and natural world, particularly in Scully's work on the old cottage, but also in his moving between such different, lived environments, along with a probing of the psychological workings of desire and identity formation. The terror they draw out in Scully, "a sense of dissolution of self in confrontation with fear and death", is close to the kind of undoing of self which Butler has been writing about, when the self is "periodically undone and open to becoming unbounded".

A coruscating series of emotional undoings characterises Scully's quest for Jennifer through Europe. Throughout, it is "desire" which characterises his search, desire as longing and loss. As he journeys, unable to grasp what is happening, what he wants, where he should be, his narrative becomes more and more unknowing, haunted, faltering. "Of course she left you – there's nothing *to* you" (167), he concludes during his drunken night-time swim in Hydra. In the early encounter with the riders, in the European journey, and in the final scene of the novel, Scully's ego is opened up to threat, change, unknowing. Again, Butler's description of the formation of the self in trauma is pertinent:

> I may wish to reconstitute my "self" as if it were there all along, a tacit ego with acumen from the start; but to do so would be to deny the various forms of rapture and subjection that formed the condition of my emergence as an individuated being and that continue to haunt my adult sense of self with whatever anxiety and longing I may now feel. Individuation is an accomplishment, not a presupposition, and certainly no guarantee.[14]

This insight is equally pertinent to the individual psychology, and more broadly ontological. It posits at a general level the continuous formation and deformation of self, and highlights the interaction of desire in the processes of identity formation. Both desire and identity are, for Butler, a struggle that never ceases, the putative, tentative telos rather than the "presupposition" of human existence.

---

13 Susan Greenwood, "The Wild Hunt: A Mythological Language of Magic", in *Handbook of Contemporary Paganism*, ed. James R. Lewis and Murphy Pizza (Leiden, The Netherlands: Brill, 2008), 220.
14 Butler, *Precarious Life*, 16.

Breath: Grief and Dancing and Becoming a Man

The Riders is, at all these levels, testing out this volatile account of desire and gender identity. However, perhaps no Winton novel stresses the struggle of desire, identity-forming and sexuality more dramatically than *Breath* (2008). This is in part because of the controversial sexual relationship between the young boy of fifteen, Pikelet, and the older, more jaded and hurt female character, Eva.

In the introduction to this volume, *Breath* is discussed partly in theological terms, as a fictive inquiry into "fallenness". Certainly, some readers and critics are morally, ethically or religiously disconcerted by the nature of Pikelet and Eva's sexual relationship, because of Pikelet's age, and/or because of the erotic asphyxiation practices involved in their sex acts. The opening scenes of the novel, involving the death of a young man through auto-erotic asphyxiation, set the context of loss in desire, and grieving for the lost boy who was about to enter manhood. The novel is concerned with this moment of transition, and about what levels of loss are involved in it, as "Sando's wide-eyed disciples" take on prototypical, and some atypical, manhood challenges:

> [H]e was training us to go to sea, to leap from the cliffs in a storm swell and put ourselves in harm's way . . . At that age we were physically undeveloped, too small to safely manage what we set out to do . . . We could have been staying back at school as army cadets, learning to fire mortars and machine-guns, to lay booby traps and to kill strangers in hand-to-hand combat like other boys we knew, in preparation for a manhood that could barely credit the end of the war in Vietnam. Sando appealed to one set of boyish fantasies and the state exploited others . . .[15]

The boundaries of manly initiation in the boys' world stretch from following Sando, the surfing guru, and all the bravery and derring-do this involves, to being formed by the state in the preparations and skills of warfare. Between these forces, and the engagement of Pikelet in sexual adventure with Queenie Cookson, and then more seriously with Eva, the boys move towards manhood and their masculine identities. Such options, usually narrow in a quiet Australian beach town in the early 1970s, have indelible effects on the different lives of Pikelet and Looney. Between the two boys, and in relation to the ways they develop their different identities, there is love, rivalry, daring, jealousy, and a desire to exceed the choices they were offered. Surfing offered something different:

> We talked about skill and courage and luck – we shared all that, and in time we surfed to fool with death – but for me there was still the outlaw feeling of doing something graceful, as if dancing on water was the best and bravest thing a man could do. (29)

The retrospective nature of this narrative adds to the paradoxes of this struggle that is never finished, the entry into adulthood, with its manly "skill and courage and luck"; but also with its putatively "feminine" aspects of "doing something graceful", of "dancing on water". The desire both to establish identity and to enter again and again into the processes of becoming, processes that are never completed, mark this novel. For Pikelet in particular,

---

15 Tim Winton, *Breath* (Melbourne: Penguin, 2008), 106. All subsequent references are to this edition and appear in parentheses in the text.

such processes are fuelled by a restless desire to be recognised as different. What each boy is craving at first is recognition by the manly hero, Sando, and to be distinct from their small community of

> local footballers with a nice leap and a tidy torpedo punt ... and those old coves with plastic teeth and necks like turtles who got pissed on Anzac Day and sang sad songs on the verandah of the Riverside before they passed out. (28)

For Butler, identity formation means that

> [t]o ask for recognition, or to offer it, is precisely not to ask for recognition for what one already is. It is to solicit a becoming, to instigate a transformation, to petition the future always in relation to the Other. It is also to stake one's own being, and one's own persistence in one's own being, in the struggle for recognition.[16]

The older Bruce Pike, telling his retrospective story, is haunted by unfinished things, by his own unfinished becoming, fuelled by his childhood friend Looney's violent and futile death, "shot in a bar in Rosarito, not far from Tijuana" (257); by echoes of Eva and Sando and their separate fates; and the loss of his own marriage and family; the ghost of his former self, aloft on the waves, "graceful, as if dancing on water"; and his melancholic, overwhelming, but warily forgiving philosophy that "[p]eople are fools, not monsters" (211). The struggle for recognition – between self and other, male and female, father and child – may be a process open to becoming, a process experienced as loss and failure, but also awash with continuing, motivating desire. The novel's last image is of Bruce, the ageing father, still longing to be recognised by his daughters:

> [I]t's important for me to show them that their father is a man who dances – who saves lives and carries the wounded, yes, but who also does something completely pointless and beautiful, and in this at least he should need no explanation. (265)

However, ethical questions and their possible answers or explanations do continue to circle in *Breath*. In the process of becoming, fifteen-year-old Pikelet learns about the sheer rapture – "exalted, invincible, angelic" (234) – of sex with Eva, and also its darkness. Through the desperate need to forget and to feel bodily pleasure, Eva, and then Pikelet, also experience their becoming as "squalid beyond imagining" (234). But the novel's narrative has space for pity, and an understanding of why Eva, injured, broken and unable to become what she desired, reaches out, *in extremis*, for comfort. Not monstrous, but foolish.

Finally, an ethics akin to Butler's Hegelian theory of becoming *in extremis* may be read in *Breath*. Butler's discourse on grief in the relationship of self to other

> may be understood as the slow process by which we develop a point of identification with suffering itself. The disorientation of grief – "Who have I become?" or, indeed, "What is left of me?" "What is it in the Other that I have lost?" – posits the "I" in the mode of unknowingness.[17]

---

16   Butler, *Precarious Life*, 31.
17   Butler, *Precarious Life*, 19.

Grief and its role in becoming, its production of "unknowingness" rather than rigid boundaries, is reworked as productive by Butler, and this too might be argued of *Breath* and its representation of grief. Pikelet, the partly willing, partly revolted participant in Eva's erotic asphyxiation practices, learns to dissimulate the strangling she requires:

> When she wanted me to choke her I learnt that I could brace myself on my elbows, give her a sense of my body on hers, without letting my full weight down. When I held her throat I made all the noise of exertion while applying less and less pressure . . . I held my palms over her neck and asked her could she feel it, could she feel it, and she could because she expected it . . . and I hovered, palms down, like some kind of boy-shaman, willing life into her, holding off the shivering darkness. (235)

This scene, its horror partly deflected by Pikelet's sense of its ludicrousness, the dog snapping at him in protection of Eva, his mixture of lust and revulsion, is nevertheless a limit point for Butler's theory of reciprocity between self and other in their desire for recognition. Butler began *Precarious Life* seeking positive discourses about grief and identity. She argues

> that each, in a different way, is compelled by the same need, the same requirement. This means that we are not separate identities in the struggle for recognition but are already involved in a reciprocal exchange . . .[18]

This is an ethical position of high order, but in the scene from *Breath*, above, we are confronted with an earthy, embodied playing out of such ethics. Pikelet is indeed solicitous of Eva's safety, but such care is depicted as equally about self-survival:

> I certainly didn't want to be the patsy left behind, the fool calling the ambulance, the one whose fingerprints were up and down her neck like hickeys (234)

Pikelet is teaching himself techniques of deception, recognising the fantasy, the simulation of intimacy, and in this he has "come to resent Eva Sanderson" (234).

However, the pathetic image that Pikelet discloses of himself as "some kind of boy-shaman", reverberates ambivalently here. As mentioned in the introduction, this is of course what Bruce Pike will become: a shaman professionally dispensing care to strangers, bringing them back to life with his techniques. His boyhood experiences of confronting death with Eva, his addiction to "scaring the shit out of myself since primary school" (234), lead him to his melancholic, thrilling work. Winton's fiction does what Butler's ethics only theoretically guess at. His novels give us a nuanced, shifting, ambivalent sense of how, in relation to others, the self becomes. Reverberating strongly with the ethics of *Breath*, Butler's thesis is set out clearly at the beginning of *Precarious Life*:

> I find that my very formation implicates the other in me, that my own foreignness to myself is, paradoxically, the source of my ethical connection with others. I am not fully known to myself, because part of what I am is the enigmatic traces of others. In this sense, I cannot know myself perfectly or know my "difference" from others in an irreducible

---

18 Butler, *Precarious Life*, 31.

way ... I am wounded, and I find that the wound itself testifies to the fact that I am impressionable, given over to the Other in ways that I cannot fully predict or control. I cannot think the question of responsibility alone, in isolation from the Other; if I do, I have taken myself out of the relational bind that frames the problem of responsibility from the start.[19]

What does Pikelet learn, about manhood, relations between genders, about being human, in his becoming a man? He does learn that woundedness is the stamp of selfhood, that humans are more fools than monsters, that responsibility is shared between self and other. But part of Bruce Pike's woundedness is his coming to understand the real consequences of isolation and deception among individuals. And he certainly stands, along with *Eyrie*'s Tom Keely, as a figure of "foreignness to myself". However, whether foreignness to self leads to a relational ethics, or whether, in many cases, it leads to a more grievous loss of self and relation, is an open question in *Breath*. The insights of Butler's ethics flicker in and out, in relation to *Breath*.

Where Butler's ethical thesis does illuminate current debates about gendered identities, and the limits of the human, is in considering the force and rhythms of becoming female, becoming male, and all in between and beyond. To read *Breath* simply as misogynistic, to see Eva, or even Sando, as less than fully human and as wounded, is a misreading – a misreading reliant on a false ontology, a simplistic, static understanding of identity formation. Feminism in the new millennium is alive to the shifting, myth-drenched mysteries of becoming and identity. It rightly measures and evaluates the political rigidities we have to work through, but it also, at its best, endeavours not to pitilessly replicate such rigidities.

---

19   Butler, *Precarious Life*, 32–3.

3
Falling

In Breughel's Icarus, for instance: how everything turns away
Quite leisurely from the disaster; the ploughman may
Have heard the splash, the forsaken cry,
But for him it was not an important failure; the sun shone
As it had to on the white legs disappearing into the green
Water, and the expensive delicate ship that must have seen
Something amazing, a boy falling out of the sky,
Had somewhere to get to and sailed calmly on.
   —W. H. Auden, "Musée des Beaux Arts"[1]

Falling
is the given, rising
the flame to which we cling
one yes after the windfall of *no*.

Like other bodies, ours
will obtain a height, but the question
remains, whether

by gliding down or by leaping and grasping
   —Philip Pardi, "Seventeen Wings", Part 1[2]

Neither "falling" nor "fallenness" appears in the list of entries or index of the *Routledge Encyclopaedia of Narrative Theory*.[3] Despite the (not exclusively) technical emphasis of the volume, this seems a strange fact, in that narratives of falling as physical or metaphysical

---

Small sections of this chapter have been adapted from Lyn McCredden, "The Quality of Mercy" (review of *Eyrie* by Tim Winton) in *Sydney Review of Books*, 6 December 2013.

1   W. H. Auden, "Musée des Beaux Arts," *Collected Poems* (New York: Random House, 1976), 179.
2   Philip Pardi, "Seventeen Wings," *Meditations on Rising and Falling* (Madison: University of Wisconsin Press, 2008), 67.

trope, and sometimes in relation to narratives of redemption or rebirth of the fallen, have informed the trajectories of so many narratives since the days of Adam and Eve, and of Sisyphus. Falling, as trope and as narrative pivot, snakes through Tim Winton's oeuvre. Through accident or choice, heroism or cowardice or necessity, many Winton characters fall from their former or longed-for status: from childhood into adulthood, from security into grievous loss, from a state of happiness or innocence to one experienced as guilt or alienation. While Chapter 4 of this book focuses on the leitmotif of redemption in Winton's fiction, the current chapter will examine the complex trope of falling, both bodily and metaphysical falling, the event or condition that precedes the possibility of redemption.

For Auden's Icarus, in his famous 1938 poem "Musée des Beaux Arts", falling is the result of human action, possibly presumptuous, prideful action fuelled by the desire to join or outwit the gods. Auden registers Icarus' fall as "something amazing", lamenting the indignity and bathos in "the splash, the forsaken cry". There is poignancy registered as the speaker witnesses those "white legs disappearing into the green / Water". But overwhelmingly, Auden places the fall within a longer historical frame, as one of so many half-noticed accidents. Similarly, for North American poet Philip Pardi, falling is part of "the given", the common human condition: "Like other bodies, ours". But it is also related for Pardi to choice and action, the poem's open question: does falling involve a downward gliding from above, from some place of plenitude or grace, or does it spring from human agency, from acts – violent or creative – of "leaping and grasping"? Both poets employ falling as physical *and* existential, asking how falling is inflected by questions of "the fall", of spiritual failure and possible punishment.

For Julia Kristeva, in her essay *Powers of Horror*, the fall of the human is inextricably implicated in her meditations on death:

> The corpse (or cadaver: cadere, to fall), that which has irremediably come a cropper, is cesspool, and death; it upsets even more violently the one who confronts it as fragile and fallacious chance. A wound with blood and pus, or the sickly, acrid smell of sweat, of decay, does not signify death. In the presence of signified death – a flat encephalograph, for instance – I would understand, react, or accept. No, as in true theater, without makeup or masks, refuse and corpses show me what I permanently thrust aside in order to live. These body fluids, this defilement, this shit are what life withstands, hardly and with difficulty, on the part of death. There, I am at the border of my condition as a living being. My body extricates itself, as being alive, from that border. Such wastes drop so that I might live, until, from loss to loss, nothing remains in me and my entire body falls beyond the limit – cadere, cadaver.[4]

In Kristeva's theoretical meditation on human fallenness, abjection plays a key role. Her essay visits different Jewish and Christian biblical accounts of the fall, and of human sinfulness, including the primary theft from the tree of knowledge, against the edicts of God. The punishment for such sin, in Jewish and Christian accounts, is a constant awareness of human mortality. The theft of the fruit of the knowledge of good and evil,

---

[3] David Herman, Manfred Jahn and Marie-Laure Ryan (eds), *Routledge Encyclopedia of Narrative Theory* (London and New York: Routledge, 2005).
[4] Julia Kristeva, *The Powers of Horror: An Essay on Abjection*, trans. Leon S. Roudiez (New York: Columbia University Press, 1982), 3.

with its attempt to be equal in knowledge to God, means that humans are punished with the very condition they lusted after: a constant knowledge of what they are and what they are bound towards. They know they are mortal, and will one day concede to death, when "my entire body falls beyond the limit". Hence the process of repression, the attempt at forgetting all that "I permanently thrust aside in order to live". Yet the sensual, lived world is full of reminders, "[t]hese body fluids, this defilement, this shit", pointing towards failure and death.

Falling: Myth and Experience

While Winton's fiction is set squarely in the contemporary, material world, and the daily, quotidian lives of struggling families and individual characters, the trope of falling has often embraced large, existential questions of purpose and human destiny. Perhaps the most famous, early literary author of the myth of "the fall" is John Milton, and his anti-hero Satan. In the opening stanzas of *Paradise Lost*, Milton places himself as author, at least in his expressed desires, as a peer of the "Heav'nly Muse", or further, as poetically, potently able to dive from the highest to the lowest parts of creation and back, dissecting God and Satan, and that in-between state, the falling human:

> Of Man's First Disobedience, and the Fruit
> Of that Forbidden Tree, whose mortal taste
> Brought Death into the World, and all our woe,
> With loss of Eden, till one greater Man
> Restore us, and regain the blissful Seat,
> Sing Heav'nly Muse, that on the secret top
> Of Oreb, or of Sinai, didst inspire
> That Shepherd, who first taught the chosen Seed,
> In the Beginning how the Heav'ns and Earth
> Rose out of Chaos: Or if Sion Hill
> Delight thee more, and Siloa's Brook that flow'd
> Fast by the Oracle of God; I thence
> Invoke thy aid to my adventrous Song,
> That with no middle flight intends to soar
> Above th' Aonian Mount, while it pursues
> Things unattempted yet in Prose or Rhime.
> And chiefly Thou O Spirit, that dost prefer
> Before all Temples th' upright heart and pure,
> Instruct me, for Thou know'st; Thou from the first
> Wast present, and with mighty wings outspread
> Dove-like satst brooding on the vast Abyss
> And mad'st it pregnant: What in me is dark
> Illumin, what is low raise and support;
> That to the highth of this great Argument
> I may assert Eternal Providence,
> And justifie the wayes of God to men.

> Say first, for Heav'n hides nothing from thy view
> Nor the deep Tract of Hell, say first what cause
> Mov'd our Grand Parents in that happy State,
> Favour'd of Heav'n so highly, to fall off
> From thir Creator . . .[5]

Milton's poetic rendition of the fall is, of course, deeply imbued with Christian theological influence, daring to take it further into an imaginative panoply of events, causes and characters. In this poem's mighty geography, readers are taken on a tumultuous rollercoaster ride of rising and falling, the poet tracing "how the Heav'ns and Earth / Rose out of Chaos", how humanity and the dark angels fell into "the deep Tract of Hell". However, it is the speaker's own psychological geography that is unique here. We are in fact presented with a consistently double map: of human and angelic disgrace and fall; as well as the poet's own servanthood in taking of this task, but equally, his towering poetic ambition. Milton "pursues / Things unattempted yet in Prose or Rhime", calling on God to "raise and support" his endeavour, "[t]hat with no middle flight intends to soar / Above th' Aonian Mount". The poet, flying skyward to assert "Eternal Providence", must remind us of Icarus, the consequence of whose fall into the green waters doesn't seem to be countenanced by this poet and his visionary expedition. But to the contemporary ear, the mad magnificence of this mapping of heights and depths speaks ambivalently, pivoting around the surreal image of God's spirit on high who "with mighty wings outspread / Dove-like satst brooding on the vast Abyss / And mad'st it pregnant". The creation of humanity figured here as God's hatchery in the "vast abyss" might also conjure the image of trillions of little hatchlings taking flight, their destinies to be determined by that great, impregnating God.

Eyrie: Tom Keely as Falling Man

In the opening scenes of *Eyrie* (2013), protagonist Tom Keely teeters on the brink of abjection. He can do very little for himself, let alone fly in search of the gods and their knowledge. When we meet him he is defeated and ineffectual, a drug-addled and lonely one-time idealist who has fallen out of his own life. He's also arguably a haunted version of his author. While it may not be productive to hunt through the novel for autobiographical hints, relating Tom to Tim, it is interesting to note in passing that as Winton ages and accrues a sustained body of work, ghosts – failures, grief-addled losers, violent men of a certain age, young men losing their innocence – haunt his oeuvre, and are beginning to stare out at us more persistently from the pages of his novels. Arguably, *Eyrie* is a darker – and often melodramatically funny – *rewriting* of the central preoccupations of Winton's earlier novels, with their volatile, struggling male figures, rather than a work that simply erupts, bleaker than the rest of his oeuvre.

This repetition of fallenness and haunting filters across Winton's works, perhaps most directly evident in *Eyrie*, but central too in *That Eye, the Sky* (1986) and in *Cloudstreet* (1991) and *Dirt Music* (2002). These three earlier novels explore traumatic falls, through accident predominantly, and the tentative redemption of families, in ways that mirror

---

5   John Milton, *Paradise Lost*, book 1, lines 1–31. From *The Milton Reading Room*, edited by Thomas H. Luxon, http://www.dartmouth.edu/~milton.

Winton's own early family history, as he has publicly discussed it. And further, there is, in *That Eye, the Sky, Cloudstreet, The Riders* (1994), *Dirt Music, Breath* (2008) and the short-story collection *The Turning* (2004), a preoccupying motif of falling, as the narratives circle around the family as a place of putative safety and innocence; but equally, as a place from which one can fall. The novels all ask: what kind of cradle is the family? How many ways can it go wrong? How do families negotiate and buffer their members from the world? What does it mean to belong or to be excluded, to fall beyond this imaginary place of plenitude? In Winton's fiction it is hardly a cosy version of family we are given, picket fence and bland stability, but an often harrowing, volatile, scouring place of birth, multiple violences, intense love, and possible redemption.

In contrast to the grandiloquence of Milton's early seventeenth-century heaven and hell, *Eyrie* is set in "good old Freo", Winton's and Keely's home territory. It is fallen Freo we are introduced to, "gateway to the booming state of Western Australia. Which was, you could say, like Texas. Only it was big . . . The nation's quarry, China's swaggering enabler. A philistine giant . . ."[6] In this swaggering capitalist world the fallen person, the outsider, the questioner of capitalist verities, is a nobody. Keely, Gemma and Kai are indeed nobodies in a brave new world of material enterprise and wealth, each having fallen violently. Tom is in personal ruins, has massive hangovers and pops painkillers; Gemma, hunched and defensive, is just managing to keep herself and her grandson physically and emotionally together; and six-year-old Kai wanders between worlds, a strange, haunting, lost child. Here they are, huddling in their sparse, low-rent flats on the tenth floor of the seedy Mirador, a kind of clapped-out, anti-*Cloudstreet* community, hardly keeping at bay the world of drugs and prison, abusive sex, greed and political violence; this is Freo as capitalist dystopia.

For the many readers who loved the pied beauty and hard-won promises of *Cloudstreet*, there is certainly less loveliness to be found in *Eyrie*. The writing is just as astute – colloquial, pithy, unashamedly Aussie, funny and searing in turns – but the world evoked is far more pocked and raddled, the tone mordant. It's as if Winton is taking a nosedive straight into the combined darkness glimpsed in his earlier novels; and here, the darkness merges into a bleak cesspit of no-hopers, victims and cringers who populate fallen Freo:

> [D]azed and forsaken at the rivermouth, the addled wharfside slapper whose good bones showed through despite the ravages of age and bad living . . . spared only by a century of political neglect. Hunkered in the desert wind, cowering beneath the austral sun. (5–6)

As with all Winton's novels, place is crucial. *Eyrie* is populated by local characters in an intimately known landscape, but place has turned toxic. In this modern day Western Australia, environmentalism is a joke, as the state rushes headlong

> to drill, strip, fill or blast . . . Oil, gas, iron, gold, lead, bauxite and nickel – it was the boom of all booms . . . Pentecostal ecstasy in the air, and to resist it was heresy. (6)

---

6 Tim Winton, *Eyrie* (Melbourne: Penguin, 2013), 5. All subsequent references are to this edition and appear in parentheses in the text.

Tom Keely is a nay-saying fallen angel, a once-influential environmentalist but now "just another flannel-tongued Jeremiah with neither mission nor prophecy, no tribe to claim him but family"(6). Tim Winton, himself an environmentalist in an über-capitalist domain, is arguably writing here out of dark places in his own experience and understanding of politics and place. *Eyrie* brings capitalist dreams of exorbitant wealth into dialogue with the seedy (and worse) effects of greed, and with the vulnerable, even pathetically impotent idealism of one-time activists. Winton's realism powerfully ventriloquises the cacophony of different classes, genders and ages. It is inflected with farce and black humour, and a constant fear, as Keely sits perched high above the town on the tenth floor of the seedy hotel, having toppled headlong out of relevance, status and all the certainties of his life.

"No Tribe to Claim Him but Family"

Against a world of corrupt politicians, capitalism on a gross scale, and the druggies and wheeler-dealers who inhabit the underbelly of this place, Tom Keely, former environmentalist now disgraced, licks his wounds. He reels and stumbles, self-medicates with pills and alcohol, and looks back blearily and ambivalently at his childhood, its putative state of grace when he stood together with his parental pillars, Nev and Doris, and sister Faith, knowing his place in the world. Can such downward-spiralling bleakness maintain a narrative, let alone the enthusiasm of Winton's legion of fans? The clue as to how and why Winton does maintain readers' involvement throughout *Eyrie* is to be found in part in the novel's phrase "no tribe to claim him but family". What kind of claim or gesture is this? It can't be a surprise to Winton's readers that he finds the core of loss, as well as of meaning and even hope of redemption, in family. This novel, like *Cloudstreet*, is staking a claim about the equally agonising and redemptive centrality of family, fallen and wounded as it may be.

But what and how does family signify in Winton's novels? Family can be sustaining, even redemptive. It is bound for the future even while anchored in the past. It works on premises different to political and state generalities. It can be an intimate bulwark against a hostile world, but it can also be a place of repeated, formative violence and loss. In Winton's fiction, families can be units of resistance against personal dissolution, even in the face of utter loss and falls from grace. But equally they carry the seeds of tragedy and violence, personified here in the figure of hard-bitten, sexually abused, and all but destitute Gemma Buck. So what kind of gesture is Winton making in lifting family up to the centre of our gaze? Is it a moral gesture, a measuring of the value of family and community against the tsunamis of state, media, and capitalist excesses? Or is family finally, as some critics would argue, a nostalgic, conservative, backward-looking, even apolitical trope? For all *Eyrie*'s narrative push towards rectifying the loss involved in family, arguably family is represented, at best, as an ambivalent place from which many characters fall headlong into lives of psychic and material poverty.

On Winton's national tour to promote *Eyrie*, the Adelaide *Advertiser*'s Deborah Bogle reported under the headline "Winton Uses Words as Way to Ponder Change":

> "Novelists and art can't effect change", says West Australian author Tim Winton. But in his new book, *Eyrie*, he paints a powerful picture of what happens when a culture embraces the notion that we are an economy first and a community second.[7]

Even if we do not take this article's version of "Winton" at face value, critical readers of Winton might be a little dismayed by Winton's further claims reported here:

> "I don't think I'd flatter myself to think I'd have any impact," said Winton. "Just because Keely gets to vent doesn't mean there's any use in me venting. I don't think that would serve any purpose. Novels aren't a means of persuasion. Fiction doesn't have answers. It's a means of wondering or imagining."[8]

What, then, we might ask, is the purpose of wondering, or imagining, or indeed fiction, if it has no impact, no persuasiveness? Surely responses to this question are not to be found only within the fiction; they may start to form in readers who are affected by the fiction. So we have to ask, is *Eyrie* a protest novel, and what kind of impact does it have? Or is it merely an apolitical pondering on the half-noticed, unimportant fall of one man? Not even a "venting" by its author (if we are to take the *Advertiser*'s version of "Winton" as transparent)? But let's trust the tale, and our readings of it, in considering the possible impact of the novel, and the fall of Keely as more than the tale of just one character.

This leads us to the novel's probing of the power of family as a troubled, destructive, and possibly redemptive institution, and its potential to nurture values other than those of free-fall capitalism.[9] *Eyrie* offers readers something more than just nostalgic wondering about a past childhood world, the bosom of family as a hiding-place, a choice of personal, apolitical withdrawal. Tom Keely is a character who has indeed withdrawn, massively and self-pityingly. But this narrative of a fall is arguably also one of re-emergence, even redemption, however tentative. Keely is drawn back by Winton from the edge of self-annihilation as the novelist probes the often unlovely relationships that exist, and are constantly under construction, between self, family and state. The novel focuses unremittingly on the nature of moral response to this human unloveliness, in the self, within the family, and beyond the family's tight borders.

Eyrie's openness to the unlovely and unlovable has a lot to do with the lessons Keely has learnt from the powerful figures of his mother and father. They are not perfect figures to Keely, but their love and practical actions of care for others stand as a constant in his life, even at its nadir. The novel is also interested in making family, making it up from outside the strict bounds of one's own class and religious or cultural origins. The odd, disjointed, mismatched trio of Tom, Gemma and Kai constitutes an alternative representation of family and survival, made up as it is of scraps of memory, human need and vulnerability, of lust, tenderness, and the human desire to care for a broken and endangered child. The novel is asking what it means to care for someone outside one's own tight little family circle, and one's self. Family intimacy and the outside world of strangers are thus tumbled together, the ethics of family depicted as relating absolutely to the social world, and vice versa.

The question of fathering and mothering is thus central to *Eyrie*. Keely's father Nev died too young, but left his son with the imprint of a very human, potent form of caring

---

7   Deborah Bogle, "Winton Uses Words as Way to Ponder Change", *Advertiser*, 21 October 2013, 15.
8   Winton cited in Bogle, "Winton Uses Words", 15.
9   See Nicholas Birns' use of the term "neo-liberalism" in his discussion of Winton, *Eyrie* and capitalism in *Contemporary Australian Literature: A World Not Yet Dead* (Sydney: Sydney University Press), 2015, 80–83.

for others. Many a night Nev had to knock down his neighbour Johnny Buck, restraining him from repeatedly monstering his own wife and children. The violence of Gemma Buck's family is seen to brutalise her adult life, and the lives of her daughter and grandson. Keely's mother Doris, by contrast, is a strong, loving, possibly over-loving figure for her son. She is a woman who lives on after her husband's death, copes, gets things done, loves not unconditionally but with effect. The Keely household is contrasted with that of the Bucks, and of other abusive neighbours, as a place of sanctuary:

> Keely thought of the hundred nights the Buck girls came knocking: summer evenings out there on the porch sobbing in their nylon nighties, the sound of glass breaking up the hill behind them. There was always screaming; their place was bedlam after dark ... The girls would just be at the Keely door, whimpering on the porch until a light went on and Doris took them in. Then the old man would go looking for his boots, gathering his wits a moment, muttering some prayer or imprecation, before trudging up the hill to deal with it best he could.
> In those days the Keelys didn't have trouble, they fixed it. By faith, with thanksgiving. And now and then, when the shit hit the fan, with a judicious bit of biffo. (33)

Class, religion, gender and family come rolling together in Winton's idiosyncratically Australian lingo – the girls from a battler household in their "nylon nighties", shit hitting the fan, the necessary "bit of biffo". This may very well be Winton's least ideologically straightforward novel, with failures erupting in all classes; religion seen not as panacea but as something involving "prayer or imprecation", but treated with ironic fondness in this passage – "[b]y faith, with thanksgiving" echoing a well-known Protestant mantra. And then there is gender. Winton has often been criticised for his lack of tact, or worse, in his representations of women. But here we have the wonderful creation Doris, who "took them in", and does so again for the adult Gemma, as well as caring for her fallen son, while getting on with her own life and career.

Everyone Falls

Everyone falls in *Eyrie*: women, men and children; drug-addled con artists, failed idealists like Keely, working-class battlers like Gemma, politicians and institutions of law and order. The metaphor of falling – from some kind of grace or human goodness or plenitude; from the law; from one's ideals; and from childhood possibilities – flows through the novel like the ever-present, murky waters of the city's river. It is there in Keely's constant nightmare of falling from the tenth storey of the Mirador; or worse, visions of Kai's tender young body falling over the flimsy railings of the balcony. Falling as accident or abject fate epitomises the narrative's evocation of human powerlessness. Kai is at the centre of this river of dread and victimhood, with his quiet, off-key questions, his imagining of himself sprawled on the concrete ten floors below, like the police outline of a murder victim; his reiteration that he won't grow old. Rather than Milton's fall, directly due to disobedience and arrogance, does Winton's *Eyrie* offer a more compassionate sense of human vulnerability and inadequacy? Perhaps the lines of cause and effect in relation to falling are not so clearly delineated in *Eyrie*. The novel does, in fact, continually measure the impact of human agency, critical forms of choice and responsibility in falling, and not just accident, but its narrative is never judgemental or dismissive.

Rather, Keely appears as someone who has been capable of openness with others, and indeed as someone who shared visions of a better society through his environmental work. But we meet him at the opening of the novel as someone who has given up on this openness, devastated and undermined by the world of money and politics. He might well be experiencing what Heidegger calls "being-lost in the publicness of the 'they'".[10] Religious philosopher James DiCenso, in his essay "Heidegger's Hermeneutics of Fallenness", writes that Heidegger equates this "being-lost" with

> an inauthentic mode of being, in which Dasein [Being] has "fallen away from itself" and "fallen into the world" . . . [but] the condition of "fallenness" does not presuppose as the antithesis against which it is measured a pristine atemporal existential state. Heidegger explicitly rejects an interpretation of fallenness as a "fall" from a purer and higher "primal status." For Heidegger, embodied existence is not contrasted with an extra-mundane state of Being. Both fallenness and its opposite, authenticity, are "existential modes" . . . they articulate alternative modes of understanding and living. The criteria for expressing judgments about these modes emerge from reflection upon the differentiation of experience itself.[11]

The fascinating thing about Winton's creation of Keely is that there is very little authorial judging of this character. Rather, Keely shares insight into his own pathetic condition, seeing it through the eyes of his mother and sister, and eventually through the better ethics of his past and his family. This insight firstly leads to self-pity at his own fallenness, but as the narrative progresses self-pity slowly gives way to agency and the possibility of renewal.

However, with what level of judgement do readers respond to the character of Gemma, who leaves her young grandson asleep alone in the flat each night while she goes to pack shelves in a nearby supermarket? We see that she does so out of necessity, taking the opportunity to seek out Keely as carer, even if in an indirect way. We cannot simply condemn such a character, and nor does the novel. Again, there is an authorial refusal simply to judge the actions of Gemma, who has been brutalised by her world.

But what measures of choice or accident cause Keely's fall? We see him at his lowest, and we see him slowly, reluctantly respond to Gemma's need. It is around this fulcrum of moral choice, in his care for the child, as well as some intermittent lust for Gemma, that we see Keely address his lost manhood. But it is a slow, sometimes farcical journey, maleness being deconstructed and partially put together again as the novel proceeds. As carer, protector, lover, father, son, brother, professional, Keely is abject. The novel's opening, with Keely suffering yet another giant hangover, leads to his seeking solace from his torturous headache, plagued by morning-after hunger and waves of nausea. Keely consequently passes out on the cool floor of the supermarket, thinking:

---

10   Martin Heidegger, *Being and Time*, trans. John Macquarrie and Edward Robinson (New York: Harper & Row, 1962), 220.
11   James J. DiCenso, "Heidegger's Hermeneutic of Fallenness", *Journal of the American Academy of Religion* 56, no. 4 (1988): 673.

> Maybe this was what it was like to die a little, to feel shriven, rescued, redeemed. Having your collar pulled, your fucking beard tugged by the roots until there you were, upright and guiltless, watching your irritated saviour scuff away in Third World footwear, pushing a loaded trolley. (16)

Told as farce, from floor level, this is the first literal fall in the novel, and there are many to come. Keely as hopeless drunk, as self-pitying middle-class boy sunk to living in the shabby part of town, is alarming and, for many readers perhaps, totally unlikable. But in him there are also sparks of desire and empathy. His former idealism continues to prickle through, breaking the crust of his present self-loathing.

Tom Keely resembles many Winton male characters – Henry Warburton, Fred Scully, Quick Lamb, Sam Pickle, Luther Fox, Bruce Pike, Vic Lang – in different ways hapless, fallen men, injured, trying and failing to perform. Critics have pointed out, and often decried, the plethora of broken and abused women in Winton's fiction, mostly victims of male violence. However, the male characters are arguably just as misshapen. It is most often men, along with fate, accident, class limits, self-harm, that are the perpetrators of women's harm; this is recognisable in Winton's novels as a form of male deficit. In *Eyrie*, while the memory of Nev stands tall, it is Doris who is still upright, strong and wise:

> His mother was a brick, a saint. Which of course made everything much worse, especially since she'd had ample time to form a view of his situation. Two years since the break-up. A whole year since his catastrophic brain-snap and all its rewards. Doris was a shrewd old bird. She didn't miss much. He did not want to suffer her thoughtful analysis a single moment but he was pretty certain he already understood it in all its loving, pitiless permutations. (40–41)

Here is Winton at his best, focalising through Keely, his thoughts a mixture of mammoth self-pity, filial wariness about being judged, and enduring love and respect for his mother. While he has to ironise and distance his mother – "a brick, a saint" – the depth of their history together is intimately acknowledged. The shrewdness of Doris, knowing her son in all his fallenness and still loving him, her prompting him to do better, even as she knows she cannot force his redemption, colours this novel. She lives in a world of brokenness – her son, the people she encounters in her social work, her own single life in old age – but she is independent, radiating a kindness and practicality which Keely admires, depends on, and would emulate if he could.

A Redemptive Tale?

At the novel's end, new possibilities for Keely have been sketched. But only sketched. This is not a full-blown redemptive tale, more a narrative of fallenness and a roadmap for what still needs to be done. Keely's attempts to "save" Gemma, Kai and himself have been piecemeal, and at times farcical. What can someone with nothing inside do for others? Some things, it seems. Keely sends his postcards with their impotent threat of gun, and cross, and law, to those who threaten Gemma and Kai, but violence remains virulent. However, such violence (including Keely's actions) is also depicted as farcical and infantile. And it has to be resisted. Faced with the violence of the drug world, Keely registers its mundanity, but also experiences its reality in the shape of Clappy, a small, boy-like thug spitting threats:

> Fuck us about, he hissed. Try that shit on. You don't know what I can do, you dumb fuck. Finish with you I'm in there, mate, with those two, and then the fun really gets goin'. (421)

Short-statured, cliché-spouting Clappy is also literally "dancing on tiptoe" to maintain his reach of Keely, and "the little bloke [lost] his footing and release[d] a hand to steady himself" (421). Assailants come in all sizes, it seems, as do victims. This almost farcical encounter between Clappy the thug and abject Keely brings the novel towards its climax, but not until one final fall. It would be unfair to reveal the novel's ending, but it's enough to say that Keely falls:

> The veiled faces retracted uncertainly and Keely understood. He'd fallen. He saw the tower beyond and the tiny figure of the boy safe on the balcony . . . The boy's face a flash – or was that a gull? (421)

Keely, falling as he pursues the thug who had threatened Gemma and Kai, is attempting to reclaim something of his manhood and purpose. It is ethical purpose, and not uncharacteristic of the old Keely before the fall: idealistic, out of his depth, risking himself in pursuit of something beyond self. However, readers will judge whether this is a scene of redemption or of farcical defeat. These two modes become entangled in this final scene. No one is superman or woman in *Eyrie*: not Nev of blessed memory, nor Doris the brick; not the institutions of police or the law, nor social workers; certainly not Keely the ineffectual. But what we do witness in Keely is the persistence of desire to retrieve that which is eminently un-saveable: the childhood of goodness personified in his father and revisited in his relationship with Kai, the endangered land and its creatures, Gemma, himself, and, most urgently, Kai, the child monstered and deprived of goodness. Does the ineffectual outcome, with its farcical fall, suggest that Keely can be read merely as a pitiful and self-deluded idealist, caught in the traps of nostalgia, a middle-class mummy's boy fallen from grace? Or is Keely a portrait of human longing, the unquenchable desire to live up to moral, political, un-self-absorbed goodness, no matter how unrealisable, how pitifully fallen? Sprawled in front of the gaping crowd, Keely hears

> Sir, there is bleeding. Are you well?
> Yes, he said with all the clarity left in him. Thank you. I am well. (424)

For this moment, Keely in all his gracelessness – fallen, sprawled, hurt and pitiful – declares himself "well". For readers seeking a resolution of the narrative's many tangled traces of self-pity, violent self-interest, falling and redemption, the ending will perplex. This isn't a novel offering answers. It's a lot darker and more unpromising than that. But it does have impact. It asks us relentlessly, in the figure of Tom Keely: how do we respond to fallenness in others, in ourselves, in our family, and in those beyond the tight circle of family? The novel is a counter measure to the moral dystopia of greed and self-congratulation embodied in Freo. It is on the side of renewal, emanating even, or especially, from the humbled state of fallenness.

The Turning and "The Born-Again Business"

The short stories of *The Turning*, published ten years before *Eyrie*, oscillate between the characters' faint hopes of renewal, and bleak representations of lives that seem to promise nothing. There is, it seems, no hope of starting again for Fay and Dyson, the central characters of "Small Mercies", their worlds stained by grief, addiction and struggle. Fay's life has been one of teenage pregnancy, abortion and drug addiction, followed by the constant back and forth to visit her child who is living with her parents in her hometown. She is ashamed, guilty, lonely and an addict. In the grip of her addiction, she reaches out to her former teenage love, Dyson, seeking comfort:

> What do you want from me? he asked.
> Respect, she said. No. Adoration. Shit, Pete, I just want a safe place to be. Someone trustworthy. I can trust you, can't I . . .
> Dyson felt hemmed in now. He was revolted by her. He couldn't help it. All that restless will, the cruelty of it made him sick.
> What are you thinking? she asked. Your face went black. What're you thinking about, me?
> Nothing, Fay.
> I used to be a prize once. I was a trophy and you had me.
> Let's go and sit by the fire, he said. Here's your coffee.
> You're uncomfortable.
> Yes.
> I came here for comfort and you're uncomfortable, she said, her face flushed.
> I don't think there's any comfort I can give you.[12]

The short story form is particularly appropriate for Winton's glimpsed portraits of lost, battling lives. We are offered brief vignettes of characters who have very few resources with which to combat their losses, bruised by lack of education and opportunity, and by poverty. Many of these characters are working-class victims of their own fecklessness and bad choices, but also struggling against huge social deprivation. However, we also see in the character of Fay a glimpse of resourcefulness, and a certain self-reflectiveness (cunning?) as she attempts to reconnect with Dyson, and to read his discomfort: "What are you thinking? she asked. Your face went black. What're you thinking about, me?" She is a drug-addicted, fallen figure, but she is also able to read the blackness in Dyson's face, his discomfort, and to understand something of her own parlousness. She has some insight into the depth of her fall, and she is not averse to pointing out that once "I was a trophy, and you had me". What remains distinctive about the ironically named "Small Mercies" is its lack of authorial judging. While Dyson judges in a visceral and paralysing way – "He was revolted by her. He couldn't help it" – the authorial voice is different, gently prising open the nuances of Fay's hopelessness without condemning her. The surprise of the story rests in the moral cowardice of Dyson, revealed as he is at the story's end, hiding behind a lie from which Fay has protected him in all the intervening years:

---

12   Tim Winton, *The Turning* (Sydney: Picador, 2004), 95. All subsequent references are to this edition and appear in parentheses in the text.

> You know they never did find out about our little secret. God knows, every other shitty thing I ever did somehow got back to them, but they never suspected that. Two days shy of seventeen. And your fuckin' mother paid for it.
>
> Oh Fay.
>
> You know how my parents are. You know what it'd do to them. It'd crush them. Break their hearts.
>
> Don't.
>
> And you, the tin god. They could blame you for everything. (98)

Fay's fallenness – "every . . . shitty thing I ever did", her attempted manipulation of Dyson and threat to uncover their secret, her fecklessness as a mother – are patent. However, the core of the narrative is not about events, but is an anatomy of falling, of the layers of cause and effect that bring different characters to their knees, whether in defeat or supplication or guilt. What Fay is threatening to reveal to her parents is not simply the fact of her abortion, but that Dyson too is fallen, "dead and cold inside". (97) In this knotted representation of blame and guilt, all actors in "Small Mercies" are implicated, equally victims and agents in their own fallenness.

However, some of *The Turning*'s brief stories do depict the path taken in order to assuage human guilt and shame. The eponymous story, for instance, traces the role of religious belief in the lives of Dan and Sherry, and their interactions with Raelene, battered and desperate "white trash" from the caravan park:

> On Tuesday she gave darts the flick again and went over to Dan and Sherry's. They seemed surprised and relieved to see her and they'd barely let her in the doorway before she launched into them about religion, about how she didn't believe a word of it and how sick of bloody hypocrites she was. She gave it to them about the Pope and George W. Bush and the priests who abused children and it just didn't help matters that they kept nodding and agreeing. She ran out of puff. Dan put the kettle on
>
> You never have any booze in this house, said Raelene, laughing to mask her awful embarrassment.
>
> That's . . . there's a reason for that, said Sherry, smoothing down her skirt.
>
> Because you're churchy, right?
>
> Actually, said Dan, it's because I'm an alcoholic. (147–8)

There is both humour and poignancy in this depiction of Raelene's anger and neediness. The list of jibes against religion are a little bit of an in-joke, as most religious believers can attest to the usual trotting out of Pope, Bush, bad priests and churchiness as accusations against belief, accusations which are in fact against institutions and do not address actual lived beliefs. For Dan, the beliefs have enabled him to surmount his alcoholism. "Turning", as a metaphor and as the title of the story and the collection, is significant. In Christian beliefs, conversion involves repentance (in Ancient Greek "metanoia" [μετάνοια]), a changing of the mind, a healing, being forgiven, or turning.

In the story "The Turning", Winton playfully, even mischievously, depicts the processes of belief and unbelief. Once again there is no condemnation in the authorial voice, but a thoroughgoing, open anatomising of Raelene's fallen, broken, human capacities. Even though, under the kindness and tutelage of Dan and Sherry, "Raelene warmed to the idea of Jesus and the business of forgiveness" (149), and was at points close to turning, "she didn't believe":

> The born-again business, asked Raelene. What's it like . . .
> Like a hot knife going into me, murmured Sherry, sounding all foggy, a woman with her pillow voice on. Like . . . like I was butter and here was this knife opening me up. That's the best way I can describe it.
> Raelene could only nod, saddened but somehow fortified in the knowledge, the confirmation this gave her, that she didn't believe. She'd come near, she was sure. From desperation, from outright need . . . For a few days she'd thought she was only an arm's length, a breath away from copping something. But there was no piercing moment, no sudden unmistakable feeling.
> You're happy, then, she asked. You and Dan?
> Lucky, said Sherry. Grateful. Very happy. (153)

Raelene's calling it "the born-again business", her wanting to know not the theology of conversion, but how it feels, the metaphor of her being "a breath away from copping something", indicate her childlike brokenness, as much as her yearning to be free of what is monstering her life. The story reveals the radical individual nature of belief and unbelief, the divergent paths that lead to falling, and to being renewed. Sherry too mixes her metaphors, describing conversion in both deeply passive and violently active language – "like I was butter and here was this knife opening me up". And the results of being a believer are that you become "[l]ucky . . . Grateful . . . Very happy". As to whether Dan and Sherry's conversion was a matter of luck, their own agency, or was a gift, the story leaves the theology open. But for Raelene, her honesty with herself and her facing the demons of her husband's violence are depicted in equally ambivalent terms. In the macabre last scene of the story we are left to ponder whether Raelene has found her own way of turning. In the middle of being raped, again, by her brutal and brutalised husband, Raelene turns to the little snow dome with the figure of Jesus:

> In the spill of light at the bedside she saw the little dome and her man upon the waves. She said his name, too, said it aloud with love enough to send a shudder through Max as he pushed her down. She knew she was safe from him now, not safe from tonight but gone from him altogether. He smelt of death already, of burning, of bile and acid. He was crying and she did not pity him. He was gone and it didn't matter when. Everything was new. In her dome it snowed birds as the van rocked, birds like stars. The moment Max speared her and tore open her insides she was full of hot and certain feeling. She was free. She had already outlived him. (160–1)

Readers are confronted with an apocalyptic scene of rape and a brutalised wife's condemnations, but also, disturbingly, with her claim to freedom and release. The narrative runs together a deeply mixed discourse of religious fervour and judgement: the icon, the calling on the name of "her man upon the waves", the feeling of safety and freedom, the imagining of a beautiful world where "[e]verything was new", with the condemning of the perpetrator to a hell "of burning, of bile and acid". This mixed discourse runs like a voiceover, while the realistic depiction of Raelene being brutally raped, speared, her insides torn open, is placed before us. Is this then the portrait of a disassociating mind giving itself over to a final release? We know that in her conversations with Sherry, and their consequent distance, Raelene had decided that she didn't believe, that she couldn't feel belief. She had wanted to feel what it was like to be born again, but couldn't. Yet now she is "full of hot and certain feeling". So what are we to make of this final moment of felt exaltation? Does Raelene's fate amount to the febrile, mistaken acquiescence of a battler, a "trailer-trash" victim with no real means of escape, physical, psychological or spiritual? Or does she find the freedom she speaks of, in her realisation that after this she must grasp the power to enact her escape? Is that escape only to be in her death? Is she, as seems likely from the violent and harrowing description of the rape, about to die?

Adding to these questions, we might notice the visceral nature of Raelene's new liberatory "belief", its mixture of revenge, hellfire and damnation projected onto Max, her repudiation of any pity for him. Along with this violent religious discourse, Raelene adds sexual longing as she gazes at "her man upon the waves": "She said his name, too, said it aloud with love enough to send a shudder through Max as he pushed her down". Her icon is Jesus of the snow dome – "[s]he liked how his chest looked, bared by the billowing robe . . . real pecs and a six-pack. Like a bodybuilder. He was ripped" (155). Raelene's resources are few. She resorts to what she knows, to her sexuality, and to a disassociation that allows her to dream, in quasi-religious terms, of wielding power, of possessing a certainty that does not exist in her life. With her father "just a hole in her life . . . no more than a shape" (154), with a brutal and emasculated husband, it is little wonder that she cannot believe in anything. But in a form of ancient religious commitment, the character of Raelene can be read as preparing herself as a kind of barbaric sacrifice: "She looked like Joan of Arc, like a bloody nun" (158). In a warped yet understandable way, the final scene empathises with Raelene and her innocence. What her brutalised mind is seeing, and enabling the reader to see, is that she had "already outlived" her oppressor, that she is so much more than merely a victim.

Winton is walking with trepidation over thin ice here, in his negotiation of gender politics. If we read this story as in any way the judgemental depiction of a female victim's complicity in her rape and possible death, or at least her failure to stop it, then we lose the immense sense of pity in the story's depiction of her. This pity is felt by the reader in Sherry and Dan's responses to her, but more powerfully it is expressed through the inwardness of Winton's creation of Raelene's psychic life: its complex knot of longings, her desire to feel, her struggle to believe, and her final febrile surrender, in a form of self-sacrifice which in no way sees her as simply weak. She is a sacrifice, but in her agency – her seeking out of Sherry and Dan, her seeking beyond her own small cultural existence for ways to surmount her predicament, and her final acceptance of her awful fate – we are not left thinking of her as "fallen". She is, rather, superior in so many ways to the repetitive violence of her world. This is one reading of a harrowing final scene, a scene in which the reader is quite entitled to register, alternatively, victimhood and brutalisation as the predominant notes.

The narrator of "Commission" has, he feels, been schooled in loss and shame. He feels anger too, and judgement of a father who disappeared without explanation twenty-seven years earlier. On a mission to find the lost father, a mission given to him by his dying mother, the narrator thinks of his father as unforgivable, fallen, beyond redemption. His mission is for his mother's sake. The sparseness of the story, with its clipped dialogue and sketchy details, evokes the repressed feelings of the son, now a man bearing all the marks of neglect. We know from minor details that this is Vic, the figure who recurs in a number of the stories in *The Turning*. The effects of being left behind in his boyhood, by a father gradually giving himself to drink, seem indelible. Vic, in this story and in others, is injured and lacking self-respect. But it is to his father that the son now offers his most ingrained accusations:

> Once upon a time it had been true. Honest Bob. He was straight as a die and what you saw was what you got. I believed in him. He was Godlike. His fall from grace was so slow as to be imperceptible, a long puzzling decline . . . subsiding into a secret disillusionment I never understood, hiding the drink from my mother who, when she discovered it, hid it from me in turn for fear I would lose respect for him. She turned herself inside out to protect him, and then me. And at such cost. All for nothing. He ran away. Left us. I grew up in a hurry. (225)

Once again, Winton probes the dynamics of family, its role as crucible of intense love and violent falling away. The narrator is urged on by love of his mother, but also by anger and lack of resolution about his father. What the boy and the young man didn't understand all those years ago is slowly unwound as father and son meet. But only in the briefest of terms, without resolution in the narratives. The son holds on to the facts, but "angry at how sick with love I was at the very sight of him" (225), and the father bows to the inevitability of going back to see his wife, of "[f]acing her" (225). Winton weaves a quiet, powerful web of motives, explanations, guilt and the beginnings of understanding in a family, members of which carry their own distinct narratives. For the boy who had become a fatherless man, it has been a life of "shame and disappointment, consoled only by order. Childless. Resigned" (229). Little does the son realise how much he mirrors his father, but readers see the two as products of the same family drama, each bearing the scars, but also bearing the same political and ethical understandings:

> I hear you're a lawyer now.
> Yeah.
> What kind?
> Industrial relations.
> On whose side?
> The little bloke.
> That's good, he said. That's good. Gotta look after the little bloke.
> Well that's the theory. (228)

"Commission" is perhaps too spare and delicate a story, both in its narrative brevity and in its content and dialogue, to theorise extensively about the state of abjection in which father, mother and son have existed. But the pun of the title leads us to think about both the material substance of the father, a police officer commissioned to execute justice, and the double nature of sin, as omission and commission. In the spare dialogue between the reunited father and son there is a poignancy, an envisioning of commonalities – "Gotta look after the little bloke" – forged despite the loss of so many years.

In the son's reunion with his father, along desert roads, peering into "humpies and dongas in long shadows of diggings and ruins" (228), the son's profession as defence lawyer is never far away: "I'd been in some desolate rooms in my time but I never saw anything so melancholy" (228) is the response of the son to the sparse sheds and humpies of the men his father lives amongst. In the mirror of each other, both men face their abject selves, fallen, dour, withdrawn, but also capable of remorse and of wanting something more, as they acknowledge their fallen selves. They are a burden to each other, prone and awkward with the knowledge they share. But there are also glimpses in the brief narrative of something retrievable, just possibly, from the rubble of their fallenness: "I didn't expect it to be beautiful here, I said for no reason other than not knowing what to say" (232).

4
Narrative Redemptions

> Summer and winter and springtime and harvest
> sun, moon and stars in their courses above
> join with all nature in manifold witness
> to thy great faithfulness, mercy and love.
> —Thomas O. Chisholm, "Great Is Thy Faithfulness"[1]

As we have seen in Chapter 3, falling – ontological, psychological, emotional and bodily – is a major preoccupation in the fiction of Tim Winton. But so too are hope and redemption. Winton's redeemable worlds are depicted centrally through human relationships, and between the human and the other than human, written in realistic, earthy prose and through Winton's often comic contexts. His redemptive fiction is also deeply political, the expression of a desire for justice in an often violent and unjust world.

More Than Democratic

In American singer Patti Smith's 1988 democratic rock anthem "People Have the Power", released three years before *Cloudstreet* was published, she envisages a redeemed world "in the form of shinin' valleys", where "the people have the power / To redeem the work of fools./ From the meek the graces shower . . .".[2] Winton's fictions share this democratic, redemptive vision, but reach further, towards a sacred source of such redemption. His writing is earthed and vernacular, yes, but it pushes towards something more. Both Smith's and Winton's works reveal a demotic, democratic edge, an earthy and earthed version of redemption, yet unlike the powerful persuasiveness of the anthem's *declarations*, Winton's novels are underscored by questioning. Even as his fiction presages redemption, his characters and his narratives continue to ask where and how a final end to suffering, and the reign of justice, could take place.

---

1 Thomas O. Chisholm (words) and William M. Runyan (music), "Great Is Thy Faithfulness" (Carol Stream, Ill.: Hope Publishing Co., 1923).
2 Patti Smith, "People Have the Power", *Dream of Life* (New York: A&M Studios, 1988).

There are glimpses of a more than human creator's sustaining and redemptive presence in Winton's work. His fiction shares with the Protestant hymn quoted above a vision of "all nature in manifold witness", an overarching belief that offers to sustain (author, character, reader) in the midst of trauma and its grim narratives. There are glimpses in Winton's work of Patti Smith's "shinin' valleys" where the work of small, marginalised human fools will be redeemed. In this, there is a democratising and universalising impulse at work in the fiction. And it is redemption for both humans and for the created world.

However, looking back over Winton's writings from the first decades of the twenty-first century, in the present context of severe climate change and the massive and traumatic displacement of peoples around the globe, readers might well ask if Winton's redemptive speculations grow paler and out of place, more fraught and fragile in their visions of justice and recuperation. A sense of ecological and geographical hope, and its limits, informs Winton's two memoirs, *Land's Edge: A Coastal Memoir* (1993) and *Island Home: A Landscape Memoir* (2015). In these two meditative and personal reflections on place and country, as Winton considers how an intimacy with the land and the sea has deeply informed his writing, redemption emerges as anything but an escapist or disembodied phenomenon. It does not simply equate with a release from the present moment or place. In these memoirs Winton engages with family, place, materiality and spirit, as he does in his novels, as immanent forces that inform a redemption already in process.

Cloudstreet's Comic Flood

Into the closing pages of *Cloudstreet* pours a comic flood: wedding, baby, families united, random evil staunched; and a death that presages redemption:

> A formation of pelicans rises bigbodied from the water, the sweet coppery water where jellyfish float and blowfish bloat and the slow-wheeling schools of mullet divide and meet without decision.
> And another crowd has gathered. I can see them in the shade of the trees, the river of faces from before, the dark and the light, the forgotten, the silent, the missing who watch Lester dance his silly longlegged jig while half choking on his roast chook... The Lambs and the Pickleses begin to dance, Oriel and Dolly, Red and Elaine, and even Chub is up off his arse and dancing. Quick and Rose have Harry between them like a sail in the wind... a mad, yokel twenty-year dance that sets the shadows moving in sight behind them where a black man leaves the trees like a bird and goes laughing into the sun with a great hot breeze that rolls the roof of the sky and tilts the leaves above them till the gathering is dizzy with laughter, full and gargling with it....[3]

The dancing and the festivity are created realistically, in creative vernacular prose; but also, less realistically, in the contrast with a flickering presence, "the dark and the light, the forgotten, the silent, the missing". This rollicking and possibly nostalgic version of mid-twentieth-century Australia is entitled "Moon, Sun, Stars", echoing the Protestant hymn "Great Is Thy Faithfulness", quoted above. "[S]un, moon, and stars" constitutes the

---

3 Tim Winton, *Cloudstreet* (Melbourne: McPhee Gribble, 1994), 555–56. All subsequent references are to this edition and appear in parentheses in the text.

narrative arc's final movement, offering us, in fact, several versions of redemption. The struggling, often warring family members are united by marriage. Harry the baby is there, belonging to them all, and there is food, drink, music and dancing. Displaced Aboriginal people are represented (some may well say simplistically) by "a black man" who is happy, but not part of the scene, who "goes laughing into the sun". So, *Cloudstreet* finishes with a hopeful vision of an idealised, earthly (white) family redemption.

Winton's comic, redeemed worlds also characteristically contain darker notes and questions. As the reader gradually realises, this final scene is narrated by the gently retreating figure of the boy-man, Fish Lamb. And, we are told, he (or a version of him) has been the one telling the story all along. He is now watching his family, as he slips away towards the water that has always fascinated him, and which once almost claimed his life. Fish sees his family and their joy, but he is restless to be elsewhere, moving "slow, slow to the water that smacks him kisses when he hits" (557). Still a mischievous boy in a young man's body, Fish enters the water, moving "past the dim panic of muscle and nerve into a queer and bursting fullness" (557). In Winton's glittering, affecting prose, Fish takes off towards a place even closer to redemption than those on shore know of, of which he can say:

> I'm a man for that long, I feel my manhood, I recognise myself whole and human, know my story for just that long, long enough to see how we've come, how we've battled in the same corridor that time makes for us, and I'm Fish Lamb for those seconds it takes to die, as long as it takes to drink the river, as long as it took to tell you all this, and then my walls are ripping and I burst into the moon, sun and stars of who I really am. Being Fish Lamb. Perfectly. Always. Everyplace. Me. (557)

Fish Lamb's death is depicted in redemptive terms. He regains, just for a moment, the man he might have been, in an earthy, elemental redemption necessitating his drinking of the river, his dying, and his becoming a part of the cosmos around him. But the scene pushes towards something more, as Fish takes on perfection: "Being Fish Lamb. Perfectly. Always. Everyplace. Me." Is it too much to claim that even the most secular, cynical or earthbound reader might be affected by this moment and its fictional redemption? Fish is lifted out of and above the earthly and earthy, given an identity beyond place and time, as readers surely want him to be.

A Believable Redemption?

After *Cloudstreet*, in novels such as *Dirt Music* (2001) and *Breath* (2008), Winton continued to probe the human need and the narrative possibilities of depicting redemption. Luther Fox in *Dirt Music* learns that a world of risk, accident and pain is inseparable from one in which lives, given over to one another, can touch redemptive possibilities. *Dirt Music* thus shares with *Cloudstreet* a vision of a suffering but finally redeemable world. At a narrative, technical level, the suffering of the protagonists is necessary to the writer, in order to make the redemption believable and fulfilling for the reader. The plot depends on the suffering. At an ontological level, Winton's fiction can be read as informed by sacred concepts: an immanent and suffering god, and characters that are simple, stripped down, vulnerable, and punished perhaps, but finally purified.

Again and again in realistic, traditional narratives, plots have to be thickened, complications put in place, sacrifices or horrors confronted, in order that readerly satisfaction at the end might be achieved. Whether it is a comic satisfaction, or a tragic one, or something in between, all that happens, together with the fictional histories of the protagonists, is traditionally, teleologically conceived, always already at the service of a culmination, an ending. And this is one reason why so much suspension of disbelief is necessary in order to read fiction. Readers know the end is coming, they are thrilled (if it's an enjoyable read) to see how all that has come before is gathered up into what happens at the end. It is the inevitability of this teleological structure that causes both pleasure for the reader, and that can raise critical unease. It is an unease not simply about the potentially blunting fact of repetitive fictional teleology, but the fact that in the end such fictional worlds are vulnerable – politically, historically, imaginatively – because they are always finally recognisable as *mere fiction*, visible as part of the fiction machine, bound to teleology, sometimes formulaic.

In contradistinction to this impulse towards narrative satisfaction and fictional redemption, what happens if we read critically from a more sceptical, poststructuralist premise? For poststructuralism there is always a more profound loss – not a redeemable or Romantic sense of uplifting or satisfying loss – at the heart of all linguistic inscriptions. Additionally, some scepticism, foreknowledge or blunting of surprise must arguably accompany any thoughtful reading of traditional novels. Poststructural approaches prompt us to see that all fictions are at one level linguistic artefacts, and thus never able to overcome the lack or loss at the heart of representation, never finally able to heal or redeem the wound of language.

If we want to argue that literary fiction can be transformative, or redemptive, how do we address this poststructural claim that lack is what finally remains, even in the most utopian or redemptive of representations? Take for example the representation of that most unredeemed figure, the ghost, wandering spirit of a remembered loved one, condemned to wander the earth, lost in time; or the ghosts of peoples who once lived in the land but have been decimated. Winton's *Dirt Music* is full of ghosts. Old ghosts haunt happy endings too, reminding us that suffering – in real or imagined communities – can never be forgotten, let alone redeemed. Ghosts – sometimes as perpetual victims, or angry vessels of revenge, sometimes as graceful, memory-full sorrowers, open, grieving mouths in time – continue to cry out, unsure, unfit or unwilling to be redeemed in language, no matter how powerfully transformational language seeks to be. A residue of grief and anger, a refusal to resolve, will surely always attend in human language, a trace of the struggle involved in making present what is absent, the loss incurred in naming and representation, acknowledged in postructuralism's eternal deferment of the sign.

But just what level or kind of haunting can readers accept? After all, loss and haunting, the very thematic stuff of plot-driven texts, is often recuperated, made redeemable by we readers who desire softer forms of mythology, happy endings, surprise restorations. Poststructural thought is concerned with a deeper, more systemic loss, perhaps an unutterable loss at the heart of language itself. As Homi Bhabha has written, after Derrida:

> [T]he image... marks the site of an ambivalence. Its representation is always spatially split... it is the representation of a time that is always elsewhere, a repetition... the access to the image of identity is only ever possible in the negation of any sense of

originality or plenitude; the process of displacement and differentiation (absence/presence, presentation/repetition) renders it a liminal reality.[4]

Even in the face of poststructural angst, its undermining of any narrative "originality or plenitude", Bhabha himself can still be haunted by a hovering desire for redemption. This is evident in his essay "How Newness Enters the World", where he describes the possibility of "an interstitial time and space", a living "in the midst of the incomprehensible".[5] These phrases are tantalising in their implicit acknowledgement of the tension between material and redemptive versions of language, as they register the horrors of the past, but also the need for continuance. Bhabha describes this space, this "continua of transformation", in redemptive, or at least hopeful, terms:

> History's intermediacy poses the future . . . as an open question. It provides an agency of initiation that enables one to possess again and anew . . . the signs of survival, the terrain of other histories, the hybridity of cultures.[6]

These are metaphors offering redemptive possibilities, but they are also potentially colonising metaphors: "To possess again and anew . . . the terrain"; signs that can be read hopefully, hybridities that enable, cultures that must change. The last scene of Tim Winton's *Dirt Music*, rather than moving into such wide, theoretical terrains, focuses inward, embracing personal catastrophe and rescue, and human relationship, as the grounds of hope, perhaps even redemption. At the end of the novel, cradled in his lover Georgie's arms, Fox, this white man who has dreamed of rebirth in an ancient land, is coming home, finally. Grabbed back from the claws of a near-death accident:

> He lies with his head against the deck and does not breathe. The sky is behind her. She's real. She's not real. The others have faces they don't seem to own, yet Georgie looked at the martyred jut of his hipbones, the twigs in his hair, the livid ulcers all down his thin leg . . .
> She looks in from the sky. Eyes wide as a fish's. Real or not, he should breathe. He feels his lips split in a smile. Soon. There's plenty of time for that.
> Georgie saw his eyes roll back and his hips lift toward her. My God, he was blue . . .
> Well, said the guide. You're the nurse.
> Yes, she thought. This is what I do.
> She fell on Luther Fox, pressed her mouth to his and blew.
> She's real.[7]

In her discussion of so-called tear jerker films, or "weepies", drawing on the work of Franco Moretti, film critic Linda Williams writes of the place of fantasy in any meeting with the other: "This fantasy of the meeting with the other that is always too late can thus be seen as based upon the utopian desire that it not be too late to remerge with the other who was

---

4 Homi K. Bhabha, "Interrogating Identity", in *The Location of Culture* (London: Routledge, 1994), 73.
5 Bhabha, "How Newness Enters the Word", in *The Location of Culture*, 303–37.
6 Bhabha, *Location of Culture*, 235.
7 Tim Winton, *Dirt Music* (Sydney: Picador, 2001), 460–61. All subsequent references are to this edition and appear in parentheses in the text.

once part of the self".[8] In the melancholic losses of some postcolonial imaginings, in the more positive, future-looking impetus of postcolonial theory's syncretic self-fashionings and empowerments, and in Winton's wilderness romance, we can see different but linked versions of this fantasy, this hope that "it not be too late". It seems that for Georgie and Luther there might still be time. There seems to be more to come, "plenty of time for that".

From a narratological point of view, however, romance conclusions to novels, with their visions of plenitude, redemption, new beginnings or fulfilments, must conclude. And equally, hope and promise often cling even in the deepest melancholic endings. This hope for redemption is, arguably, analogous with postcolonial theorists such as Homi Bhabha and their desires to premise futurity, to mark out a utopian cultural space of transformation – with a will to newness, communal and individual empowerment, refigured agency, even in the anonymous jaws of history. History becomes redeemable for both novelist and theorist. Both must impossibly finish, have done with or rewrite what came before, in order to enter the future. In the end, for writers, readers and critics, redemptive desires, if they are harboured, are built on the fantasies of human imagination and its infinite possibilities and inventiveness, its embrace of change and a sense of grace in the face of the horrors that impossibly must be transformed.

However, *Dirt Music* also inaugurates many questions about Winton's fictional and redemptive desires. What, for instance, do we make of another reading of *Dirt Music* as a *white* romance, the story of white desire for belonging in Aboriginal Australia? Winton is certainly not alone amongst Australian novelists in seeking to understand and represent white belonging in this place. For non-Indigenous novelists writing across the 1980s and into the 2000s, the decades of Aboriginal land rights and cultural renaissance, the constant challenge was to approach issues of belonging, place and identity without stepping (or tumbling) into cultural appropriation and "aboriginalisation".[9] David Malouf's novel *Remembering Babylon* (1993), Andrew McGahan's *The White Earth* (2004), Kate Grenville's *The Secret River* (2005), Gail Jones' *Sorry* (2007), and many other novels by non-Indigenous Australians, struggle with questions of how to belong, and who should belong, in Australia. Each has generated heated postcolonial debate about white belonging or non-belonging.

In *Dirt Music*, Luther Fox's journey can be seen as one of attempted aboriginalisation, of seeking to move off into Aboriginal country and away from the grief and violence of white culture. But how deeply inscribed by the Aboriginal other is this novel? The white hero and heroine find the beginnings of redemption, possibly, with each other, in a romance. However, we need to ask whether *Dirt Music* is merely providing an exotic, Australian outback as backdrop, at the expense of any real acknowledgement of Aboriginal presence or contestation of place, in its narrative of romance and redemption. Or worse, such white romance can be read as possible only through the repression of that other, greater grief and violence to which the land has been witness. Much depends on the reading of Fox's sojourn in the land, and what he comes to know, being read by the land, as well as in his meeting with the quasi-Aboriginal figures he encounters. Are we able to read the beginnings of Fox's redemption as, in part, his learning to live in and through the land

---

8   Linda Williams, "Film Bodies: Gender, Genre and Excess", *Film Quarterly* 44, no. 4 (Summer 1991): 12.
9   See Nicholas Birns on "Concern" in *Contemporary Australian Literature: A World Not Yet Dead* (Sydney: Sydney University Press, 2015), 121–55.

as both other and as nurturer? Does the representation of the white man's losses mirror Aboriginal losses of family, home, music, future? Or does Winton's fiction in *Dirt Music* usurp such catastrophic loss in its narrative push towards (white) transformations? Part of what Fox learns is that this is, after all, *not* his land. His stories are elsewhere.

Beyond Limits: Risk-taking, Yearning, Hoping

Winton's fiction, even in its darkest moments, has a comic vigour which traces the energy and hope of its characters, impelled as many of them are to take risks, possessing a desire to go beyond limits, to excel, to achieve, to be different, to challenge, to compete, to soar, to cheat death. We see this desire in *Breath*'s Pikelet and Looney, young boys holding their breath below the surface of sea and creek, daring each other to take risks, to come back. We see it in wounded Eva still wanting something beyond her reach, trying to regain the rapture of her early sporting achievements, longing to push beyond her confinement. Winton's novels probe the spiritual, as well as the physical and psychological dimensions of this desire for "going beyond". They hold up a mirror to an arguably secular Australian culture, a mirror in which to comprehend human fallenness, but also to acknowledge human longing for redemption, for newness, new vigour, through confrontation with terrifying human trauma and death, and the redemptive power experienced on return from such extremes. Winton has spoken often of the religious dimensions of such experiences.

In a 1996 interview with Australian poet and literary critic Andrew Taylor, Winton was asked about religion in his work, and in Australia. He replied:

> Australia is such a resolutely irreligious culture. Given our origins, the European origins in this country, it should be no surprise that Australians are pretty doubtful about men in uniform and authority and suspicious of the church. In America you can rely on some common religious understandings, some spiritual givens, if you like. Here the soil is pretty thin and bitter. There is no religious life without the central necessity of imagination. That historical Australian hostility to the imagination has wounded our culture, I think. It's hard writing against that flow, particularly when it's joined and reinforced by the anaesthesia of consumerism.[10]

In his stance towards Australia as "resolutely irreligious" Winton has, of course, many Australian literary predecessors, among them Patrick White, whose probing of suburban life and its failures of imagination is carried out in tumultuous novels which excoriate Australia and its lack of spiritual depth, novels such as *Riders in the Chariot* (1961), *The Solid Mandala* (1966), *The Vivisector* (1970) and *The Eye of the Storm* (1973). Winton in this interview parallels imaginative and religious life. He sees them both under threat from what he calls "the anaesthesia of consumerism". This stance is echoed in Winton's own anti-consumerist activism and environmentalism, beliefs and actions he publicly links to his religious faith. A literary life inflected by religious belief is indeed an unusual trajectory for a contemporary Australian author, although leading poet Les Murray and North America-based Australian poet and academic Kevin Hart are similar to Winton

---

10 Andrew Taylor, "An Interview with Tim Winton", *Australian Literary Studies* 17, no. 4 (1996): 375.

in the ways their self-proclaimed religious faith is experienced as inseparable from their imaginative practices.

As with these earlier writers, Winton has garnered accusations of religious essentialism, with some critics seeing his fiction as infected by masculinist representations that spring, supposedly, from his "white" Christian heritage. In what might be interpreted as criticism of his open religious declarations, Winton is accused of failure to represent adequately the minorities in Australian society, particularly women and Indigenous Australians. Further, some see as nostalgic his vision of a supposedly more innocent, earlier Australia.[11] Winton's public discussion of his religious beliefs, it might be argued, has fuelled critical unease. One read of the parodic, anonymous blog *The Worst of Perth*,[12] and its article "Sunburn on the Groyne", reveals the opposition Winton attracts, even as – or in some cases because – he remains a highly popular author in Australia, and increasingly so internationally. In examining the nature of the criticism directed at Winton's fiction, variously targeting his essentialism, misogyny, nostalgia, opportunism, and pre-eminently his status as a narrow, white-settler writer – we are, equally, learning something about broader responses to religious sensibility in Australia.

If Winton can be accused of being a narrowly "religious" writer (or worse, a "Christian writer"), it's important to consider how many other Australian writers can be placed in a similar category. In the same interview with Andrew Taylor, Winton discusses Australian literary predecessors who had a concern for the sacred:

> Randolph Stow and Patrick White, Frank Webb . . . Kevin Hart, Les Murray . . . I could see the dents in the wall where people had been before, if you know what I mean . . . And I suppose you could see the bruises and cuts on their foreheads to prove that they'd been really banging their heads, that the effort had taken a toll. I guess I was trying to find a language for this human yearning.[13]

Beyond these Australian (male) writers, Winton also names American novelist of the mid-twentieth century Flannery O'Connor as a major influence on him. It is O'Connor's imaginative representation of a Southern American sacred context and language with local roots[14] that Winton invests in. Winton's fiction, like O'Connor's, broadens the scope of "religious writing", placing his own work within a genealogy of religious writers, and indeed in the tradition of all artists "trying to find a language for this human yearning". However, and regardless of Winton's own broadening of the category of religion, or the sacred, the overarching argument remains: many of the criticisms levelled against Winton continue to stand in for critical disapproval or distaste of his religious stance. Such an argument needs further substantiation.

---

11   See Robert Dixon, "Tim Winton, *Cloudstreet* and the Field of Australian Literature", *Westerly* 50 (2005), 240–60.
12   "The Wintoning Project," *The Worst of Perth*, 30 April 2011.
13   Taylor, "Interview with Winton", 376.
14   Jon P. Peede and Joanne H. McMullen, eds, *Inside the Church of Flannery O'Connor: Sacrament, Sacramental, and the Sacred in Her Fiction* (Macon, Ga.: Mercer University Press, 2008).

Australian Sacredness?

If fiction writers and poets in Australia have found it "tough" confessing religious faith, as Winton writes, then concomitantly, literary critics interested in "the sacred" across the latter half of the twentieth century found a cold welcome. It is true that from the late 1980s onwards, Australian scholarship about the category of the sacred, in the context of literature, has produced some groundbreaking critical work: Kevin Hart's *The Trespass of the Sign: Deconstruction, Theology and Philosophy*;[15] and David Tacey's *The Edge of the Sacred*[16] and *Re-enchantment: The New Australian Spirituality*.[17] More recently, political and cultural scholar Roland Boer has been prolific in this field, evident on his blog, *Stalin's Moustache*,[18] and in his multi-volume series *Criticism of Heaven, Criticism of Earth, Criticism of Theology*, and *Criticism of Religion*.[19] In 2009, Bill Ashcroft, Frances Devlin-Glass and I published the critical volume *Intimate Horizons: The Post-Colonial Sacred in Australian Literature*.[20] A central argument of this latter work is that a puzzling gap exists between many academic critics and creative writers around the category of the sacred, with critics lagging behind poets and novelists in their awareness and acknowledgement of religious or sacred sources of the creative imagination. Further, we argued in *Intimate Horizons* that there exists a deep blindness in white-settler Australians and their expressions of growing respect for Indigenous sacred knowledge, in relation to ancestors and to the land, while they often seem unable to engage with European or non-Indigenous accounts of the sacred. This is a fairly brief description of the complex state of affairs across the last decades of the twentieth century in Australia, in relation to diverse sacred discourses.

However, there is now a growing *international* scholarly engagement with the field of literature and the sacred, with many international scholars invoking and examining "post-secularism" or "re-enchantment", in scholarship including J. D. Caputo's *The Prayers and Tears of Jacques Derrida: Religion without Religion*;[21] Slavoj Žižek's *On Belief*;[22] Charles Taylor's *A Secular Age*;[23] Luce Irigaray on the embodied divine, including her concept of the "sensible transcendent";[24] and Pericles Lewis' *Religious Experience and the Modernist Novel*.[25] While multidisciplinary humanities work on the sacred (in feminist studies,

---

15 Kevin Hart, *The Trespass of the Sign: Deconstruction, Theology and Philosophy* (New York: Fordham University Press, 1989).
16 David Tacey, *The Edge of the Sacred: Transformation in Australia* (Melbourne and Sydney: Harper Collins, 1995).
17 David Tacey, *Re-enchantment: The New Australian Spirituality* (Melbourne and Sydney: HarperCollins, 2000).
18 Roland Boer, *Stalin's Moustache* blog, https://stalinsmoustache.org.
19 Roland Boer, *Criticism of Heaven: On Marxism and Theology* (Leiden, The Netherlands: Brill, 2007); Roland Boer, *Criticism of Religion: On Marxism and Theology II* (Leiden, The Netherlands: Brill, 2009); Roland Boer, *Criticism of Theology: On Marxism and Theology III* (Leiden, The Netherlands: Brill, 2010); Roland Boer, *Criticism of Earth: On Marx, Engels and Theology* (Leiden, The Netherlands: Brill, 2011); Roland Boer, *In the Vale of Tears: On Marxism and Theology V* (Leiden, The Netherlands: Brill, 2013).
20 Bill Ashcroft, Frances Devlin Glass and Lyn McCredden, *Intimate Horizons: The Post-Colonial Sacred in Australian Literature* (Adelaide: ATF Press, 2009).
21 J. D. Caputo, *The Prayers and Tears of Jacques Derrida: Religion without Religion* (Bloomington: Indiana University Press, 1997).
22 Slavoj Žižek, *On Belief* (New York: Routledge, 2001).
23 Charles Taylor, *A Secular Age* (Cambridge, Mass.: Harvard University Press, 2007).
24 Luce Irigaray, *Key Writings* (London: Continuum, 2004).

Indigenous studies, anthropology, philosophy, literary studies and cultural studies) is slowly growing in Australia, and more so internationally, we must still probe the arguably palpable academic aversion to the "religious turn" in Winton's work.

Robert Dixon, while not overtly critiquing Winton's religious or spiritual concerns, describes Winton's writing as nostalgic, pre-modern and pre-global, terms which, this chapter argues, can be read as standing in for a suspicion about the "primitivism" of a religious, regional, local and anti-cosmopolitan sensibility. Dixon is primarily writing about Winton's most popular novel, *Cloudstreet*:

> Winton is quite explicit ... about the novel's nostalgia for lost places, for an Australian accent and culture that are pre-American, pre-modern, pre-1960s ... This goes a long way toward explaining the popularity of the novel, at least for a certain generation of readers, the baby boomers, who were the major cultural force in the 1990s, when the novel was published. But nostalgia is by its very nature conservative: it prefers the past to the future; it is at best ambivalent about modernity; it prefers the local and the traditional to the global.[26]

Dixon's criticism is deeply invested in the value of modernity and global cosmopolitanism, and stands against the national or traditional, which are held by Dixon to be parochial and even tribal. These terms are highly reminiscent of secularist discourses that opposed religion in the early part of the twentieth century. It is indeed a complex knot of allegiances being wound together here in Dixon's criticism, with nostalgia, conservatism, preference for the past, anti-modernity, traditionalism and the local all made to stand for the kind of retrograde and parochial position that Winton supposedly embodies, at least in *Cloudstreet*. It's not a big step to see Dixon's stance as including, though only in a partly conscious way, Winton's religious sensibility as part of this set of preferences.

In response to Dixon's championing of a global, secular sensibility, we need, in the context of Winton's work, to consider scholarly discussions of "post-secularism", which has been "out of the box" as a concept for at least two decades. For example, the contributing editors of the 2012 social science volume *The Post-Secular in Question* write:

> [B]y many measures there is, in fact, a religious resurgence of global dimensions, but this resurgence is not taking place with much uniformity around the globe. Rather, it is taking many forms – not all of which fit into an easily codifiable definition of "religion" ... A growing unease with "Enlightenment fundamentalism" and broadening scepticism about scientific naturalism ... has also made it easier for academics to take religion seriously again ...[27]

We are indeed in a rapidly evolving historical and intellectual moment, and need to ask how Winton's writing relates to these new scholarly encounters with religion, sacredness and spirituality in Australia. While it is possible to trace the theme and the narrative

---

25 Pericles Lewis, *Religious Experience and the Modernist Novel* (Cambridge: Cambridge University Press, 2010).
26 Dixon, "Field of Australian Literature", 247.
27 Philip S. Gorski et al., ed., *The Post-Secular in Question: Religion in Contemporary Society* (New York and London: Social Science Research Council and New York University Press, 2012), 2–3.

impetus towards redemption in his novels, it is also important to examine the fuller context of Winton's fiction, asking what kinds of ontology, and indeed theology, can be read as emerging from his oeuvre. Broadening the category of "religion", the term used almost universally by American scholars, this volume argues that the term "sacred" is a more useful and capacious category with which to think about Winton's work and new directions in theological scholarship. It is a term that echoes the work of early twentieth century ethnologists, as well as that of postmodern anthropologists such as Michael Taussig, in *What Colour Is the Sacred?*[28] "The sacred" embraces a range of discourses and understandings beyond the institutional claims of "religion" on the one hand and, on the other hand, it embraces much more than the narrowly personal, subjective connotations of "spirituality".

In Winton's novels and short stories, the desire for connection with sacred forces, and for redemptive promise (overlapping though not identical categories) is evident, as we have been arguing, in tension with the human propensity for risk-taking, an imaginative ranging out beyond the known, even when the characters are largely unconscious of the sacred dimensions of their actions. However, as well as risk-taking and a moving out beyond the quotidian, in many Winton novels the everyday and the known are also sources of sacred meaning-making: in, for example, the earthy dynamics of the Flack family in *That Eye, the Sky*, and in *Cloudstreet*'s ordinariness made strange. However, to complete the circle, Winton's vision of ordinariness, simplicity and earthiness is always brought into relation with something beyond or greater than the human, forces sometimes engulfing and traumatic, at times epiphanic and potentially redemptive.

In a 1986 essay on Winton, "Burning Bright", critic Brian Matthews broached these sacred motifs in Winton's early works, arguing:

> It is as if, with the creation of Ort [in *That Eye, the Sky*], Winton has finally cleared the ground. Both *An Open Swimmer* and *Shallows* are fictions in wihich key images threaten to assume visionary significance or presence and thereby to illuminate in an unexpected way: it is a process of transmutation in which the ordinary and familiar attain another status, another kind of presence, because of the intensity of the atmosphere in which they exist or the way in which, for a moment, they are being perceived. *That Eye, the Sky* manifests Winton's version of Wordsworth's "spots in time" – those instants where quite ordinary scenes become enigmatically momentous, epiphanic, in a way that mere logic cannot explain.[29]

Matthews is here, in this early critical essay on Winton, somewhat tentative and exploratory in his designation of Winton's visionariness. Winton's work for Matthews is at once "threaten[ing] to assume visionary significance or presence"; it "illuminate[s] in an unexpected way"; it's a transmutation of the ordinary and familiar; it "exists or is perceived"; it is an instant, and is "enigmatically momentous, epiphanic", "beyond mere logic". The critic, it might be argued, is calling on the literary historian's toolkit of periods and genres to invoke Winton's Romantic roots, as a shorthand way of signalling the larger sacred resonances of his fiction.

---

28 Michael Taussig, *What Colour Is the Sacred?* (Chicago: Chicago University Press, 2009).
29 Brian Matthews, "Burning Bright: Some Impressions of Tim Winton", *Meanjin* 45, no. 1 (March 1986): 88.

Winton throughout his writing life has been exploring different kinds of language – Romantic, abject, sublime, comic, sensual – in order to explore the relationship between the human, the material, and the more than human. His fiction has developed both linguistically and ideologically from *That Eye, the Sky*, through *Cloudstreet* to *Dirt Music*, *Breath* and *Eyrie*, and they are developments that are not yet fully appreciated or understood critically. The earlier novels certainly envision "sacredness" as emerging from, but also at home in, the ordinary and familiar. In the creation of Ort, the child narrator of *That Eye, the Sky*, Winton creates a vehicle of representation that can claim all the innocence and gullibility, the humour, as well as the pain and trauma of a young boy grieving for his father severely injured in a road accident. It is in the extremity of violent accident, coma and hovering death that Ort seeks other explanations, besides mere brute randomness, for what has happened to his reality. Winton has Ort seeking meaning in the parodic episode in which Ort and his mother attend church (discussed in Chapter 1); in response to the equally farcical and strange ministrations and compassion offered by fallible prophet Henry Warburton; as well as in Ort's appeals for a response from the bush and from the night sky arching over his home and family. None of these potential sources of meaning is conclusive in the novel. Winton brings *That Eye, the Sky* to its lyrical, ambivalent ending with a wild form of sacred language teetering on the edge of Ort's hysteria, and the narrative possibility of the father returning to the living. Again, this scene is spoken in the voice of the traumatised but practical, earthed child, examined in Chapter 1.

Breath: What Does Risk-taking Signify?

In *Breath*, published twenty years after *That Eye, the Sky*, the extremes of risk-taking, with exhilarating and sometimes traumatic consequences, are generated differently, in a bleaker language reaching for sacred possibilities. From the opening scene, with its cutting down of the young man who has hung himself, having gone too far in sexual experimentation, we dissolve back through the memories of Pikelet to the underwater games of two adolescent boys, and to the growing dangers of surfing the big waves, as Pikelet and Loonie follow their hero Sando in his extreme sport. We witness the wilder sexual play of Eva and Pikelet, with representations of paedophilia and autoerotic asphyxiation. There has been robust critical debate about the characterisation of Eva.[30] *Breath* ravels together the many forms of risk-taking – the extreme testing of the self – that are shared by all the central characters. What does self-testing indicate about human desires? What kind of phenomenon is this that sends young boys, and surf champions, and lonely, wounded women, out to confront the limit experiences of their own bodies and desires?

Pikelet is from the beginning someone discontented with the ordinariness of his life – his embarrassing parents, the small town he lives in, and his own prowess as a surfer. He wants to shine in the eyes of his guru, Sando, but it is his friend Loonie, and not Pikelet, who achieves Sando's favour and who succeeds in taking on the biggest risks. Narratively entangled in Pikelet's memories of his childhood risk-taking is his adult,

---

30 Colleen McGloin, "Reviving Eva in Tim Winton's *Breath*", *The Journal of Commonwealth Literature* 47, no. 1 (2012): 109–20; Hannah Schürholz, "'Over the Cliff and into the Water': Love, Death and Confession in Tim Winton's Fiction", in *Tim Winton: Critical Essays*, ed. Lyn McCredden and Nathanael O'Reilly (Perth: UWA Publishing, 2014), 96–121.

retrospective account of living as an adult with his broken marriage, his patchy fathering of his daughters, and his vocation as a paramedic confronting trauma every day. But does the fact of human risk-taking point beyond itself, to something more fundamental in human ontology?

Larger psychological, ontological and theological questions in the novel probe what is happening when humans seek to take such risks, to test the limits of the known world. One tentative reply to these questions in *Breath* is that it is the thrill of accomplishing a return, the possibility that meaning will be given or made in such acts, a fuller significance imbued, a new constitution of the self revealed as its limits are tested. This is, arguably, akin to the desire for ecstatic return, resurrection, redemption, of creating new beginnings as old limits are transcended. At the beginning of *Breath*, as the two boys on the edge of manhood play their game of dare, we read:

> Easy, is it? Said a voice hot and close in my ear.
> I jerked aside with a shout. Loonie bawled with laughter.
> Brucie Pike, he said. You're all talk.
> Am not.
> Are so.
> Am not.
> Well then, Pikelet, you better prove it.
> So I showed him what I had. We dived all the rest of that day, kicking down time and again to the opaque depths of the Sawyer River to hold our breaths so long that our heads were full of stars, and when we finally climbed out, spent and queasy, the bank plunged and canted beneath us in the evening twilight. That was the first of many such days and we were friends and rivals from then on. It was the beginning of something. We scared people, pushing each other harder and further until often as not we scared ourselves.[31]

Breath, perhaps more than any other of Winton's works, conjoins risk-taking with ancient human desires – individual and communal – for meaning-making, and a transcendence of self. Risk-taking in *Breath* is a confrontation with the edge of things, with the abyss, with the limits of causality, a refusal to accept mere accident as explanation. It is a gambling with the random, a human thrusting for control. In Winton's fiction, risk-taking combines fear and exhilaration, and the pitting of self against non-human forces, even the possible demise of the self. But of course when young boys are enchanted with the prowess and grace of older men – in this case Sando and the older surfers – "death was hard to imagine when you had these blokes dancing themselves across the bay with smiles on their faces and sun in their hair" (28). The angelic hovers here, in the shining image of the surfers, and the multiple forms of risk and beauty that seduce the young boys.

In an essay on risk in *Breath*, North American critic Nicholas Birns argues convincingly that "Neoliberalism, extreme sports, and erotic asphyxiation are all manifestations of the quest for 'a rebellion against the monotony of drawing breath', of the desire to always be exceptional or interesting."[32]

---

31 Tim Winton, *Breath* (Melbourne: Penguin, 2008), 17–8. All subsequent references are to this edition and appear in parentheses in the text.
32 Nicholas Birns, "A Not Completely Pointless Beauty: *Breath*, Exceptionality, and Neoliberalism", in *Tim Winton: Critical Essays*, eds McCredden and O'Reilly, 276–7.

However, there is arguably more to this desire to be exceptional. Critically, we are invited to probe further the causes and nature of risk-taking as Winton depicts them. It is possible to read Winton's recurrent explorations of risk as including a fascination with the economic risks of neoliberalism, and there is certainly also more than an aesthetics of surfing and risk-taking. There is joy and beauty – as well as terror – in the young boys' confrontation with the ocean, as they pit themselves against the inhuman, or the more than human, colossus of the waves. Edmund Burke's influential thesis on sublimity[33] argued for the interconnectedness of terror and beauty, something which is reflected in Winton's conception of the sacred, the desire and fear involved in leaping beyond the restrictions of the self, into freedom: "dancing themselves across the bay with smiles on their faces and sun in their hair". While there is consequence and aftermath to risk-taking for Winton's characters – the return of traumatic experience, the rising up again of the past into the future, the realisation of failure and brokenness – there is also flickering promise, voiced at the novel's end by the older Bruce Pike: "Out there I'm free. I don't require management . . . [I'm] a man who dances . . ." (265).

In Bruce Pike's adult reference to his childhood passion, and all that it taught and gave him over a lifetime, there is a sense of self and beauty, a refusal to be ashamed, which is captured in this final image. Readers are offered a kind of earthy transcendence, a form of humble redemption. In *That Eye, the Sky*, *Cloudstreet*, *Dirt Music* and *Breath*, Winton's poetics of redemption involve a reaching out in literary language for an understanding of the sacred forces of meaning-making hovering within and beyond the human. These are forces that are inextricably intertwined, incorporating the material, the bodily, the aesthetic, the human, and the more than human. In these novels, Tim Winton explores what might variously be termed the sublime, the other than human, the sacred, seeking a language with which to encounter the sacred forces, to plumb with increasing intensity the limits of human life, in both imaginative and religious terms.

---

33 Edmund Burke, *A Philosophical Enquiry into the Origin of Our Ideas of the Sublime and Beautiful* (Oxford and New York: Oxford University Press, 1990).

5
"Liquid Elites and Bonded Shame": Winton and Class Identity

In his 2013 essay, a memoir entitled "Some Thoughts about Class in Australia: The C Word", Tim Winton argued that "something fundamental has changed in our culture", in our understandings and even our willingness to talk about class structures in Australia:

> Concerns about the distribution of wealth, education and health are difficult to raise in a public forum without needing to beat off the ghost of Stalin. The only form of political correctness that the right will tolerate is the careful elision of class from public discourse, and this troubling discretion has become mainstream.[1]

Winton's essay is anecdotal, passionate and provocative, rather than systematic. Its concerns about class origins and the need to remember them are close to what Marianne Hirsch, in her work on the related context of memory amongst ethnic and migratory groups, describes as "postmemory", a phenomenon that "strives to reactivate and re-embody more distant political and cultural memorial structures by reinvesting them with resonant individual and familial forms of mediation and aesthetic expression."[2] "Some Thoughts about Class in Australia: The C word" blends childhood memories with cherished but volatile class images of Australia "then" and "now"; and it also speaks with a strong voice advocating in the present for the lower echelons of Australian society who are caught in "domestic hardship: poverty of choice, poverty born of constraint, the poverty that is working servitude or the bonded shame of unemployment".

It is arguable that the authorial persona of Tim Winton, lodged in the public imagination through Winton's self-imaging, and through his characters, is located squarely in his working-class origins. But in this essay he also describes growing up in the lucky 1970s, when further education became, for a brief moment, possible for nearly all classes, and when many, including Winton, took up that life-changing opportunity. Hence, the essay is concerned with class and its changing demographics in Australia across the last

---

1 Tim Winton, "Some Thoughts about Class in Australia: The C Word", *Monthly*, December 2013, http://tinyurl.com/Winton2013.
2 Marianne Hirsch, *The Generation of Postmemory: Writing and Visual Culture After the Holocaust* (New York: Columbia University Press, 2012), 33.

five decades, but it is also about "authentic" identity, and particularly Winton's felt identity, as working class, and the ethical call he feels to advocate for

> the poor, who make up almost 13 per cent of Australia's population . . . the welfare class: the sick, the addicted, the impaired and the unemployed, who only exist in the public mind as fodder for tabloid TV and the flagellants of brute radio . . . the working poor. These folk, the cleaners and carers and hospitality workers . . . labour in the shadows in increasingly contingent working situations. Described as "casuals", the only casual element of their existence is the attitude of the entities that employ them. Often on perpetual call or split shifts, their working lives are unstable. Many of them women, a significant proportion of them migrants, they have little bargaining power and low rates of union representation.[3]

The Future of Class in Australia

At the end of 2015, the time of writing this book, Australia was embarking on a significant moment in its history, with the publication of Justice John Dyson Heydon's report into trade unions.[4] In the context of a conservative federal government probe into the role of unions and workers, based on this commission's findings, a broader social debate began, with class relations a constant subtext, if not *the* text. In Winton's description above of Australia's working poor and the unemployed underclass, it is possible to hear the kinds of passionate motives, both conscious and unconscious, informing so many portraits of working-class life in his fiction across the last thirty years: characters such as Raelene and Max in "The Turning",[5] Fay in "Small Mercies", "fifteen and feral-looking" (251) Boner McPharlin in "Boner McPharlin's Moll", the unnamed house cleaner and her son in "On Her Knees", the Larwoods in "Cockleshell", and *Eyrie*'s[6] Gemma Buck and her grandson Kai are all depicted as members of this group of struggling, working-class characters.

However, another informing motivation for his writing surfaces in Winton's essay. This is Winton's awareness of his own self-conscious migration between classes:

> [A] child of the working class who has prospered to a degree unimaginable to my parents and grandparents, and done it in the arts, I am conscious that my own trajectory is atypical.[7]

Winton in the essay places himself in relationship to other writers such as Tom Keneally, Richard Flanagan and Christos Tsiolkas, who have belonged to, but have also experienced and depicted a distance from their working-class origins; or at least a tension, registered in their literary works. While Winton registers this "atypical trajectory" away from his

---

3   Winton, "Some Thoughts about Class in Australia".
4   John Dyson Heydon, *Royal Commission into Trade Union Governance and Corruption: Final Report* (Barton, ACT: Commonwealth of Australia, 2015). https://www.tradeunionroyalcommission.gov.au.
5   Tim Winton, "The Turning", in *The Turning* (Sydney: Picador, 2004), 133–61. All subsequent references are to this edition and appear in parentheses in the text.
6   Tim Winton, *Eyrie* (Melbourne: Penguin, 2013). All subsequent references are to this edition and appear in parentheses in the text.
7   Winton, "Some Thoughts about Class in Australia".

working-class origins, he also distinguishes himself, on the other side, from the privileged class position of writers like Patrick White:

> The great laureate was invariably presented to the world as an oddball, but in truth White's trajectory embodied the rule. Our purse-lipped Jeremiah was a scion of the squattocracy. His was a life of inherited mobility. He began writing in spats and ended up scowling contentedly in a cardigan and beret, and to that extent he conformed to a pattern very familiar indeed. He was, whether he knew it or not, the norm.[8]

In this somewhat reductive portrait, Winton clearly is eager to dissociate himself from what he sees as the privilege and pomposity of the great writer, White, "scowling contentedly in a cardigan and beret" and thinking himself a rebel but in fact (in Winton's eyes) living out "the norm" for his class: inherited mobility; early, desultory "writing in spats"; and a blindness to the privileges he enjoyed. Perhaps the man who lived through a world war in Europe and the Middle East, and who came out as homosexual, the lover of a "foreigner" in a period when this was not easily acknowledged, experienced a mobility of class and gender that was a little more precarious than Winton here sees. But what is equally fascinating is the psychology and the affect of class discourse which Winton displays, whether he knows it or not.

As Winton himself argues in the essay, class experience in childhood leaves powerful imprints on the adult: "I watched my grandfather work until he was in his 70s. Sometimes I carried his Gladstone bag for him".[9] Arguably, what ripples beneath the surface of Winton's memoir of class is a desire not to be, and not to be identified as, a class traitor. It is highly important to him, it seems, that he remember and honour his working-class origins, and while he realises that he has moved into a different class as a writer, he still wants to define himself as a writer belonging with, if not in, the working class. He tells us that "[f]or years I worked in a residential high-rise where the looks on people's faces in the lifts and on the walkways ranged from wry resignation to unspeakable entrapment".[10] From this experience as an outsider amongst his own class he realised that,

> Like the expatriate whose view of home is largely antique, I was a class traveller who'd become a stranger to his own. For all my connection to family, for all the decades I'd spent in fishing towns among tradespeople and labourers, the working class I knew was no more. My new neighbours were living another life entirely.[11]

The narrative here veers from personal anecdote about class identity to a generalising account about the changing experience of being working class in Australia, past and present. Winton registers the "new" working class as more resigned and neglected, "living another life entirely" (meaning different from the one he recalls from childhood, and, ambiguously, from his own increasingly middle-class existence). Hence Winton is also registering his own distance from his origins, and a certain sense of inauthenticity, being a "class traveller", a member of the mobile, moneyed, articulate middle class.

---

8   Winton, "Some Thoughts about Class in Australia".
9   Winton, "Some Thoughts about Class in Australia".
10 Winton, "Some Thoughts about Class in Australia".
11 Winton, "Some Thoughts about Class in Australia".

Writing Class

So, we are led to ask how Winton writes class in his fiction. One answer is that sometimes it is forthright and polemical, and sometimes subtle and poignant, but it is usually reflected in the kind of vernacular language employed by his characters. For example, in the short story "Commission" (217–33) from *The Turning* (discussed from a different angle in Chapter 3), class is registered subtly, in a subtext that poignantly measures the differences, including class differences, between son and father after twenty-seven years of separation. The son belongs in the city, and must drive out of his cosmopolitan life in order to find his father, who is reportedly living well beyond the city, in the desert, "up past Kalgoorlie" (218). We learn that the son is a lawyer who wearily deals with "drunks and junkies [who] take everything out of you, all your patience, all your time and will" (219). As he searches for his father the son finds it "hard not to be angry at the prospect of dealing with the squalor again" (219). There is an understandable impatience and anger in the son at having to retrieve his disloyal father, but our empathy for the son is undercut by the brief details about the young man's fastidious self-consciousness. Inquiring from an "old cove" along the way about his father's whereabouts, he feels himself being inspected by the old man, feeling "awkward standing there in my pressed jeans and pullover. The old fella considered my brogues with interest" (220).

"You in strife?" asks the old man (220), comically turning the tables on the son and his self-righteous mission. The old man draws him a map of where to find the father, the young man noting: "he took up a blank pad and the stub of a pencil whose lead he licked before drawing a map" (220). The young man is depicted as mobile and moneyed, one of those members of the middle class described in Winton's essay, but he lacks the middle-class confidence noted by Winton, because of the woundedness of his origins in a dysfunctional working-class family, a woundedness partly beyond his agency: "There was no point in being furious at my mother for needing this, but I couldn't help myself" (219). This character is unnamed in "Commission", a story written with spare, almost allegorical precision. He turns out to be the character Vic Lang, recognised in the other stories of *The Turning*: "the copper's kid, [who] is dux of the school and doesn't even stay for graduation" (2). The character of Vic appears in most of the stories of *The Turning*, named and unnamed, sometimes only briefly referred to, sometimes centre stage. So what do we make of Winton's preoccupation with traumatic experience in working-class life, reflected in the young man's complex sense of the past – his being burdened and dismissive, at once – especially when we recall the opposite response in his essay, an honouring and cherishing by Winton of his working-class origins?

It is illuminating to compare the literary text and the film adaptation of *The Turning*, each film episode a separate story from the book, made by a different director. In the film adaptation of "Commission", directed by David Wenham, the father is played with muted sorrow and dignity by Hugo Weaving.[12] The class differences between father and son are subtly highlighted, in small details such as when the policeman father discusses his son's job as a lawyer, and the comment by the father that it is a shame to get the son's good car dirty while they drive along the desert roads. Rather, it is the hard-won dignity of the working-class father that steals the film episode, in part because of Weaving's charismatic

---

12 Robert Connolly (creator), *The Turning* (film). Directed by ensemble. Produced by Arenamedia and Screen Australia, 2013.

and dignified acting. While the adult son suffers a complex mixture of emotions in regard to the father who left them without explanation twenty-seven years earlier, the father is clear-eyed, fully aware and contrite regarding his shameful behaviour, and immediately prepared to return with the son to "face" his dying wife. The film is brief, nine or ten minutes long, and is constructed around several economical, poetically understated dialogues in which the father does not seek to justify himself, but calmly narrates his early life as an honest policeman in what he came to believe was a totally corrupt police force. He acknowledges his culpability and shame in being driven to alcoholism, leaving his family, and living, hermit-like, far from the city. In this way, both the film and the short story narrate with pathos the integrity of a fallen, working-class man. His spare, makeshift hut, rudimentary living conditions, and his hard-won reputation for honesty amongst his feral companions in the desert can be read as a justification, if not a redemption, of the man.

The closing frames of the film depict the father, now clean shaven as if self-shriven, sitting calmly in the early morning light, "a battered cashbox in hand which he held like a man entrusted", ready for the trip back. He seems like the combined archetype of struggling bushman and working-class hero, both prevalent in Australian mythologies. The film can be read on many levels: as a nostalgic heroising of the working-class man (faulty, but having raised himself up), in comparison to the son's begrudging and regretful nature. But this reading does not account for the fact that the reader or viewer, along with the son, registers the damage that has been done by the father's actions, testified to in the son's wounded bitterness. However, story and film adaptation also portray a working-class man of some integrity, martyred by his idealism, living a monastic life in sober repentance, as much as he is characterised by any disloyalties. The suggestion hovers that he left the family for their protection, as well as through what he believes was his own cowardice in being unable to cope with the corruption of his colleagues.

Finally, the son, who cannot help but reach out in love to his father, begins to acknowledge the old man anew:

> You read a lot, I see.
> Yes. It's an education. But my eyes are going.
> We'll get you some glasses, I said.
> What time d'you want to leave?
> Oh, first thing.
> Fair enough. (232–3)

The father is being incorporated, tentatively, back into his son's life; but the old man has his eyes doggedly fixed on the future meeting, the shame that must be faced, and ignores, or cannot acknowledge, the son's gesture. The matter-of-fact bluntness of the old man's dialogue reminds us of his class position, its lack of embellishment, and again reinforces his simplicity and lack of deception, producing empathy for him. This too could be read as sentimentalising the working-class man of integrity and authenticity. There are, obviously, many readerly responses to such representations of class, and the story deftly weaves together a number of these.

In *The Turning*'s "Boner McPharlin's Moll", we are presented with a rawer, less palatable portrait of working-class victim than we find in "Commission". Through innate intelligence and a university education, the narrator, Jackie, is able to transcend the kind of confining, working-class life that her school boyfriend Boner goes on to lead, and their lives diverge: "I went east for postgrad work and then left the country altogether. I did the things I dreamt of, some diplomatic stints, the UN, some teaching, a think-tank" (284). It is indeed mobility, education, status and money that define the older Jackie as a class traveller. But as a thirteen-year-old rebel, she moves outside her own petit bourgeois origins, attracted to "the local bad boy . . . in his Levis and thongs . . . that truckin stride . . . like a skater's wade, swaying hip to hip with his elbows flung and his chest out . . . the embodiment of rebellion" (251).

Boner's decline from poverty into drugs and a life of degradation is traced across the years by Jackie, his friend who never quite abandons him, despite his criminal and mental incarceration, which shrivel him in her eyes into "a wild, twisted little man; an ancient child, fat and revolting" (289). The story of Boner and his decline lacks all sentimentality. It probes the nexus of poverty, class and lack of education, seeing Boner as the deprived embodiment of such social forces; but Boner is also depicted as possessing agency, as drug runner and informant for the police, and not mere victim. Criminality, and the way it congeals around impoverished conditions such as the McPharlins' with its elusive promise of more, is a constant theme in *The Turning*. It is exactly what Vic Lang, the policeman's son, has learnt to recognise and to contest as a lawyer.

The Turning is a series of fragmentary tales, and might be experienced as puzzling by first time readers or viewers. However, it is possible to read the entirety of *The Turning* with Vic Lang as its recurrent character, and as drawn together in its probing and assessing of a working-class childhood and the imprints it leaves on the adult. In almost all the stories Vic is the narrator, or is referred to, either as the schoolboy in a small country town, feeling an outsider because his father is the newly appointed policeman, or because he is academically bright, and potentially heading towards university; or as the older lawyer, suffering from the neglect of his father, and from his own redeemer complex. However, it is important to note that while the stories of *The Turning* evaluate working-class life in a range of ways, nostalgically, critically or positively, it is mostly in ways that register the formative trauma and painful narrowness of working-class life. For example, in "Long, Clear View", the unnamed narrator, an adolescent boy whom we realise is Vic, watches the small town to which his family has come as the new policeman's family. The boy's narrative is factually apocalyptic, but emotionally realistic:

> From your parents' window you look out on the strange town. Down there people are quietly stealing, cheating, lying. They're starving their pets and flogging their kids and letting them hang in their wardrobes and burn in cars and choke to death in beachside toilets. And when legs are broken nothing happens, no charges are laid. It's as if things like this are suddenly ordinary. You can't believe how close you came to fitting in here. Everything you know and all the things you half know hang on you like the pressure of sleep. (201)

These are the febrile thoughts of a child turning into a man, bearing the weight of working-class lives (his and other people's), and his father's job in a small country town. The residents of this "strange town" are caught in patterns of corruption and lack of choice. In the boy's mind it is all the same – "people", "they" – all acting in the same ways, with no ethical, public consequences. Through the boy's eyes nothing changes in this world. The boy from the city has to negotiate a nexus of social conventions that make him the outsider: "At school there are new boundaries you can't even see, lines between farmkids and townies, blackfellas and whites, boys and girls, gestures you just don't get" (189). In this self-awareness, the child is already becoming a class traveller, moving beyond his origins in his desire to transcend these conditions – the lack of mobility and opportunity for a better life – that he witnesses in the town. The final image is of the boy sitting in his parents' bedroom, cradling a rifle to his cheek as he stands guard, cocking his weapon, holding it "for as long as it takes to have everyone home safe" (204). It is a haunting and revealing image of how the boy is being shaped by the clenching narrowness and fear in his life. The impact of social stratification in "Long, Clear View" is depicted as visceral, embodied and complex.

In the final story of *The Turning*, "The Defender", we again meet Vic, now in later life. He is a defence lawyer, a sick, scarred man suffering from shingles and a nervous breakdown. He is haunted by his boyhood, by memories of the violence – racial, familial, criminal – which stalk him into his life as lawyer, knowing "what other lawyers called him behind his back. The Redeemer" (310). It's interesting to ponder what is being made of Vic as a class traveller. He is depicted as someone who never really fitted neatly into working-class, small town life, but who also cannot continue to carry the burden of fighting for life's losers, those needing redemption. Gail, his wife, has a complex attitude to him, made up of pity, guilt, impatience and love. In this way she may well be reflecting a reader's attitude to this crippled, working-class man. She honours his ethical life, but is also exasperated by the woundedness imposed by his childhood:

> Do you realise that every vivid experience in your life comes from your adolescence? You should hear yourself talk. You're trapped in it. Nothing you do now holds your attention like the past. Not me, not even your work, these days . . . I'm just part of some long, faded epilogue to your real life. (302)

It is not by chance, but part of the schema of the story, that the friends Vic and Gail are driving to visit are from a different class background to Vic. Their names – Daisy, Fenn, Keira, the baby – tell us as much, along with their genteel country life, Dad capering around in his "floral boardshorts" (303) on the lawn with his kids. They are impractical, live beyond their means, have soft, plump bodies and an inherited orchard. It is not the kind of world in which Vic grew up. Vic is stranded in his adult life, with lack of direction, a childless marriage and an emotional distance, even from Gail, whom he loves. The young boy with the gun in "Long, Clear View", who had shouldered the responsibilities of manhood in his father's absence, who as a lawyer bears the burden of protecting and redeeming the vulnerable, has emerged into adulthood, but is scarred and lost. The last image of *The Turning*, and the last we see of Vic, is of a man battling ghosts. He is taking part in skeet shooting on his friends' lawn, able but reticent to use the gun: "He led, but did not fire. He thought of the boy lurking behind the curtain" (317). But strangely, as Vic takes up the rifle and fires, we are left with an ambiguous, resonant image: "He blasted away, pull after pull after pull, until he was covered in sweat and they were out of ammo and he realised that darkness had fallen around him and he was happy" (317).

The last word here causes us to consider what it is, exactly, that has given the man release, even if it is momentary. Vic is, with all his wounds and hauntedness, a working-class survivor. Our sympathy is with him, even if it is qualified. Winton's working-class man is even a hero *because* of his woundedness, and because he has not ultimately given up his origins.

Eyrie as Working-Class Lament

Vic may or may not be the creative seed of another working-class boy who becomes a lawyer with a cause and who bears the wounds of his past, Tom Keely in *Eyrie*. Unlike the brief, fragmented stories of *The Turning*, *Eyrie* has the length of a novel in which to develop a more extended portrait of how education, wealth and class characteristics are formative of lives and relationships. In the first pages of *Eyrie*, the narrator, a self-lacerating critic of the state and its environmental degradations, describes his hometown through bleary, prophetic eyes:

> Port of Fremantle, gateway to the booming state of Western Australia. Which was, you could say, like Texas. Only it was big. Not to mention thin-skinned. And rich beyond dreaming. The greatest ore deposit in the world. The nation's quarry, China's swaggering enabler. A philistine giant eager to pass off its good fortune as virtue, quick to explain its shortcomings as east-coast conspiracies, always at the point of seceding from the Federation. Leviathan with an irritable bowel. (3)

Sociologists and fiction writers both deal with social inequality, and the role of capital and class in shaping individual and collective lives. Literary critic Terry Eagleton has long combined Marxist and literary approaches, his faith in Marxist critiques of capitalism still alive in his most recent volume, *Why Marx Was Right*.[13] While Eagleton has been a dogged and consistent interlocutor of power, in both literary and ideological terms, he has a number of critics who challenge his sustained Marxist approaches. For example, British philosopher Roger Caldwell takes up his position, in his essay on Eagleton's work, at some distance from Eagleton's faith:

> Marx's vision of history is one of class-struggle and exploitation – whether of slaves in ancient society, serfs under feudalism, or workers under capitalism. Throughout history essential needs have been denied to the majority because of the economic systems they have been forced to endure. Moreover, in the age of capitalism the worker lives in a state of alienation, having become a mere commodity in the labour market. And since the profit-motive reigns supreme, the result of ever more aggressive competition and tighter profit margins can only be the increasing misery of the workers ... [However] there is Marx's assertion of the inevitable breakdown of capitalism due to its supposed internal contradictions. As with the End of the World, we have had many advance notices, but the World, and capitalism, are still with us. In fact, although Marx is confident that the inner contradictions of capitalism are such that it will eventually implode of its own accord, he is notoriously unspecific as to the processes that will bring about its death-throes. Then there is the revolution that is to follow capitalism's demise: what guarantees do we have that power will end up in the hands of the proletariat, as opposed to, say, a militarised elite who will enforce a new authoritarian form of feudalism on the population? If so, the transition to Marx's goal of a truly classless society might be indefinitely deferred.[14]

---

13   Terry Eagleton, *Why Marx Was Right* (New Haven, Conn.: Yale University Press, 2011).
14   Roger Caldwell, review of *Why Marx Was Right* by Terry Eagleton, *Philosophy Now* 96 (December 2015). http://tinyurl.com/Caldwell2015.

5 "Liquid Elites and Bonded Shame": Winton and Class Identity

In his tongue-in-cheek account of the claims and the failures of Marxism to predict the future meaningfully, Caldwell summarises what he sees as inadequate in the grand narratives of the old nineteenth-century economic philosophy. Caldwell seeks to puncture the lack of real-world follow-through on the great promises of Marxism. He does not, however, engage substantially with the major players he names: capitalism and its internal contradictions; power, both capitalist and proletarian; class and the dream of a classless society. His sardonic tone is more than countered, arguably, by Winton's memoir on class, and *Eyrie*'s deeply jaundiced representation of Western Australia's swaggering, philistine greed, its victims scrambling for survival. The real-world dramas of capital and class continue despite Caldwell's irony, and it is the novelist in this instance who is committed to an empathetic representation of little people being trampled under the weight of über-capitalism. Caldwell's attitude does little to address the conditions Winton powerfully represents.

However, in sociology's methodological toolkit there are many other tools when it comes to looking at how class might be conceived of, and addressed. Sociologist Floya Anthias, in a recent essay on class, constructs a compelling and multi-layered argument about social stratification, arguing for a fluid, differentiating mode of viewing class. She writes:

> The social divisions of ethnicity, gender and class can function to reinforce the material inequalities of individuals or interrelate to produce contradictory locations ... where human subjects are positioned differentially within these social divisions ... This indicates that they cannot be looked at in terms of a view of social divisions as constituting permanent groupings of individuals. It is more useful to see individuals as subject to the effectivities of a range of processes in terms of positionality and identity.[15]

Anthias argues for a multi-layered and mobile model of human subjectivity and agency, one in which class, gender and ethnicity are seen as contributing to contradictory identity positions. Rather than class as "permanent groupings of individuals", Anthias writes that such terms as "class" continue to be necessary for sociology, and for broader social debates, but that they must be seen within fluxive contexts in which "a range of processes" intersect in the formation of individuals and collectivities. This structure complements Winton's imaginative creation in *Eyrie* of a volatile interconnectivity between state, capitalist interests and individual subjectivities. "Leviathan with an irritable bowel" is his bleakly comic description of such a voracious and suasive capitalist reality. Of course, Winton's fictional account is a more imaginatively detailed discourse than Anthias' can be, as he traces the coercive and destructive effects of the new social divisions which have erupted "through good fortune" and not virtue, in the early twenty-first-century state of Western Australia.

---

15   Floya Anthias, "The Concept of 'Social Division' and Theorising Social Stratification: Looking at Ethnicity and Class", *Sociology* 35, no. 4 (2001): 852.

Eyrie as Parodic Thriller

Eyrie is written in the hybrid detective genre perfect for tracking this swaggering volatility, up and down the chain of social existence in this place, at this time. The novel is constructed in the form of a parodic thriller, where all the central figures are seen to be scooped up and hollowed out by the forces of greed and corruption. Middle-class Tom Keely is effected substantially, through his daring to point out publicly and loudly the contradictory effects of such grabs for land and wealth; and Gemma Buck, his erstwhile childhood neighbour, is caught in other ways, pincered by a childhood of violence and abuse, poverty, crime, and the fact of being a woman, a mother and a grandmother. The portrait of Gemma is written in strong class and gender terms from the beginning. In a context of economic "pentecostal ecstasy", where the government gave away fresh, easy permission "to drill, strip, fill or blast" in the "boom of all booms" (5), what are the lives of little individuals worth?

In one of their first conversations, the class and economic gap between Gemma and Tom is pinpointed in their different modes of speech:

> Gemma looked at her fork, shrugged.
> These days you're just a bit more . . .
> More what?
> I dunno. Posh.
> Keely laughed; there was nothing else for it. Though it didn't sound as mirthful or unfurled as he'd hoped.
> Fuck off, she said, mildly.
> Posh? Me? You must be on drugs.
> Don't talk to me about fuckin drugs.
> Gemma, I'm unemployed. This is it, he declared, waving at the armchair, the bookshelf, the TV, the portable CD player, the obsolete iPod. Apart from the battered laptop beside him on the laminated table, there was nothing else . . .
> You went to uni and that.
> True.
> And there you were all the time, on the telly, on the news, in the paper. In ya house by the water in Freo – bet that place had character.
> He lifted his hands in surrender.
> Just cause you don't have a job and you look like shit, doesn't mean you're not flash.
> Alright . . . I hear what you're saying . . . (96–7)

Beginning in their common childhood memories, this conversation traces the awkwardness that lies between them now, a gulf created by Keely's access to "uni", money, public status, mobility, and a very different family life. The gap is also revealed in Gemma's language, punctuated with "dunno", "fuck off", "fuckin", "and that". Winton's dialogue measures the painful nexus of class, economic, family and gender deprivations that have led Gemma to her current position. But we also register the fact that Gemma is spot-on in her blunt analysis of Keely's demurring about his privilege: "Just cause you don't have a job and you look like shit", Keely's reply – "Alright . . . I hear what you're saying" – an admission of her insight. He recognises Gemma's self-knowledge about her parlous position, something Keely himself does not seem to possess, or be able to utilise.

5 "Liquid Elites and Bonded Shame": Winton and Class Identity

However *Eyrie* is read, Keely's ambivalent, fallen position (discussed in Chapter 3) is connected to his stranded position, between classes: "Just another flannel-tongued Jeremiah with neither mission nor prophecy, no tribe to claim him but family" (6). He is someone who has railed against gross consumption and its connection to the environmental blitzkrieg in his state, but he is also someone who is pained by the loss of his personal material accoutrements – his Freo house, his public status, his supposedly secure job and life. Even his family – meant to "claim" him – look on at his fall in consternation, but also love, wondering, too, where and how he might belong. It is interesting to note here that it is family that Winton stresses, both Keely's childhood home and the new, unorthodox family he begins to create with Gemma and Kai. His fathering of Kai leads Keely to a new beginning, learning how to belong again. He ends up not being ashamed of Gemma and her working-class accent and appearance, as she suspected he was, and by loving Kai like a son. Class does not disappear in this novel's concerns, but forms a part of those "*contradictory* locations" of identity that Keely begins to probe in himself.

Density and Volatility: Class in *Cloudstreet*

In *Cloudstreet*, published twenty-two years earlier, the density and volatility of class position was already a major focus, represented retrospectively in terms which might be called nostalgic, and framed within a comic genre. Class is probed in detail, as part of the complex social stratification of family, economics, education and gender. It is depicted in the very economic set-up of the house and its inhabitants' struggle to survive as shopkeepers, and joint inhabitants in a community of necessity. Class is also an informing context in Rose's attempts to understand her family origins, and in her first job at the telephone exchange

> Rose found it difficult to distinguish Darleen, Merle or Alma by voice alone because they sounded so alike. They spoke with a cackling kind of pegnosed lilt and laughed like they were being dug in the ribs by a shovel. They were roughmouthed and irritable, with the eyes of rouged cattle.[16]

Rose is equal in class status to Darleen, Merle and Alma, but there is something special about her, the novel seems to be saying. She is proven in character, first of all, by not being a class traitor, being happy at work, "exhausted from not laughing" (239) at the girls' jokes. However, her class loyalty is most fully confirmed on the awful night she is asked to accompany her educated boyfriend, Toby, to a party among university types:

> There was a photographer from the Daily waiting on the steps of the Dalkeith mansion when Toby and Rose arrived starched to the gills . . .
> Who are these people, anyway?
> Oh, uni people, old money, the usual literary establishment.
> What's the editor's name again?
> George Headley. He's edited *Riverside* since the ivy started growing.

---

16 Tim Winton, *Cloudstreet* (Melbourne: Penguin, 1991), 239. All subsequent references are to this edition and appear in parentheses in the text.

> This must be important to you ...
> Rose crept in behind Toby. A jazz combo played in the hallway. A buffet table filled the dining room and forced its trestle way into the huge, dark, heavy-panelled living-room. Leather furniture, jarrah bookcases, elephant's feet, hatstands, squarish paintings on the wall squeezed Rose into her dress. From the huge windows she saw the slick lawns, the gleaming backs of cars, and below it all the lightmoving river. (391–2)

Winton sets the class scene with this litany of palpable privilege as old as time. The solidity and seeming permanence of this world is no match, however, for Rose's pride in herself, and in her family and class origins. She is spritely as she moves amongst these "uni people, old money, the usual literary establishment", carrying sandwiches and wine as requested of a female; but she also registers "the lightmoving river", with its refracting, mobile difference to such stolidity. Toby, in contrast, is snivelling in his desire for recognition from these "uni people", who egg him on, facetiously, cajoling him into describing his next poetic production:

> Toby's giggle mounted another sentence: Well, well, well, actually I've been thinking about some very comic, funny, funny material inspired only today. Rose, tell them about where you live. Tell them about the lady in the backyard who lives in a tent. Tell them about the slow boy you used to love.
> Rose shook in sick surprise. Toby went on in desperation.
> You see, fellows, I'm working up this grotesquerie about ... well there's this shopgirl and a famous writer ... (393–4)

The novelist of *Cloudstreet* constructs a victory for working-class pride, as Rose strides out of the party and out of relationship with Toby, accompanied by the overwhelming realisation that her life may be problematic, not blessed with the heavy-panelled living rooms and slick lawns of Dalkeith, nor the quick, ironic wit of Toby's uni friends, but nor does she dwell in what Toby describes as grotesqueries. It is a turning point for Rose, and leads her eventually to marriage with the working-class man Quick Lamb. Winton offers such victories, in fiction, to his working-class characters, while erstwhile Marxist commentators and their fellow travellers such as Roger Caldwell offer much bleaker scenarios of class identity in a capitalist era.

Winton's portrait of Quick Lamb and of his perfect, working-class qualifications for marrying Rose Pickles, can be found midstream in the novel, as Quick is described on one of his many fishing expeditions:

> The boat sat well in the water, evenly hipped and clean painted. In their rowlocks, the oars knocked and creaked with business. The working, operating feel of things pleased Quick Lamb. There was nothing more warming than the spectacle of something proceeding properly after a due amount of work. He was like that with rifles, with motors, drum reels, or some fancy roadhouses's new flushing toilet. If you didn't know how they worked, then things weren't worth having – something the old girl used to say. (284–5)

With its onomatopoeic stress on the density and sturdiness of well-trimmed gear – hipped, painted, rowlocks, knocked and creaked – its list of useful machinery, and its emphasis on working, work, worked, this passage is giving Quick Lamb his credentials. Rather than the fripperies of uni men, Quick is a quiet, adept working-class man, warmed by the proper running of his equipment and his knowledge of how it operates. These traits of a working-class man – practical, earthed, a hands-on do-er – are amplified in the following passage, where Quick becomes the extraordinary fisherman, his body full of the sensations, "clear and momentous" (285), of his task, "the sky like a fine net letting nothing through but light and strangeness" (285). As he fishes,

> [t]he first bite rang in his wrist like the impact of a cover drive, a bat-and-ball jolt in his sinews . . . They thumped in the bottom round his ankles, the size of big sliver slippers . . . He dragged in four fish, two hooked and two biting their tails . . . Now the boat vibrated like a cathedral with all these fish arching, beating, sliding, bucking, hammering . . . and in the end he stopped casting and lay back in the smother and squelch of fish as they leapt into the boat of their own accord . . . (286)

It is an Australian epiphany we are reading in this scene, with its fishing, its cover drive, bat and ball, and its melding of the ordinary and the corporeal, with the mystical.[17] The fish don't only bite, they leap into Quick's boat; they are a beneficence, a sign of Quick's being blessed, bona fide signs of his worthiness as a practical man open to the world beyond the simply material. In his boat that "vibrated like a cathedral" (however that might be), Quick is, of course, also a Christ-like figure, a "fisher of men", able and willing to care for his brother, Fish, and his future family. The scene is a comic reversal of "the one that got away". Quick's vision of "the figure of a man walking upon the water" (286) does not induce the expected piety, but laughter, as he tells himself to get "sensible again" (286). It's a kind of delirium he falls into, as his boat sinks; he "[keeps] on seeing figures" all the way back to his caravan, falling into a vision or dream:

> [T]here they all are, down by the river laughing and chiacking about, all of them whole and true, with their own faces in a silver rain of light fused with birds and animals. Lester, Oriel, Hat, Elaine, Lon, Red, Fish, himself, and people he doesn't know: women with babies, old people, men with their sleeves pinned, barefoot children, all moving behind a single file of other people the colour of burnt wood . . . (288)

This is, firstly, the *dream* of Quick, a lost man who is finding his way back to where he authentically belongs. It also depicts a classless place (with working-class inflections), with its chiacking and its men with "their sleeves pinned", but also its utopian bringing together of old and young, white and black, in one single gathering. Contemporary Marxist philosopher Bertell Ollman, discussing Marxist utopianism, writes with a number of reservations about dreaming: "[D]reamers are not utopians, only dreamers. They become utopians by adopting a mode of thinking in which dreams, hopes, and intuitions play a bigger role in constructing their vision of the future than their analysis of the present."[18]

---

17 At the time of writing, marine biologists from the University of Melbourne had just discovered twenty new species of freshwater fish in the Kimberley region of northern Australia. It is serendipitous that they decided to name one of these species after Tim Winton.
18 Bertell Ollman, "The Utopian Vision of the Future (Then and Now): A Marxist Critique", *Monthly Review* 57, issue 3 (July–August 2005). http://tinyurl.com/Ollman2005.

Under this rubric, we might also recall Marx's critical but not dismissive description of utopianism as "the anticipation and imaginative expression of a new world".[19] Novelists like Tim Winton provide imaginative meat on the bones of such anticipatory utopianism. While some have criticised what they see as the backward-looking or nostalgic register of *Cloudstreet*, the lyrical way in which this scene crosses between the past, the present, and a comic, utopian version of the future might better reflect many readers' experiences of this novel. Quick's dream is personal *and* social, embracing himself, his family, "and people he doesn't know", "other people the colour of burnt wood". It is Winton's contribution to envisioning another kind of Australia, beyond the narrowly tribal or familial. While the vision of races coming together is arguably little more than hinted at, this passage, together with the opening and the closing scenes of the novel, repeats a kind of working-class utopian dream (see Chapter 4 for a full discussion of the novel's close) with people of all ages and races, workers, Indigenous, mothers and men, coming together in leisure and friendship, "laughing and chiacking about, all of them whole and true".

"Whole and true", the utopian dream of rest and of plenty, is what energises Quick to take up a new direction, allowing his dreams to trigger the future. It is a moment when Winton and his creation, Quick Lamb, become mirrors of each other, as the imaginative capacity to change the world is celebrated. Fiona Morrison writes of this autobiographical element in *Cloudstreet*, although she equates Winton to Wax Harry, the baby of Rose and Quick who brings the two families together, both Wax and Winton being born in 1960:

> *Cloudstreet* offers a story of something like that of Winton's own family, and in this sense it works as an origin story that unites two very interesting strands. One of these is a broadly comic vision committed to carnivalesque rambunctiousness, bodily presence and versions of reconciliation, which are, at the same time, plucked from countervailing instances of fragmentation, division and alienated absence . . . The intensity of the reincarnated speech community is memorial in its scope and certainly equals the intensity with which Winton records the inner lives and visionary experiences of the stereotypically less articulate working-class people, particularly the men . . . and its powerfully local speech community provides the engine of this novel.[20]

Morrison is a strong guide to *Cloudstreet*'s construction of an Australian, mid-twentieth century working-class vernacular, and its connection to Winton's projected working-class identity and values. She sees the novel's "metaphysics of presence",[21] its use of vernacular, its working-class sense of authenticity and a belief in the possibility of wholeness, as strands running in parallel in the novel. She argues further that "the texture of the speaking community is . . . everywhere to be found, and this is the powerful and ambiguous point of collision between speech, writing and a mediating consciousness".[22] The vernacular Morrison is describing operates in a number of ways, through direct speech, the reported thoughts of the often tongue-tied characters, and the free indirect speech of the narrator.

---

19   Karl Marx and Frederick Engels, *Selected Correspondence* (Moscow: Progress, 1975), 172.
20   Fiona Morrison, "'Bursting with Voice and Doubleness': Vernacular Presence and Visions of Inclusiveness in Tim Winton's *Cloudstreet*", in *Tim Winton: Critical Essays*, ed. Lyn McCredden and Nathanael O'Reilly (Perth: UWA Publishing, 2014), 50–51.
21   Morrison, "Bursting with Voice", 51.
22   Morrison, "Bursting with Voice", 52.

In this way we are given far-reaching access to the thoughts and values of the working-class characters who cannot necessarily express them in dialogue.

Morrison also confronts the prickly question of Indigenous speech, and the way in which the novel leaves Indigenous characters mainly silent, or gnomic, or laughing as they fade away. This creation of a mainly white vernacular may leave readers uneasy about the muted presence of Indigenous characters, a privileging of white working class in the context of Indigenous suppression. On the other hand, Winton's creation of specifically non-British, postcolonial uses of vernacular language also playfully offers white-settler Australia a different, home-grown mode of language to that of imperial Britain. These postcolonial issues of language and place will be addressed more fully in Chapter 7 of this volume.

Cloudstreet's Hybrid Languages

A kind of hybrid language combining the mystical and the sensual, working-class vernacular and lyricism, ripples through *Cloudstreet*. As Morrison argues:

> Winton's effort is to secure a sense that the Australian working-class man is not merely the subject and spokesperson of ethnographic "local colour" humour or even bleak colonial realism but the locus of full poetic apprehension.[23]

Winton's form of poetics carries a powerful ideological freight. It seeks to clear a space for working-class language and to claim an authenticity for working-class life. No matter how far such "authenticity" might be considered nostalgic, or fabricated out of utopian dream, it is an unmistakable characteristic of *Cloudstreet*, and of Winton more generally, and possibly a reason for the novel's popularity. Morrison closes her essay by quoting Scott Hames on Scottish vernacularity. Hames sees that language

> is about heritage and authentic roots, and where there is a prevailing rhetoric of revival of cultural self-presence rooted in claims about authenticity and obsessed with an aesthetics of embodiment.[24]

There is arguably a similar neo-Romantic or utopian drive informing *Cloudstreet*, a need to invent the working-class world that Winton fears is disappearing. By giving this world – rooted in 1950s Australia – a literary *and* popular form and accent, Winton is an imaginative dreamer, like his character Quick Lamb. Winton laments the loss of this world, but also gives new imaginative form and energy to the traits and values of working-class life that he believes were formative of his own identity, values that he does not want to see gone forever.

However, it is revealing to ask just what the content of "working-class" life, traits and values is in Winton's fiction. In his essay on class he describes his childhood world having passed, and the working class he once knew disappearing with it. What does he go on to argue positively *for*? For a replenishment or re-evaluation of such values

---

23 Morrison, "Bursting with Voice", 66.
24 Scott Hames cited in Morrison, "Bursting with Voice", 71.

in the contemporary world? To this end he quotes current statistics, and describes the conditions of the working and unemployed poor in Australia, and in *Eyrie* he charts the overwhelming destructiveness of twenty-first century-capitalism and mining in his home state. He also argues that right-wing forces have overseen a "careful elision of class from public discourse, and this troubling discretion has become mainstream".[25] But again, what is the content of Winton's "working class" in relation to what Anthias has described as a fluid and complex nexus of factors, rather than "permanent groupings of individuals"?[26] One response to this would be to say that Winton describes what is *not* working class, but middle class (mobility, education, moneyed choice, and, in the case of *Eyrie*, poetry, non-manual labour, irony). Hence, it could be argued that Winton's "working class" may be represented more in its absence in *Eyrie*.

If we accept the shifting nature of all class groupings and definitions, this means that Winton and other artists are constructing an object of imaginative importance, part-imaginary, part-factual, placing it before a readership which itself will be reading through their own class lenses, assessing what they see or refuse to see. This does not mean, of course, that the notion of working-class values and traits is unreadable, or is not needed. Rather, such an "object" is constantly, imaginatively, passionately requiring to be reassessed and drawn back from mere nostalgia. And this dialectic of fact and imagination, reality and dream, is what Winton conducts so powerfully in his work.

---

25 Winton, "Some Thoughts about Class in Australia".
26 Anthias, "The Concept of Social Division", 852.

6
High and Popular: Straddling the Fiction Market

In 2002, literary journalist Jason Steger offered the following snapshot of fiction sales in Australia:

> The fiction market is not small beer... in 1999–2000 Australians bought 1.1 million new hardback novels worth $17.8 million, 1.2 million trade paperback novels for $13.9 million, and also spent $42.6 million on 8.5 million mass-market novels. In that period, 36 new hardback, 155 new trade paperback, and 1089 new mass-market novels were published.[1]

Since 2002, the terms "hardback novel", "trade paperback novel" and "mass-market novel" have become somewhat anachronistic, as e-publishing, and the growing hybridisation of popular and literary writing, paperback and hardback, have accelerated. Fiction, as a cultural phenomenon, has long hovered between the categories of popular entertainment and that controversial term, "the literary work". In debates about the values and roles attributed to different kinds of fiction, "entertainment" or "popular" fiction often suggests action and plot-driven, genre-based and with a biggish audience, as well as non-challenging/familiar. "The literary" is equated with the intellectual, aesthetic, challenging, and linguistically, formally innovative.

In 2008, critic Beth Driscoll described the Australian federal government's Books Alive program, which put some of the $75 million earned each year from the GST on books into a campaign that "whips up enthusiasm for recreational reading":

> Books Alive... models an entertainment-driven version of literary practice. Rather than fostering thoughtful reading, Books Alive participates in the blockbuster culture of contemporary publishing, of marketing hype and mass sales that just may be the key to literature's survival.[2]

---

1 Jason Steger, "The Truth of Publishing Is Stranger than Fiction", *Age*, 13 June 2002. http://tinyurl.com/Steger2002.
2 Beth Driscoll, "On Culture, Cash and Books Alive," *Australian*, 26 July 2008. http://tinyurl.com/Driscoll2008.

At first, Driscoll seems to draw a brisk, definitive line between the popular and the literary, aligning the former with market practices and with reliance on "blockbuster" values. However, this is arguably Driscoll's way of seducing "literary types", making them feel comfortable that literary values are being upheld, and that they are still seen as "thoughtful". She then proceeds to muddy the waters that swirl around the categories of popular and literary:

> It is a reality that building a market for literature is essential. Literature cannot exist without people prepared to buy it, without vibrant bookstores and well-patronised libraries. Research done before the campaign indicates that one-quarter of Australians rarely read for pleasure.
>
> In the first year of Books Alive, book sales increased by about 15 per cent compared with the same period in 2002, and organisers claim that the campaign has put 1.2 million books in the hands of readers. Books Alive's project of creating a market for literature is truly valuable.[3]

Not all will agree with this diagnosis of literature and its relationship to the marketplace. Of course it's good to promote literacy, as Driscoll points out, and Books Alive does emphasise (and market to) children as readers. But she warns that "Books Alive's popularity-oriented approach flattens culture, mixing literary fiction with true crime and promoting them all like blockbuster films".[4] Driscoll's critique of a flattened culture, elaborated in her 2014 monograph *The New Literary Middlebrow: Tastemakers and Reading in the Twenty-first Century*,[5] is brave because it dares to define, or at least give the wide parameters, of not only the popular (of which many are writing today) but of "the literary". And of course these two categories are never definitively separate. Driscoll argues:

> Traditionally, prose innovation and intellectual weight have been the foundation of literary reputations. The Books Alive panel, in contrast, selects books it describes as "thumping great reads". The campaign's slogan ... embraces the devouring, escapist values of pulp fiction – books "you can't put down" – rather than the close, thoughtful reading we associate with the classics.[6]

However, "books you can't put down" may also include those being read closely and thoughtfully. Sometimes novels can offer several or all of these possibilities – entertainment and thoughtfulness, genre and fine writing; yet the critical distinction between "the literary" and "the popular" still fascinates, still causes debates across the globe, amongst scholars, general readers and reviewers. Canadian literary scholar Paul Swirski has argued that, for his profession, "the opinion persists, often as part of an unarticulated and thus unexamined set of background beliefs, that popular fiction has no merit and thus no place in literary studies".[7]

---

3 Driscoll, "On Culture".
4 Driscoll, "On Culture".
5 Beth Driscoll, *The New Literary Middlebrow: Tastemakers and Reading in the Twenty-First Century* (London: Palgrave Macmillan, 2014).
6 Driscoll, "On Culture".
7 Peter Swirski, "Popular and Highbrow Literature: A Comparative View", *Comparative Literature and Culture* 1, issue 4 (1999): 2. http://dx.doi.org/10.7771/1481-4374.1053.

Blurring the Lines: Literary and Popular Fiction

Tim Winton has been characterised as both "literary" and "popular"; the author of books for children and adults, his fiction is placed on school and university curricula, and selected by reading groups across the country. He has a national and international profile, so it is safe to say that his novels are popular – that is, well promoted nationally and internationally, sold in large numbers, at least among literary-inclined readers (students, teachers, other professionals, middlebrow readers) in China and Australia, the UK and the USA. However, Winton's writing arguably flouts this binary of popular and literary. His oeuvre embraces multiple forms and genres: children's books such as *The Bugalugs Bum Thief* (1991); laconic short stories and novellas of childhood and the rites of passage which usher a young boy into adult life, such as *That Eye, the Sky* (1986) and his later, more melancholic or brooding short stories and novels, *The Riders* (1994), *Dirt Music* (2001) and *The Turning* (2004), *Breath* (2008) and *Eyrie* (2013). *The Riders* and *Dirt Music* are dark fables representing loss and grief, the threat, trauma or failure hovering in the lives of children, traumas which often impact on adult life. This darkness also marks Winton's collection of short stories, *The Turning*, a mood captured by director Robert Connolly's film adaptation.[8] Winton's latest novel, *Eyrie*, can also be described in the same way; but it is not as if the darker, more brooding, existential aspect of Winton's oeuvre occurs only in the late works. It is there from the beginning.

This dark mood is not simply the result of the author growing up, or older. What can be made of this tension between trauma and comedy, loss and celebration, in Winton's fiction? Where and how do the popular (the entertaining, the blockbuster, the rollicking, the comic) and the literary (challenging, often disquieting, linguistically innovative) lock horns in Winton's work? This chapter examines two connected issues about Winton's work: how the categories of popular and literary can be deployed usefully in relation to his oeuvre; and the tension between the "sunnier", iconic, often humorous strain in Winton's writing, and a more negative undertow which informs many of his works. We need to ask whether there is any correlation between these two aspects, the designation of popular and literary, and the tension between the sunny and the melancholic. This inquiry arises as a concern about what "literature" is and might be in the context of a globalised book market, of which Winton is a part, and the ubiquity of multiple forms of popular entertainment in the twenty-first century.

One way of approaching these interweaving sets of questions is to examine the reception, both scholarly and general, of Winton's latest novel *Eyrie*. *Eyrie* was shortlisted for, but did not win, the 2014 Western Australian Premier's Award, the state's top prize, but it did win the People's Choice Award in that same competition, voted on by the public from the shortlist. Not in agreement with this popular vote, UK journalist Catherine Blyth reviewed *Eyrie* for British daily *The Telegraph* under the headline "Overextended and Underdeveloped: A Heartfelt Story of Disillusionment and Salvation Fails to Soar".[9] Blyth argues that the novel is a failure because, well, it's about failure, in both theme and narrative

---

8 Robert Connolly (creator), *The Turning* (film). Directed by ensemble. Produced by Arenamedia and Screen Australia, 2013.
9 Catherine Blyth, "Overextended and Underdeveloped: A Heartfelt Story of Disillusionment and Salvation Fails to Soar", review of *Eyrie* by Tim Winton, *Telegraph* (UK), 18 June 2014. http://tinyurl.com/Blyth14.

structure: "*Eyrie* is like being stuck in a lift with an unusually eloquent one, receiving a lecture on humanity's vileness while you wait for a story to get things moving".[10] The inference here is that readers don't want vileness, and they certainly don't want it in a story that has no narrative drive, no action. Blyth sets up the narrative trajectory of the novel in this succinct way:

> Tom Keely, a lapsed environmentalist, is hungover, again. Jobless, wifeless and childless, he measures out his days in booze, painkillers and bad breakfasts. Outside it is "hot enough to kill an asbestos sparrow", so mostly he lurks in his eyrie, a tiny flat in a benighted tower block. It is 2008 and mineral-rich Western Australia ... is being eviscerated for China's industrial revolution.[11]

It is a racy, apt summary and offers us glimpses of Winton's humorous, vernacular skills through direct and indirect speech. Self-contradictorily, Blyth tends here to make us see that there is a great deal going on in the novel: international deals in the economy and with the environment, and other kinds of melancholic, personal deals at the individual level. So where does the problem seem to lie, for Blyth? It is to what she sees as the narrative "torpor", the failure to solve anything, that Blyth objects:

> Tension is generated through longing and fear, sometimes beautifully: a beating is remembered by "the exploded feeling in his cheek". There are insights into corruption and the pilfering of the stricken land. But Winton's hovering over so many fascinating avenues, while refusing to nose down them, grows frustrating.[12]

This reviewer wants to read action and solution. With her own dose of vernacular language, Blyth wants the author to "nose down" the many avenues set up by the narrative; to stop hovering and stalling, stop "frustrating" the narrative-hungry reader.

This scenario is a possible starting point for an understanding of how the differences between the popular and the literary might be considered. However, before the question can be thought about in these terms, it's helpful to list fully the elements and qualities that Blyth is calling for in a good read: more action, something resolved, a "nosing down" into all the possible "fascinating avenues" raised in the novel but not pursued. Does Blyth's stance amount to a call for more "popular" techniques (action, colour, narrative drive, keeping readers entertained), and less heavy, thoughtful, literary material, less self-reflexivity? In response, I would agree with Swirski in his complicating from the outset the distinctions between popular and literary fiction. Swirski's passionate argument, firstly to his own peers in literary scholarship, offers empirical and polemical evidence that the distinction between the popular and the literary is a wavering, unfixed one. He concludes his argument in this way:

> Much of popular fiction can stand on its own feet next to many works hailed as lasting triumphs of Western literature. Much more deserves to be treated as the only thing it tries to be: gripping but ephemeral entertainment without aspirations to bowl over the literary

---

10 Blyth, "Overextended and Underdeveloped".
11 Blyth, "Overextended and Underdeveloped".
12 Blyth, "Overextended and Underdeveloped".

establishment. Some of it is demonstrable shlock, which makes the task of educating the readers who persist in buying it all the more worthwhile. But to tell a good popular novel from a bad one, or a good popular novel from a bad classic, we need to approach contemporary literature – in whatever form or genre it chooses to manifest itself – with an unjaundiced eye and a critical apparatus of sufficient refinement.[13]

Swirski here is writing in defence of many kinds of writing along the popular/literary spectrum, and of their diverse cultural value. He does not deny that there are distinctions to be made between the two poles, but he also probes the many commonalities and intersections between them. He's not afraid of describing some writing as "schlock", whether literary or popular, or somewhere in between. What he does call for is an astute critical reading that can evaluate a work, discussing its comparative values and achievements, in a dialectical manner, across the popular–literary divide.

The *Telegraph* reviewer of *Eyrie*, in criticising its "overextension" (this seems to imply overaestheticisation, and/or too many ideas with not enough plot satisfaction) and lack of action, seems to come from the opposite camp to Swirski. Whether consciously or unknowingly, Blyth is calling for what are traditionally popular, entertaining, action-led fictions, decrying the do-nothing, verbally overpowering but underachieving hero:

> [T]his novel is the sequel to a gripping unwritten tale, in which Keely took on big business and lost his beliefs. By contrast, as a meditation on the salvation business . . . [t]he cheap thrills of heroism are called into question, but it is all a little worthy, and the treatment feels both overextended and underdeveloped.[14]

In other words, the reviewer wants more action hero in her hypothetical prequel (taking on big business, losing your beliefs), rather than what the critic calls *Eyrie*'s "meditation on the salvation business".[15] However, what happens if readers are interested in language and in the *substance* of belief (lost or found), in thinking about values, and in questioning the expected, ubiquitous and popular action-man hero? Does this mean such readers are highbrow, literary, and potentially scornful of popular writing?

Parodying the Genre

What is fascinating about this review is that it fails to notice that the novel is actually a funny, provocative parody of the action-man stereotype, but also more sweepingly of the genre of crime fiction, with its who-dunnit formulas. *Eyrie* weaves together self-reflection and internal monologue with pithy representations of the underbelly of crime and petty thuggery, the recriminations of the underworld drug scene, seeing them as part of a network of political and social corruption fuelled by big, fast business. This is Winton's drama of spiritual self-questioning. In other words, *Eyrie* is a novel by a strong writer at the top of his career, playing fast and loose with both popular and literary themes and forms, using a wide range of narrative and genre techniques. The existentialist drama of

---

13 Swirski, "Popular and Highbrow Literature".
14 Blyth, "Overextended and Underdeveloped".
15 Blyth, "Overextended and Underdeveloped".

Tom Keely, who blunders from hero to loser, from idealist to misanthrope, from activist to passive victim, to (not so secret) agent, makes this, in my reading of *Eyrie*, a highly developed, playful *and* serious production. Is it popular or literary? Does it matter? Is it Blyth's sequel to her much more exciting, hypothetical prequel? It depends where you are looking for your excitement.

It is just so in many of Winton's novels, in which we are reading about the aftermath of loss and trauma. Meditation, self-reflection, interior drama, are the stamp of many of Winton's works, rather than immediate action. The beautiful early novel *That Eye, the Sky* achieves its narrative "drive" through its emotion recollected in tranquillity, its pathos and retrospectivity even as it is narrated in the present tense by Ort, the young boy who fears he is losing his father after a near-fatal accident:

> It took me and mum ages to put him to bed ... We had to roll him and drag him like a feed sack, push him, pull him. There's his heel marks in the dust on the floorboards in the hall. How are we gonna keep it up? How? What do we do to get him fixed? He's not bad you know. He's done nothing bad. My dad kisses me good night and he puts his fingers in my hair and tells me stories and shows me how to do things that you don't normally think of ... [16]

That Eye, the Sky creates a moment in time impacted by loss and fear, the recollections narrated by a child who will carry all the sadness – his father's accident, his mother's grief, the family's seeking and not finding solace – into an unclear future: "What do we do to get him fixed?" This moment in time is crafted carefully, with its movements back and forth between past and present almost imperceptible. Its rising fear and loss of control is told in childlike vernacular – the boy's passionate defence of his father's goodness; his recounting in sensuous terms his father's fingers touching him, his father's special storytelling voice. Present, past and future are woven together here in a prose that touches chords of nostalgia, but goes beyond this. Published in 1986, *That Eye, the Sky* captures a late hippy, urban-fringe, bush-dwelling moment of time that readers in the 1980s and thereafter may well register for its "pastness", but equally, it is memorable for the child's hope and efforts to create and sustain a future of value for his family.

Whether this novel, and many other of Winton's brooding, even meditative works, can be dismissed as "nostalgic", readers and critics will determine. While very little happens in this moment – as the father lies in a coma, as the self-proclaimed prophet and miracle worker Henry Warburton farcically stumbles and fails at all he takes on, and as the church members can offer no real welcome or solace – a great deal actually does happen, including a child's imagining the possibility of miracle and resurrection. However, in terms of action and plot, this desire for miracle does not "nose down" all avenues in terms of action. Rather, miracle is only suggested in a child's excited language, as the novel ends:

> Everywhere, in through all my looking places and the places I never even thought of – under the doors, up through the boards – that beautiful cloud creeps in. This house is filling with light and crazy music and suddenly I know what's going to happen and it's like the whole flaming world's suddenly making sense for a second ... (150)

---

16 Tim Winton, *That Eye, the Sky* (Melbourne: McPhee Gribble, 1986), 50. All subsequent references are to this edition and appear in parentheses in the text.

6 High and Popular: Straddling the Fiction Market

In a rapid-fire stream of consciousness narration Ort witnesses what is about to happen: the impossible, the hoped-for, and even resurrection, just as the novel ends. *That Eye, the Sky* is simultaneously humorous and vernacular, epiphanic, lacking in action, but promising much. Is it popular or literary fiction? Or both? The novel can be read as genre writing, as bildungsroman, adolescent fiction, or adult fiction with a child narrator. It doesn't seem to matter, as the novel falls into the same "category" as Mark Twain's *The Adventures of Huckleberry Finn*, a childhood favourite of Winton.

As well as being somewhat divided about the genres of Winton's fiction, scholars of Australian literature certainly do not agree when it comes to the value of Winton's overall contribution, and long may it be so. After all, values – both aesthetic and ontological – need to be put into question in such debates. Robert Dixon's discussion of nostalgia in *Cloudstreet* is not altogether dismissive, but it does swing around the term "nostalgia" as a hinge word, variously deployed as positive and negative.[17] While nostalgia might be enjoyed by many, especially in popular cultural consumption, most critical uses of the term suggest that it is sub-intellectual, sentimental, or merely emotional, as opposed to thoughtful or future-oriented. It is often seen as a preference for the past over the future, a shunning of modernity and the global for the (presumably) comforting avenues of the past, tradition, and the local. I want to suggest that the genre-mixing playfulness of *Cloudstreet*, its cutting back and forward between farce and realism, between magic realism (the talking pig!) and documentary (the Nedlands murders), between nostalgia and plain old shame at the shabbiness and failures of the past, between the popular and the literary, make *Cloudstreet* a lot more playful, richer, and less sentimental than Dixon and others have seen it as being.

Where, for instance, on the spectrum of popular and literary, nostalgic and future-oriented, do readers place the character and story of Fish Lamb, the brain-injured boy who never grew to manhood? Fish is loved, tolerated, cared for; but he is also an aching burden in the lives of his family members, a boy stuck in childhood. He will never know the full promise or pain of his future life. His boyhood accident and its consequences are the beginning of suffering and disbelief in his religious family; but they are also the source of wonder and longing invoked by the novel for something better than the partial, hurt world, a longing which circles round and round in this novel and is never simply nostalgic. The disembodied narrator at the end of the novel observes Fish in the backyard, where he talks to his pet pig:

> Down in the yard at Cloudstreet, down there in the halls and channels of time Fish and the pig exchange glances... But I can't read your face. I stare back at you in the puddles on the chilly ground, I'm waiting in your long monastic breath, I travel back to these moments to wonder at what you're feeling and come away with nothing but the knowledge of how it will be in the end. You're coming to me, Fish, and all you might have been, all you could have hoped for... No shadows, no ugliness, no hurtings, no falling down angry. Your turn is coming.[18]

---

17   Robert Dixon, "Tim Winton, *Cloudstreet* and the Field of Australian Literature", *Westerly* 50 (2005), 240–60.
18   Tim Winton, *Cloudstreet* (Melbourne: McPhee Gribble, 1991), 529–30. All subsequent references are to this edition and appear in parentheses in the text.

Readers are momentarily made to stop and wonder who this intimate, ghostly narrator is, and realise with a shock that it is Fish himself, speaking from another, imagined dimension. The scene is in a broadly realist genre (vernacular dialogue, inner monologue/stream of consciousness, domestic setting), but it arguably bursts out of this generic classification. There is farce here too, as the boy exchanges glances with his talking pig, but this passage disturbs any purely literary, aesthetic reading. There is also an ontological, meditative questioning in the writing, as it looks both backwards and forwards along "the halls and channels of time", suggesting the not-yet, the possible emerging from the impossible, in its longing, with its extended sentences and their "long monastic breath". Readers are asked to flow with the strangeness of the narrative: an internal monologue of a damaged boy, grown into an awkward adult body but deprived of full life, who is being addressed by another self, one who exists, whole, beyond the shadowed, hurting world.

It is the inner monologue of a no-longer existing character who sees more than all the living characters, and offers up a prayer, a hope, a dream of fulfilment, of: "Being Fish Lamb. Perfectly. Always. Everyplace. Me" (558). There is little action, but a kind of quotidian, comic, vernacular meditation, writing that draws on both popular and literary techniques woven intimately together, so that it seems irrelevant, or just inept, to place the novel in one strict category or the other.

Cloudstreet is often described as Australia's favourite novel in readers' polls, such as the survey of the Australian Broadcasting Commission's viewers' *First Tuesday Book Club*.[19] The novel's popularity is evident in the fact that it was made into a television mini-series and adapted for the stage. For Australian playwright Nick Enright, co-author of the stage script of *Cloudstreet*, "[p]eople get that look in their eye, that *Cloudstreet* look". For him, the novel has "leapt the fence in Australia, it's in the bloodstream of the nation".[20] Enright's poetic metaphor – "the bloodstream of the nation" – is arguably seeking to surmount the polemics surrounding definitions of popular and literary. The playwright draws the two together, and many viewers would agree that the stage play, highly popular for the duration of its performances in Australia, Britain and the USA, does just that.

Cloudstreet, as well as *That Eye, the Sky*, also addresses the second question raised at the beginning of this chapter: how to consider the sunny, celebratory, poetic and epiphanic elements in Winton's writing, in comparison to the darker, more melancholy aspects. Fish Lamb is a poignant, lumbering, painful creation, but finally his fate is reconciled, with a dignified gesture towards hope in death. Fish's longing for the element of the water is a form of renewal in baptism. Just so, the character of Quick Lamb, who grieves for his brother, and is his childhood guardian, understands in his depths the pain of human existence. He is deployed by Winton to reconcile all the characters through his marriage to Rose, the daughter of the "other" family, and through the birth of their child, "Wax" Harry, in what could be called a full-blown comic, celebratory dénouement. *Cloudstreet* employs all the popular, fulfilling elements of comic narrative. Traces of tragedy can be found, such as the fate of the Indigenous characters, earlier inhabitants of the house in Cloudstreet, and of the wider land, but they are muted (some critics would say not adequately developed) in the narrative undertow towards white narratives of reconciliation and rebirth.

---

19 Andrew Cattanach, "10 Australian Books to Read Before You Die – *First Tuesday Book Club*," Booktopia blog, 5 December 2012. http://tinyurl.com/Cattanach2012.
20 Nick Enright cited in Fiona Morrison, "Figures of the Many and the One: Genre and Narrative Method in Tim Winton's *Cloudstreet*," *Sydney Studies in English* 25 (1999): 133.

6 High and Popular: Straddling the Fiction Market

These darker elements hinted at in *Cloudstreet* are present in more startling, less reconciled ways in later Winton novels and short stories. It is arguable that *Cloudstreet*, together with its adaptations, was a popular as well as literary pinnacle for Winton. Between 2001 and 2013, Winton published four demonstrably darker works: *Dirt Music*, *The Turning*, *Breath* and *Eyrie*, none of which offers comic conclusions, though the three novels arguably turn, tentatively, towards hope. While the wide popularity of *Cloudstreet* has not been repeated, Winton has achieved critical success, winning Australia's top literary prize, the Miles Franklin Literary Award, four times, for *Shallows*, *Cloudstreet*, *Dirt Music* and *Breath*, and being shortlisted for the Man Booker Prize (UK), for *The Riders* and *Dirt Music*.

What follows, then, from the fact that in the latter half of his career (and in some of the earlier works) Winton has produced a range of darker works that focus on trauma, loss, failure, grief and regret? The collection of short stories, *The Turning*, deals with Vic Lang, possibly Winton's most unreconciled character. Winton remains a top-selling author but his reputation still swings between " popular" and "literary" amongst critics. (See Chapter 8 for a discussion of popularity in terms of sales figures in Australia, the UK and America.)

New York-based reviewer Alison McCulloch has a very different reading of the relationship between Winton's dark and comic elements. In her review of *Eyrie,* McCulloch writes of the novel's central character, Tom Keely, who is a failure in multiple ways, personally and politically:

> His is a familiar plight in the literature of despair, but it's one that Winton has made over anew for this time and place. And in his hands, with his distinctive Australian voice and vernacular, this disquieting story also has the power to surprise and delight – perhaps even inspire.[21]

"The literature of despair"? Is it a step too far to describe Winton's later work in this way? Or, if this seems a reasonable description of certain strands in Winton's work, what then does this suggest about readers' reception of its "disquieting" power? Do literary readers want to be disquieted, challenged, confronted (as against those seeking entertainment)? Some do, and, it seems, McCulloch is one of them. Of course readers are a diverse cohort. Some want the challenge of such disquiet – which may lead to "surprise and delight", or not – but other readerly responses to *Eyrie*, for example, include: "life's black enough, I want to read for escape"; or "I don't want to be depressed by what I read"; or, like Blyth, "I want plot, narrative, action"; or, "I need to like the characters in order to be involved". These kinds of responses are commonplace amongst readers.

However, Winton continues to be awarded prizes, and to be read in large enough numbers for it to be argued that there are readers out there, Australian, Chinese, American, Canadian and British, who read Winton as both popular and literary: for the vibrant – and yes, often disquieting – plurality of his fictional techniques: his lyrical, aesthetically rich prose; its generic weaving and ducking; its moving, challenging squadron of characters – surfers, lovers, beachcombers, losers, drunks, hurt and abused women,

---

21 Alison McCulloch, "Decline and Falling", review of *Eyrie* by Tim Winton, *New York Times Sunday Book Review*, 25 July 2014. http://tinyurl.com/McCulloch2014.

leftover hippies, loving mothers, lonely wanderers; its vernacular humour; its meditative insights, and yes, its skating close to nostalgia at points.

Island Home: The Genre of Memoir

In 2015, Winton published *Island Home: A Landscape Memoir*. Its very genre, memoir, suggests non-fiction, but it employs many fictional techniques: repeated image, lyrical place-making, a narrative voice that is of course "Winton", but is both close to yet distinct from many of his fictional characters. The memoir's opening chapter, "County Offaly, 1988", takes us back to *The Riders* and Ireland. Without very much self-reference, Winton tells us of the months he spent in rural Ireland, and how his young son coped with the move from Australia at the age of two. Like so many of Winton's fictional characters, the little boy is central to the opening recollection, his voice offering a perspective that some may consider merely nostalgic. After an icy "savage afternoon" out in the "long, lumpy fields", father and son sit by the fire:

> Later by the fire he sets aside his hot chocolate to stare at the snapshots of home pinned to the wall. All the suncreased faces of friends and family. Daggy hats and bare chests. Dogs in utes. The endless clear space behind people, the towering skies and open horizons. He lingers over the dreamy beaches and mottled limestone reefs at low tide, sculpted dunes at sunset.
>
> Is it real? he asks, cheeks rosy, hair in cockscombs from the towel.[22]

In the hands of a lesser writer, this passage has all the ingredients of nostalgia – pastness, a small child missing home, innocent memories of a loved, absent place and people, idealising of that place – "endless clear space...open horizons...dunes at sunset". However, Winton turns this brief, suggestive piece into a meditation on the centrality of land, place, home and belonging. His imagined audience is surely a wide one, as he reaches out towards Australians, and fellow-travelling Europeans, who want to consider what being Australian might mean, but more fully how we might think about being situated in local, intimate, complex place. The popular and the literary converge here, in a rich, unbounded way.

Literary critics, as Swirski has argued, need to become more adept at reading books that refuse to settle down into either "popular" or "literary" categories, into either the literature of sunny, surfing celebration, or the literature of despair. Winton's writing disturbs these pure categories. As a master craftsman of prose he is able to weave in and out, and beyond, such fixed and static binaries. He is able to take the reader with him because he doesn't forget either end of this spectrum along which fiction continues to move. He is, in summary, a writer of literature in a global reading marketplace.

---

22 Tim Winton, *Island Home: A Landscape Memoir* (Melbourne: Penguin, 2015), 3–4.

7
Becoming, Belonging

> In the semi-arid range country where I live these days the heavens draw you out, like a multidimensional horizon... In our hemisphere the sky stops you in your tracks, derails your thoughts, unmoors you from what you were doing before it got you by the collar.—*Island Home: A Landscape Memoir*[1]

Tim Winton has won a reputation as an Australian novelist of local and national place, and of belonging,[2] a Western Australian with a rich imaginative grasp of city and country, small town, beach, ocean and desert, and of the ways in which place shapes personal and communal ontology. However, it should be recalled that Winton is also a writer of urban and suburban place (*Cloudstreet* (1991), *Eyrie* (2013)), as Evie Wyld reminds us in her 2014 *Guardian* review of Eyrie:

> Some readers will be surprised that a novel from the twice-Booker-shortlisted author takes place around a tower block, so successfully has he made himself the poet laureate of the wide sky, the red dirt, the salt and thick estuarine mud of Western Australia in his previous work.[3]

Wyld's list of Winton's places might be supplemented in two ways. First, by adding creek, bush, coast, beach, surf, open sea; and secondly, by noting that the nature of place and belonging that Winton probes is not a simple, bucolic or unproblematic one. In fact, Winton is the Australian prose poet of marginal places, and, drawing on his own childhood experiences living in small towns, of their sometimes narrow, cramped mindsets. Discordance in such places is a recurrent creative spur in Winton's oeuvre; the lyricist of waves and watery depths, small farming communities and lonely beaches also

---

1 Tim Winton, *Island Home: A Landscape Memoir* (Melbourne: Penguin, 2015), 18–19. All subsequent references are to this edition and appear in parentheses in the text.
2 See Salhia Ben-Messahel, *Mind the Country: Tim Winton's Fiction* (Perth: University of Western Australia Publishing, 2006).
3 Evie Wyld, "Tower Block Blues", review of *Eyrie* by Tim Winton, *Guardian*, 30 May 2014. http://tinyurl.com/Wyld2014.

turns out to be a trenchant critic of small town mentalities, as he depicts the struggle in so many characters to become and to belong. What can we make of Winton's double approach – lyrical and unsettled – to becoming and belonging in place?

How and Where to Belong

Dirt Music (2001), for example, charts the narrow confines of White Point and its denizens, the Buckridges, the Foxes, Georgie Jutland, and the town's many legal and illegal fishermen, along with the trauma that leads Lu Fox out beyond the Point, in search of escape and solace in uninhabited places. In a wry 2002 *Guardian* review of *Dirt Music*, Australian expatriate writer Peter Porter wrote:

> For years now Australia has been the last frontier. Those who flock to its scattered wild places come from all over the planet, not least from within Australia itself. The crowds at Darwin or Broome, or scouting through the Red Heart, are as likely to start out from Macquarie Street Consulting Rooms or Collins Street Legal Chambers as from Detmold or San Diego. Only a few will be ecological pilgrims: most are attracted by the combination of rugged landscape and hi-tech convenience. Nature may still be bleaker there than anywhere on earth, but its visitors can expect the latest in aircraft, refrigeration, personal hygiene and haute cuisine . . .[4]

Porter's chary eye on the popular modern sport of frontier tourism is humorously judicious, but it also forgets (or doesn't know) that many Australians who live in Australia, daily registering the material realities of country in multiple ways, have a growing, grounded awareness of the *unsettled* and dynamic nature of living in this land. Of course there is not *one* register but many, but Australia is recognised by her peoples: its impinging deserts and droughts, its volatile weathers and vast distances, its small town–big city differences, and its unique mix of Indigenous/white-settler/multicultural/refugee inhabitants. Not all Australians have visited Coober Pedy or Uluru or the Kimberleys, but everyone living here is constantly reminded in the media, in school curricula, and on local television and film of the differences that constitute "Australia". Attitudes towards place in Australia are many too, but there is a growing recognition of the need to think about human and non-human interaction here.

Revered feminist and ecologist Val Plumwood was a strong proponent of the dynamic interaction between land and humans. She argued passionately in 2009:

> A rigid division that makes us choose between human and non-human sides precludes a critical cultural focus on problems of human ecological identity and relationship . . . It assumes a fallacious choice of self/other, taking an us-versus-them approach in which concern is contaminated by self-interest unless it is purely concern for the other. Most issues and motivations are double-sided, mixed, combining self/other, human and non-human interests, and it is not only possible but essential to take account of both. Both kinds of concerns must be mobilised and related.[5]

---

4   Peter Porter, "Rednecks of the Outback", review of *Dirt Music* by Tim Winton, *Guardian*, 8 June 2002. http://tinyurl.com/Porter2002.

Porter's ironic account of a global tourism that seeks out frontier places, expecting the provision of modern facilities, is understandable. However, a newer, richer awareness such as Plumwood's is growing in Australia, and is related to the impact of global warming and a sense of the finiteness, fragility and wildness of land forms and weathers, as well as concern for the fate of Indigenous inhabitants of such so-called frontier places. Plumwood's is a pragmatic stance, not speaking from absolute idealism or absolute pragmatism, but from a philosophy that understands the desires of humans seeking after experience of place: the need to acknowledge intimate relationships between human and non-human, the needs and actions leading hopefully to a belonging *in place*. As Porter was aware, this fuller awareness is not a tourist's way of belonging.

The argument of this current chapter, then, is ultimately that Tim Winton is the poet of *non-belonging* who also dreams, and finds imaginative form for, the possibility of belonging, for Indigenous and non-Indigenous Australians, for the working class and class travellers. This argument may seem counter-intuitive to fans and critics of Winton, many of whom see him as a local or regional writer with a strong, celebratory sense of belonging in the Australian landscape. However, if we think of *Cloudstreet*, for example, that rambunctious, popular allegory about finding and making home, it is at its core preoccupied with transience and the constant necessity to reimagine what has been lost, or never known for white-settler Australians; and with centuries-long displacement for Indigenous Australians. *Cloudstreet* as a comic, larger than life narrative of reparation for what has been lost by the Lambs and the Pickles makes it so satisfying, at least imaginatively, but it is also a novel about ghosts and monsters, loss and hauntedness.

Indigenous Belonging, White Belonging

The representation of Indigenous displacement in *Cloudstreet* is not a central narrative in the novel, but it continues to be a contentious focus for some critics. Michael R. Griffiths, in his essay "Winton's Spectralities, or, What Haunts *Cloudstreet*?" writes:

> [B]oth the house and its narrative, are then constitutively haunted by the dispossession of Indigenous peoples in Australia and the history of child removal more particularly. And if what the Pickles inherit and the Lambs find themselves occupying is a house inscribed irreparably in this history – as a synecdoche of family as nation – *Cloudstreet*'s spectrality inscribes the political community it allegorises, rendering it inseparable from this history of dispossession.[6]

Griffiths details the many forms of ghostly unbelonging in *Cloudstreet*, beginning with the girls who had lived in Cloudstreet when it was a home for Aboriginal children, including the "shadow girl" who committed suicide in the house. And then there are the novel's living Indigenous figures, "the corporeal and yet prophetic figure of the 'black man'... both ghostly and present"; and the "ventriloquised figure of Aboriginality"[7] who appears

---

5 Val Plumwood, "Nature in the Active Voice", *Australian Humanities Review, Ecological Humanities* 46 (May 2009). http://tinyurl.com/Plumwood2009.
6 Michael R. Griffiths, "Winton's Spectralities, or, What Haunts *Cloudstreet*?" in *Tim Winton: Critical Essays*, ed. Lyn McCredden and Nathanael O'Reilly (Perth: UWA Publishing, 2014), 81.

to Quick on his nomadic travels away from Cloudstreet, and who urges Quick, in a strange reversal of roles, to go home (not to Britain, but to Cloudstreet). These figures, and the wistful pastness of the smiling Indigenous figure – "a black man [who] leaves the trees like a bird and goes laughing into the sun"[8] – disappearing into the ether at the end of the novel, lead some critics to be uneasy with what critic Nathanael O'Reilly describes as the normalising depiction of white inheritance in a stolen, haunted, land.[9] I would argue, too, that the inheritance experienced by the white Pickle and Lamb families, while vastly different from the experiences of Indigenous figures in the novel, is represented as a speckled, spectral, unsettled sense of place and belonging. Oriel in her tent, and the figure of Fish with his shadowed identity, are synecdochal figures of unsettledness; and in another way, so is the figure of the Nedlands Monster. His narrative supplies a haunted, violent subtext throughout the novel. The murderer is finally captured not as an embodiment of evil but with "the hopeless look of him ambushed and frightened and suddenly not winning... just a frustrated man with a harelip who's gone back to his lifetime of losing" (502). These are not figures of colonial supremacy, but of stuttering vulnerability and wrong-footedness in a place that refuses them identity or belonging.

Winton is driven to seek out the foundations of restorative belonging in multiple ways across his oeuvre: ideologically (and arguably not always successfully) in his depictions of Indigenous and non-Indigenous difference; through his probing of the shifting relationships between human and non-human; and always through his opening up of the tentative, fallen, unfinished, and possibly redeeming processes of becoming. While the narrative of *Cloudstreet* finishes with a comic and satisfying celebration, it is also haunted, as Fish goes back to the water, and the struggles of Cloudstreet continue to echo long after the narrative ends.

So, many Winton characters, whether situated in the city, suburbs or country, do not belong. They are, more often than not, out of joint and out of place, nomads literally or internally. As well as the Indigenous figures and ghosts, Oriel, Fish, Quick, Rose, Dolly, the Nedlands Monster, and others in *Cloudstreet*, there are iconic Winton battlers such as Queenie Cookson in *Shallows* (1984), Jerra Nilsam in *Minimum of Two* (1987) and *An Open Swimmer* (1982), Ort and his family post-trauma in *That Eye, the Sky* (1986), Lu Fox and Georgie in *Dirt Music* (2001), Pikelet and Eva in *Breath* (2008), Vic and many of the other characters in *The Turning* (2004), and Tom Keely, Gemma Buck and Kai in *Eyrie*. The feeling of exclusion experienced by such characters is probed for its causes, which include the blindness of class hierarchy, colonial unease, personal or communal trauma, individual psychological reticence, or family dysfunction. None of these characters easily belongs. Many of them are class travellers, or idealists who trip and fall, or questers who want to belong but who are also grappling with the unsettling processes of their own becoming.

The poignant ending of *The Turning* short story "Big World" draws with it this complex tangle of belonging and becoming: of knowing and not knowing what life will offer. Biggie Botson, with "a face only a mother could love",[10] and his mate, the unnamed

---

7 Griffiths, "Winton's Spectralities", 85.
8 Tim Winton, *Cloudstreet* (Melbourne: McPhee Gribble, 1991), 556.
9 See Nathanael O'Reilly, "Postcolonial Issues in Australian Literature", in *Exploring Suburbia: The Suburbs in the Modern Australian Novel* (Amherst, NY: Teneo Press, 2012).
10 Tim Winton, "Big World", *The Turning* (Melbourne: Penguin, 1991), 4. All subsequent references are to this edition and appear in parentheses in the text.

narrator, are drifting between boyhood and manhood, and are momentarily caught up beyond the human, in the non-human "big world" of nature and transience. They are enjoying the last freedoms of their adolescence, escaping north in a "gutless old Volksie" (4). At day and story's end, "two mad southern boys still wearing beanies in March" (5) stand watching their fizzling car,

> taking in the vast, shimmering pink lake that suddenly looks full of rippling water. We don't say anything. The sun flattens itself against the saltpan and disappears. The sky goes all acid blue and there's just the huge silence. It's like the world's stopped . . . Right now, standing with Biggie on the salt lake at sunset, each of us still in our southern-boy uniform of boots, jeans and flannel shirt, I don't care what happens beyond this moment. In the hot northern dusk, the world suddenly gets big around us, so big we just give in and watch. (14–15)

An understated, deflationary humour pervades this lyrical moment, as the young men register their pipe dreams of escape fizzling out in the shape of a collapsing old Volksie. As they stand gazing there is a realisation (in the narrator, the narrative, the reader?) that time wavers and warps around them, beyond their control. The vast, rippling, illuminated lake at sunset provides the boys with momentary peace, and a fitting sense of their own smallness in the big world. They are two working-class boys without much clue, but in this final image they seem to be embraced and transfixed, as "the world suddenly gets big around us". The present tense narration contributes to this sense of embrace, of time pausing. However, it is also the intelligence of the narrator that enables the reader to see his own growing sense of self. He is able to observe and measure the world outside himself, with a wry perspective on the comedy of their callow situation. The narrator's sense of becoming entails an intuitive understanding of the immensity of life beyond human self, stirred as he is for a moment by the huge acid blue sky and the beauty of the salt lake at sunset. Biggie and his mate are hardly part of the luxury-seeking crowds streaming to the frontier described in Porter's review of *Dirt Music*. They do not expect or look for bourgeois comforts, and they cannot express their understanding of this quiet moment in the embrace of the "big world", but Winton can, and offers it to his readers.

Gender Belonging

As discussed in Chapter 2, *gender* unease brews in the unfixed and sometimes turbulent crucible of becoming man and woman. Such turbulence also troubles the broader processes of becoming. Cited in Chapter 2, critic Bridget Grogan argued that:

> [A]t their most complete and tender Winton's men embrace transience and the inevitable loss this entails; simultaneously, they acknowledge the wide beauty of the temporal world and the love of and for others that is both impermanent and yet eternal . . .[11]

---

11 Bridget Grogan, "The Cycle of Love and Loss: Melancholic Masculinity in *The Turning*", in *Tim Winton: Critical Essays*, ed. Lyn McCredden and Nathanael O'Reilly (Perth: UWA Publishing, 2014), 217.

This is a very different emphasis to place on Winton, if we are intent on seeing him as the comic genius of *Cloudstreet*, and that novel as a rollicking, celebratory allegory of place and belonging, even of nostalgic, national belonging. What Grogan is suggesting here, which this chapter also argues, in its examination of place and the processes of becoming and belonging, is that Winton is no straightforward pantheist of place and nature, no simple country boy extolling the values of small town life. The interchange between nature and humanity is an often fraught, tangled and traumatic one in Winton's novels. Nature is sublime, in the Burkean sense discussed in the introduction: "[T]hat state of the soul in which all its motions are suspended, with some degree of horror".[12] It teaches some stern and trenchant lessons about temporality, about fierce, material, non-human power, and the demand that humans bend the knee. "Becoming", in this framework, is an entering into the irreducibility or unfinishedness of the self and its relation to others, including the non-human other. From Judith Butler, we heard also in Chapter 2: "I am not fully known to myself, because part of what I am is the enigmatic traces of others. In this sense, I cannot know myself perfectly or know my 'difference' from others in an irreducible way".[13] For so many of Winton's characters – Queenie, Dolly, Rose, Pikelet, Eva, Vic, Lu, Tom, Gemma – this processual understanding of the self involves relationship to places which are either antagonistic, or act as foils to human idealism, or where humans seek to lose the self, experienced as burden.

Uniquely compounding this process for white-settler and lately arrived Australians is the realisation that they live in a huge, diverse country, one in which they are not native. Winton through this perspective echoes poet Judith Wright, for whom "two strands – the love of the land we have invaded and the guilt of the invasion – have become part of me. It is a haunted country".[14] The knowledge that we do not own or even belong naturally in this place is unsettling, and has been the focus of poets and postcolonial theorists writing from many angles. The violent history of white settlement inevitably establishes the parameters of attempts to belong here, constantly (and properly) inflecting non-Indigenous relations to land and place.

Winton's fiction moves back and forward, between non-belonging and desire for a future of belonging, and is written right in the heart of this postcolonial moment. As the authors of *Key Concepts in Post-Colonial Studies* argue in regard to postcolonial modes of belonging and becoming in settler colonies:

> In this sense they [the non-Indigenous] are simultaneously both colonized and colonizer. Settlers may seek to appropriate icons of the "native" to their own self-representation, and this can, itself, be a form of oppression where such icons have sacred or social significance alienated by their new usages. On the positive side, as settlers themselves become indigenes in the literal sense, that is, born within the new space, they begin to forge a distinctive and unique culture that is neither that of the metropolitan culture from which they stem, nor that of the "native" cultures they have displaced in their early colonizing

---

12 Edmund Burke, "Of the Passion Caused by the Sublime," in *The Works of the Right Honourable Edmund Burke, Vol. 1 (of 12)* (1757; Project Gutenberg, 2005), part 2, sect. 1. http://www.gutenberg.org/files/15043/15043-h/15043-h.htm.
13 Judith Butler, *Precarious Life: The Powers of Mourning and Violence* (New York and London: Verso, 2004), 32–3.
14 Judith Wright, *Born of the Conquerors* (Canberra: Aboriginal Studies Press, 1991), 30.

phase. The new culture may, and indeed often does, involve borrowings from both of these prior social and cultural forms.¹⁵

Postcolonial theories of displacement, hugely different for Indigenous and non-Indigenous peoples, are closely aligned with Winton's fiction in their acknowledgement of unsettled belonging. In novels such as *Shallows* and *Dirt Music*, as well as *Cloudstreet*, *Breath* and *Eyrie*, there is a pervasive unease and loss experienced by the central characters. Together with colonial unsettledness, this unease is often triggered in Winton's fiction by large existential forces – accident, death, the wildness of nature – which shape and challenge human agency. These forces are not separate from colonial unease, but can be seen to act in concert for white-settler Australians: Queenie Cookson's traumatic witnessing of the barbaric capture and flaying of whales; Fish's near-drowning in the sea, and Oriel's living in her tent afterwards; Lu Fox's seeking refuge in the wilderness, prophet-like, after the tragedy of his family's death; all are written with a haunting sense of white unsettlement and displacement, where such forces – the sea and its creatures, the land's distances and risks – can and do obliterate the would-be dominators, and even those who are innocent, usually children such as Ort, or Fish, or Bird, or Pikelet.

Luther Fox's "going native", seeking out the wilderness in order to escape and to re-find himself, is haunted by memories of his wilderness childhood, and particularly the fate of his mother in a storm as they hunted together for eggs:

[T]here was no blood on her that he could see, just spilled yolks and sinister, glistening albumen smeared up her bare legs. The sheared point of the bough was in her chest but he didn't yet understand that she was dead. He would be ten in a few days.¹⁶

His mother, a lover of the wilderness and the earth, is killed by it in this scene which entangles birth and death. But it is another, earlier childhood memory that indicates the complex processes of Lu's struggle to become, suspended ontologically as he is between his father and his mother:

And here he is again bringing a snakeskin in from the creek to show them. She holds up the papery tube and smiles.

Look, Wally, she says. Look how good the world is, look at the things it leaves us. It means us no harm.

The boy senses he's stumbled into a debate in progress.

Doesn't count, mutters the old man, hardly looking up. It's an illusion, a dream we have to pass through.

But look!

Things. Stuff. Just things.

And the smile on her face as she sits back in her chair with the book open on her lap and the hair shining with each happy shake of her head. Holy, she says with a hint of teasing. Holy, holy, holy.

---

15 Bill Ashcroft, Gareth Griffiths and Helen Tiffin, *Key Concepts in Post-Colonial Studies* (London and New York: Routledge, 1998), 212.
16 Tim Winton, *Dirt Music* (Sydney: Picador, 2001), 360. All subsequent references are to this edition and appear in parentheses in the text.

> Shit and gristle, that's all. It doesn't matter.
> Holy. Tell him, Lu.
> Standing there openmouthed between them, wondering if bringing it home has been a mistake. (361)

Fox is haunted by both the lovely, evanescent things of his childhood, his mother, "hair shining with each happy shake of her head. Holy . . .", and by the raw, bitter facts: "But there she is in the end with a tree through her. And the old man all that time dying with those blue fibres in his lungs. God's good earth . . . the world is holy? Maybe so. But it has teeth too" (362).

Fox's mother has revealed to him the holiness of the non-human world, but he has learnt from "the old man" equally, that accident, transience and death reign. The land of his childhood turns traitorous, combining with chance to undermine human sovereignty; and the adult Lu is pictured remembering all this as he shelters in the midst of a cyclone. Are we dealing here with postcolonial unease, or existential trauma? It is hard to disentangle these conditions here. In *Dirt Music*, the two speak to each other as compounding elements of Australian becoming, most particularly for non-Indigenous Australians in Winton's novels.

Place and Belonging

In *Dirt Music*, place and its role in becoming are not monolithic. Home is made up of the different childhood houses remembered by Luther and Georgie, and it is the coasts, desert vastness, lush northern islands, and cyclonic weather of their present story. As Lu Fox makes his way north, beyond people and his past, trailing his grief and loneliness, he hitches his way through Western Australian mulga country, granite breakaways, rocky escarpments, horizontal monotony, until

> [a]t Mount Magnet the young blokes set him down at a corner that feels like a crossroads of some moment. This is the end of the south. Farm fences are gone and soil has long been replaced by dust or grit. The Indian Ocean is hours to the west. On the roadsign, towns have three- or four-digit distances. He tries to imagine the gibber planes and the red dunes to the east, the impossible amplitude of the continent. They say it's empty and the idea draws him but he can't get his mind around it. Thinks of the north the old man spoke of with pride and fear in his voice, the rugged stone ranges, the drinking that made the boozy south seem temperate, the cattle herds pounding red dust skyward and the seasons discounted to plain Wet or Dry. (221)

Winton is able, in Fox's present-tense inner monologue, blended finely with a broader, topographical imaginary voice, to sketch out the "impossible amplitude" of the place. For Fox, there is indeed a suspension of ego, and a confronting of the horror and beauty of survival in the land. Phrases such as "gibber planes and the red dunes to the east" are a combination of mapped facts and a wilder imaginary experience of place as harsh and hardly knowable. This place also mirrors Lu's confused desires. In his grief he wants to be swallowed up by the emptiness, "the idea [that] draws him", but memories of his boyhood and his father's account of a wild, other place up north infuse and draw him. Further, while this passage runs parallel to Lu's inner witnessing of place, it also becomes an account of white colonisation and its limits: "This is the end of the south. Farm fences are gone and soil has long been replaced by dust or grit". What comes into view is the pre-colonial desert world beyond known seasons, European methods of cultivation. However, there is still the cattle-herding of the settlers, a world beginning to be trampled by settlement. But this is a place largely beyond the colony's mere replication of the imperial world, its farm fences and cultivated soils, a new place that Lu Fox, trailing his feral European name with him, reaches for in his current turmoil.

In this respect, Lu is an unlikely modern day version of Voss, or at least some aspects of Voss, from Patrick White's 1957 novel. In *Island Home*, Winton describes his first reading of White's novel:

> In *Voss*, Patrick White's expeditionary hero ventures out into the hinterland to conquer distance. He aims to master country and fill its apparent emptiness by his sheer presence, with his ego and his sense of European destiny. In the end he's swallowed operatically by desert, a victim of his own ignorance. *Voss* was a turning point for me, a sign of what might be possible in writing poetically about figures in landscape.[17]

Dirt Music reflects the influence of *Voss* in one way, through its poetic depiction of a European Australian man pitting himself against distance and the "apparent emptiness" of Australia's vast, uncharted places (although one cannot imagine Voss strumming on a homemade guitar). Both Voss and Fox have their egos to deal with, Voss' gargantuan, and in the end self-devouring, Fox's crippled, almost blown apart by his grief. But Lu Fox does find in the deserts and islands a hard-won healing. Both authors conjure the land from some experience of it, but also from European (and religious) literary tropes of desert prophet and hermit, seeking some kind of truth in the wilderness. But as Fox comes towards the end of his travels, he realises, as perhaps Voss partially does, that he doesn't belong in that place. Fox is described lyrically, immersed in the land: "[T]he midden and the beach and the boabs are pearlescent. His hands, his feet, are lunar. He's washed in cold light. Transparent . . ." (418–19), but he is also not *of* the land. His process of grieving and loneliness have been schooled by this place, but he doesn't belong here, running short of food, and registering another kind of loss as he realises:

> He is not a nomad, he can't even imagine such a life. It's not just exhaustion that disqualifies him but his instinct to linger, to repeat, to embellish. A way of living isn't enough. Fox has to stay, to inhabit a place. It's as though his mind can only settle when he's still. He feels he's dragging a life and a whole snarled net of memory across foreign country. None of it lives here; it doesn't spring from here and it will neither settle nor belong . . . he knows now that he'll die out here; he'll eat himself alive like a body consuming its own wasted muscle. (419)

For anyone looking for a smooth ontological synthesis between Indigenous and non-Indigenous Australians and their ways of belonging, *Dirt Music* does not offer such a panacea. Luther Fox has been taught by the land, but part of what he has learnt is that

---

17 Tim Winton, *Island Home: A Landscape Memoir* (Melbourne: Penguin, 2015), 150. All subsequent references are to this edition and appear in parentheses in the text.

he does not belong there *in the same ways* as those who have travelled it for centuries, hunted in it, lived and died in it, and endowed that relationship with sacredness. What the novel does do is bravely step back from white *indigenisation*. For Winton, the differences between Indigenous and non-Indigenous need to be acknowledged and appreciated. There are political and ontological reasons for considering respectfully the cultural realities of Indigenous peoples, and there are political and ontological reasons for considering how non-Indigenous peoples in Australia might grapple with their becoming and belonging. This is the contribution of *Dirt Music* – that it writes from white-settler, European Australian perspectives, honouring the differences between peoples, and moving forward in the process of white belonging.

Dirt Music: Postcolonial Erotics and Literary Ancestors

For some, the narrative of Georgie Jutland and Luther Fox might seem to reduce to postcolonial erotica. The hero has gone out beyond himself, tested his body and soul almost to extinction, learnt much, and now lies in the saving embrace of his lover:

> Georgie looked at the martyred jut of his hipbones, the twigs in his hair, the livid ulcers down his thin legs . . . Georgie saw his eyes roll back and his hips lift toward her . . . Luther Fox began to convulse . . . She fell on Luther Fox, pressed her mouth to his and blew. She's real. (460–1)

For some readers, perhaps of a strictly ideological bent, there is lack of equivalence between the fate of one lovelorn hero and the lessons he learns, and the fate of those others (mainly invisible in *Dirt Music*) who have lived and died Indigenous in the land. Some might even argue that to superimpose a white love story onto a postcolonial journey is to grossly devalue the latter. At one level, this kind of critical stance involves making clear decisions about the relative value of high and popular literature, and placing love stories well below stories of national, ideological import. The juxtaposition of the two in *Dirt Music* is certainly challenging. But it is, after all, *dirt music*, a levelling and dialogical evaluating of forms of writing as well as forms of ontology. The novel is also one of Winton's redemptive narratives, or so it seems from this brief, inconclusive but hopeful reunion between Luther and Georgie. Such a reunion has been prepared for through the novel's closing chapters by the way in which Winton interweaves place and lovers. It has been the thought of Georgie that Luther clings to throughout his exile, the man (and the novelist) infusing the land with the body and presence of Georgie:

> Now and then he sees her at the shore, sees himself there, too. They're like trees. They *are* trees . . . He touches her, breathes in her nutty odour, shudders as his hip brushes hers. He presses his brow against her bark . . . warm-blooded even after dark and its skin so smooth, its clefts so sculpted. (404)

Winton gives himself writerly latitude here (and some amusement?) as the woman's body fuses with the land, and with the fantasising Luther, "[a] ragged man with flayed shanks whose sudden tiny cry in the night is no louder than the gasp of an open oyster" (405).

In *Island Home*, Winton writes not only about the influence of *Voss* on his writing, but the importance of fellow Western Australian novelist Randolph Stow. Winton describes the figure of Heriot, in Stow's 1958 novel *To the Islands*, and Heriot's fate makes a stark contrast with the final moments of *Dirt Music*:

> On the face of it, his trajectory is not unlike Voss's. An angry failure, perhaps even a murderer, he journeys out into the remotest bush in what looks like an act of self-destruction. But the teacher finds himself brutally taught, strangely protected and militantly controlled by the country he blunders through. At the end he relinquishes the idea of an object. He surrenders to immensity and merges with the landscape, turning a European *failure to arrive* into a tragic antipodean acceptance, even an apotheosis. To me it's a visionary work. Stow is still the marker for me, the distant knoll by which I take my bearings. (151–2)

What surprises here is the number of similarities, but also the number of differences between Winton's and Stow's visions. What Winton admires about Stow's work is the older novelist's austere, uncompromising treatment of Heriot, his placing of the anti-hero symbolically in terrain where his sense of belonging is totally stripped from him, as he journeys into the "remotest bush", to be "brutally taught, strangely protected and militantly controlled by the country". In the end of *To the Islands*, there is only Heriot and his surrender "to immensity", the realisation of his "failure to arrive". There is something of this brutal lesson too for Luther Fox in *Dirt Music*, but it is significant that Luther trails grief rather than guilt into his journey. His longing for release from memory and loss humanises and, arguably, romanticises him, in a way that Heriot is not. Winton does say in his memoir that Stow stands as "the distant knoll by which I take my bearings", pointing to both the debt he feels to the older writer but also the differences Winton registers. The grand, even tragic resonance of Patrick White's *Voss* and Randolph Stow's *To the Islands* emerges from two novels published in 1957 and 1958 respectively. Winton's is a different vision, and a different moment in history. It might be neater to attribute these differences to authorial style or disposition, but surely the changes across the last five decades in national discourses about place, becoming and belonging, and the struggles of Indigenous and white becoming, have something to do with such differences.

"The Irreplaceable Organic Estate"

Winton writes in *Island Home*:

> At last it seems we've begun to see past Dampier's infernal flies, to behold in our remarkable diversity of habitats, landforms and species the riches of a continental isolation that so long troubled us. Things once seen as impossibly homely, weird or simply perverse are now understood as precious. The irreplaceable organic estate informs our aesthetics and politics, our notions of pleasure and recreation. In short, it shapes our mentality. Not only have we started to integrate and internalise all these lessons, we're learning to appreciate the fragility of what sustains us. (111)

The other movement in the processes of becoming and belonging, particularly for European Australians, is evident in this passage, and is recurrent in Winton's fiction and activist writing. It is a broad and possibly idealistic claim about the general awakening of Australians to the value of "the irreplaceable organic estate". However, as this chapter has been arguing, such prophetic confidence needs to be understood as being in dialogue with the unsettled nature of white Australia. Winton can make these claims to a new awareness, but he is still, in his latest fiction and his memoir, radically aware of the distance still to travel. For all those who share Winton's optimism and sense of history here, there are those who refuse to acknowledge or value such lessons. But Winton's work is soundly in the spirit of Christopher Hitt's fine and influential essay "Toward an Ecological Sublime", which balances dumb awe at nature and wilderness, and a knowing humility in the face of earth's non-human imperatives:

> In an age of exploitation, commodification, and domination we need awe, envelopment, and transcendence. We need, at least occasionally, to be confronted with the wild otherness of nature and to be astonished, enchanted, humbled by it. Perhaps it is time – while there is still wild nature left – that we discover an ecological sublime.[18]

Eyrie, Winton's latest novel, seems to be in dialogue with this ecocritical approach, and with *Island Home*, the two books being published close to each other. *Eyrie* powerfully imagines the ongoing, destructive vigour of capitalist and urban cultures of greed that desecrate human and non-human alike. In *Eyrie* we witness the osprey in its eyrie, as Keely takes Gemma and Kai on the river to see the bird. Compared to the cramped and wounded inhabitants of the seedy Mirador hotel, the osprey appears

> [a] severe, stately bird, watchful, poised, tensing . . . Osprey, said Kai. The creature tilted its head, twisted slightly, then gathered itself. It rose, languid, powerful, to reach into the air. Osprey, said the boy.
> It climbed without effort, wheeled up past the supplicant fingers of clifftop trees and retreated to the shadows, leaving only a harsh cry to signal its presence . . . The boy blinked skyward.
> Keely refrained from commentary. The act itself was enough. The boy and his grandmother craned their necks, watching the sky, waiting for more.[19]

The child is learning what he sees, rehearsing the word, watching. It is something that Keely, debilitated as he is, can give to the boy: a wonder and respect for what is beyond their own small, human selves. This healing gesture, and indeed the broader ethics of Winton's fiction and its vision of place and becoming, entails growing up, living in and reading the country as imperative for white Australians, some of which in part can be learnt from Aboriginal Australians. *Eyrie* explores the ways in which non-Indigenous Australians begin and continue this necessarily vexed process. Kai has lived only in books, loves books about the natural world, but here he begins learning how to translate the living

---

18   Christopher Hitt, "Toward an Ecological Sublime", *New Literary History* 30, no. 3, Ecocriticism (Summer 1999): 603–23.
19   Tim Winton, *Eyrie* (Melbourne: Penguin, 2013), 87–8. All subsequent references are to this edition and appear in parentheses in the text.

world informing the books, to be in relationship with it. It is not by accident then, that Winton emphasises child characters and their need to become and to belong. Winton's ongoing question, in his adult and children's literature, is about how much guilt and non-belonging children, Indigenous and non-Indigenous, can be asked to carry.

So if children have the right to belong, do adult white-settler Australians? What work (disciplined thinking, imagination, policy-making, changing of discourse) is needed in order for non-Indigenous Australians to enter into a sense of belonging, or at least the processes of self-reflection and becoming? In *Island Home*, Winton is direct in his criticism of white Australians who

> are keen to preserve what they view as artefacts of antiquity, [but who are] far less passionate about the sacred power and ongoing cultural role these [Aboriginal] sites retain for living people . . . making a trophy of another people's living culture. (149–50)

He is here calling for an openness to the knowledges and cultures of Indigenous Australia, cultures which embrace the human and the more or other than human, what is lived, believed, practised, handed on. The imposition of European culture as only museum culture, or preservation culture, seems to be what he has little time for.

So Winton focuses on the ways in which European Australians, as well as Indigenous Australians, need to share in a living place, with an openness towards learning relationship to the land:

> There are of course, many places in Australia where this primal energy has been known since time immemorial and where it continues to be refreshed by ritual visits and ceremonial relationship. My acquaintance with these kinds of places is largely restricted to the far north Kimberley, home to the world's oldest extant tradition of icon painting. In rock shelters throughout coastal archipelagos, behind mainland beaches and out into a rugged hinterland the size of California, the conjoined pasts of people and country endure and continue in sites of rare power. (147–8)

Winton's approach here is audacious, and yet also humble. It is audacious in depicting himself as having the right to be in such places of "primal energy", and as possessing the ability as an outsider to experience these "sites of rare power". But he is not claiming aboriginality, or special access. He humbly describes his relationship as an "acquaintance", as "largely restricted". He is bearing witness to places of power that he has not constructed or lived with, but which speak to him, enabling him to recognise his own smallness in the face of "the world's oldest extant tradition", "the conjoined pasts of people and country". He seeks to be in relationship to the Wandjina and their rock art, whose "fragile persistence . . . is something to treasure and to celebrate" (149).

In her astute review of Peter Read's works on Indigenous and non-Indigenous belonging, ecological literary critic Emily Potter examines the three volumes that make up Read's trilogy: *Returning to Nothing* (1996), *Belonging* (2000) and *Haunted Earth* (2003).[20] Read has played a very important non-Indigenous role in debates around white belonging to land and place in Australia, and Potter both signals her admiration for Read's work and

---

20 Emily Potter, "The Anxiety of Place: Peter Read, *Haunted Earth*", *Colloquy: Text Theory Critique* 9 (2005): 124–9.

asks a number of questions of it, questions which might equally pertain to Winton's fiction. Potter concludes her argument:

> Rather than pursue the possibilities for a postcolonial nation through a view of unordered and shifting ecological relations amongst humans and non-humans, Read comes to rest on the unproductive comparison between indigenous and non-indigenous presence in place, a comparison that, in the end, requires parallel equivalence rather than networked specificity to be the tool of settler belonging. The anxiety that non-indigenous Australians live thinly on the land is what seems to most haunt this book, as it does *Returning to Nothing* and *Belonging*. It is perhaps by looking beyond depth as the site of affective meaning and towards the tremors and vibrations of the earth's surface that fear can be replaced by hope. For here, in the irreducible tactile, aural, and visual encounters that occur between self and other, the future opens up.[21]

Potter applauds Read's endeavour to understand the dynamics of white-settler belonging, but she separates herself from any notion of "parallel equivalence" between non-Indigenous and Indigenous belonging. The difference, she argues, needs to be maintained. But at the same time Potter agrees with one strand of Read's argument, that white-settler hauntedness and the desire to belong must be addressed as parts of an ongoing process, envisaged as "the irreducible, tactile, aural, and visual encounters that occur between self and other". This idea of irreducible process reminds us of Judith Butler's call to "know my 'difference' from others in an irreducible way".[22] This irreducibility is seen as an enabling contingency in Potter's argument, as it is in Butler's, and not merely as an anxiety which considers white-settler becoming to be somehow lesser or thinner, but also not one of "parallel equivalence" to Indigenous Australian belonging.

White Un-belonging

Bruce Pike in *Breath* might be read within these same parameters, where becoming is seen as processual, entailing the irreducibility or unfinishedness of the self, and the consequent need for developing an ethics of relationship to others. Pike's melancholic sense of failure, and his experience of not being fully known to himself, are traced back to their roots, with breath being the novel's dominant metaphor of becoming. Not knowing oneself has both negative and positive consequences in *Breath*. It may be debilitating and weakening, aligned with immaturity and gaucheness, but from another perspective it can be claimed as an ongoing freedom to become that needs to be embraced. The narrative of Pike's life can be read from both these angles, and much of the novel sees Pike in the negative frame, but with the potential for positivity, as he learns to understand his own difference and irreducibility as "the site of affective meaning", learning to engage non-judgementally with, in Potter's words, "the tremors and vibrations of the earth's surface . . . in the irreducible, tactile, aural, and visual encounters that occur between self and other". The final paragraph of the novel gives us a perfect picture of this space of freedom, experienced in the non-human world of the ocean, but also in relationship to his daughters, as "a man who dances."[23]

---

21 Potter, "Anxiety of Place," 128.
22 Butler, *Precarious Life*, 32–3.

Pike's drama is existential, the story of a man who falls at each hurdle on his way to manhood. But how does the presence of the sea intercede in *Breath*? Winton makes the ocean, and surfing, not just backdrop but the core of Pikelet's becoming, integral to his need to belong. Around ocean, and learning to surf, this child of English migrants who are scared of the sea sets out on the process of becoming a man, and of belonging. In the introduction, we examined the strange family formed by Sando, Eva, Loonie and Pikelet. The adolescent Pikelet "basked in Sando's attention and treasured these brief moments of esteem" (154). The novel is narrated in retrospect by the adult Bruce Pike, who has had to learn to let go of many boundaries of self. Through his precipitous and unorthodox sexual relationship with Eva, in Sando's careless, charismatic fathering, and in Pikelet's realisation that Sando's favourite is Loonie and not himself, Pike grows into a melancholic man. But it is to the ocean, its challenges and blessings, that Pike returns in memory, and in this final present-tense moment. The ocean is where he can accept the unfinished and irreducible nature of his becoming. It is important to him that his daughters watch him on the waves, seeing past his pragmatic, everyday self to "a man who dances . . . who also does something completely pointless and beautiful".

But this final moment of pleasure and pride has been earned in the lessons Pikelet has experienced with Sando, out in the deep, as human and non-human enter into a dance that is terrifying:

> Sando paddled on up to the channel in tight to the reef where the swells humped prodigiously but did not quite break. At a loss and scared of being alone, I followed. He paddled and propped, paddled and propped, checking and adjusting his position all the time. He motioned me closer as a fresh set lumbered in. At first all I saw was a series of dark lines in the distance and then these swells became a convoy, bearing down on us, increasing in size and speed with every passing moment until they became distinct waves that warped and wedged so massively that I found myself looking uphill into great sunstruck rides. You could feel the whole skin of the ocean being drawn outward to meet them, and it was impossible to resist the conviction that we were about to be mown down, even here in the depth of the channel. (114)

The boy's intimate, watching relationship to the ocean (similar to that of an author), his being equally terrified and committed to observing and honouring the ocean, carries the reader along. We are impelled to feel the terror of the boy attempting to be a man, trying to satisfy his mentor, charting the movement and the power of the waves as they "lumbered in", "dark lines . . . a convoy, bearing down on us . . ." There is of course something of the daredevil boy seeking approval, but there is also the measuring of the self in relation to the non-human ocean, "the distinct waves that warped and wedged".

It is hyperbolic to compare Pikelet to Voss or Heriot, but there is the same pitching of the self into the arms of the non-human, natural world, with terror and with ecstasy, in all three characters. Here, it is one of Winton's many young boys, unmanned in the wild, gigantic embrace of the sea, but then differently becoming, amongst

---

23 Tim Winton, *Breath* (Melbourne: Penguin, 2008), 265. All subsequent references are to this edition and appear in parentheses in the text.

> [m]ountains of water [that] rose from the south . . . rumbled by, gnawing at themselves, spilling tons of foam, and the half-spent force of them tore at my dangling legs. There was just so much water moving out there, such an overload of noise and vibration . . . (116)

It is too simple to claim that Pikelet learns to belong through this experience. It is not a belonging, or a sense of having finally become someone, that Pikelet achieves. Rather, it is an experience akin to what Potter describes as "the irreducible, tactile, aural, and visual encounters that occur between self and other, [in which] the future opens up". In his detailed observance of the non-human world and its power, Pikelet has established one of those moments of becoming – not complete, not resulting in a sense of comfort and home – in which the fragile human form learns to bow before what is greater, to acknowledge a force "that stops you in your tracks, derails your thoughts, unmoors you" (19). Pikelet here is not unlike his creator, a man who dances, who makes something beautiful, though not pointless.

8
Winton's Narratives: Market, Reading, Impact

> [N]arrative is present in myth, legend, fable, tale, novella, epic, history, tragedy, drama, comedy, mime, painting (think of Carpaccio's Saint Ursula), stained glass windows, cinema, comics, news item, conversation. Moreover, under this almost infinite diversity of forms, narrative is present in every age, in every place, in every society; it begins with the very history of mankind and there nowhere is nor has been a people without narrative. All classes, all human groups, have their narratives, enjoyment of which is very often shared by men with different, even opposing, cultural backgrounds. Caring nothing for the division between good and bad literature, narrative is international, transhistorical, transcultural: it is simply there, like life itself.
> —Roland Barthes, *Image Music Text*[1]

In the Roland Barthes of the mid-1960s there is a mighty struggle going on over how to think and write about narratives. What is *their* story? In what kinds of texts, and in what ways, do they inhere? In his influential essay "Introduction to the Structural Analysis of Narratives", words and the narratives they make are to be regarded linguistically, in structuralist mode. They are to be anatomised, treated in a pragmatic or some would say narrowly instrumentalist way; and equally, they are seen as universalisable. But what of *specific*, intimate narratives?

Narratives are made up of words (as well as found in music and imagery and multiple other texts), but narrative keeps escaping into a wider ambit for Barthes, out the door and into "the very history of mankind [sic]". The later, poststructuralist Barthes was always lurking in the structuralist, but in Barthes' 1966 essay there is still this mighty struggle going on between a universalising understanding of narrative, something shared by all and visible in the structure of narratives, and a much wilder, deconstructive concept: narrative as "Caring nothing for the division between good and bad literature". So what is narrative,

---

1 Roland Barthes, "Introduction to the Structural Analysis of Narratives", in *Image Music Text: Essays*, selected and translated by Stephen Heath (London: Fontana Press, 1977), 79. First published in French in *Communications* 8 (1966).

how do we see it behaving or misbehaving, fifty years on? What kinds of narratives are there, and what kinds of impact can narrative be said to have, culturally and socially? Can narrative be separated from its reception, and from the multiple, unruly semiotic effects of texts in the world, those free-floating texts Barthes also tells us about?

The Impact of Winton's Narratives

There is a series of interlocking questions about Tim Winton's narratives that this book has not yet addressed adequately: what *kinds* of narratives has Tim Winton produced? And what kinds of impact can his fiction claim? Further, what do we know about Winton's readership? There are not, of course, purely empirical responses to any of these questions. However, we might start with something as basic as comparative sales figures, which are an (imperfect) indicator of the size of Winton's national and international audiences, and one clue to impact. From there, we need to map the recurrent or overarching preoccupations of his narratives, helping us to speculate further about the impact of his fiction, not just in quantitative terms, but culturally, ideologically and ethically.

It continues to be a matter of speculation as to what kinds of impact a particular author, and fiction more generally, can lay claim to. In Chapter 3, we saw Winton stating in a 2013 newspaper interview that "[n]ovelists and art can't effect change";[2] but there he is, on various hustings,[3] and in his memoir *Island Home*, speaking up for political and community change in approaches to Indigenous Australians, refugees and the environment, his national audience listening because he does have impact as an activist, but also as a novelist. The two arguably travel together in Winton. Of course, Winton might not want to stand solidly behind his earlier newspaper claim that novels don't have the kind of impact which effects change.

Critic Astrid Erll presents another view of literature's impact, describing the joint work of texts and readers, and the changes they can effect in cultural perceptions, practices and even in reality.[4] If Erll's approach to narrative sounds idealistic in its understanding of the reach and impact of literature, then Mikhail Bakhtin's theoretical work on narrative is positively utopian, pointing to the need for critics and readers to consider "the impulse that reaches out beyond" mere words, connecting literature to a "living impulse" and not just to the "naked corpse" of words.[5] Bakhtin's highly influential concept of the dialogic imagination, of the relationship of words to the world, argues for a strong, theologically inflected understanding of the impact of the literary in cultural and political debates.

So what kinds of impact might we consider when thinking about the scope of literary narrative? This is a crucial question for many humanities scholars as the value of literature, and of literary studies as the disciplinary site where literature is analysed, is again being

---

2   Deborah Bogle, "Winton Uses Words as Way to Ponder Change", *Adelaide Advertiser*, 21 October 2013, 15.
3   Tim Winton, "Tim Winton's Palm Sunday Plea: Start the Soul-Searching Australia", *Age*, 29 March 2015. http://tinyurl.com/winton2015.
4   Astrid Erll, "Cultural Studies Approaches to Narrative", in *The Routledge Encyclopedia of Narrative Theory*, ed. David Herman, Manfred Jahn and Marie-Laure Ryan (Oxfordshire and New York: Routledge, 2005), 88–93.
5   M. M. Bakhtin, "Discourse in the Novel", in *The Dialogical Imagination: Four Essays*, ed. Michael Holquist, trans. Caryl Emerson and Michael Holquist (Austin: University of Texas Press, 1981), 292.

scrutinised from many sides. The value of studying literature in Western cultures has come under repeated fire, not only from those educators emphasising pragmatic or skills-based education, but also from families paying for their children's education and expecting jobs and professions as a direct result, and from those who have always questioned, or never seen, the value of an education in the humanities. Literature is not where the dominant players in society hang out; literature, with its messy ambivalence, but also its critical questioning of the status quo and of the dominant structures and values of Western capitalist society.

Further, literature has come into competition across the twentieth and into the twenty-first century with other forms of media and their modes of presenting narrative and meaning-making, with film and television pre-eminently, and from social media, and digital storytelling, including games, videos, blogging, and other online personal and conversation sites. Reflecting on the trajectory of literature in the contemporary world, the always provocative British novelist and social commentator Will Self recently opined about the nature of reading and writing:

> Let's think about reading – about what it's like to read. And after we've thought about reading for a while, let's consider writing – and what it means to write. There are many ways of reading: we scan, we dip, we skip and we speed through texts we know to be intrinsically dull, searching out the nuggets of information we desire as a bent-backed prospector pans for gold. In contradistinction: we are lost, abandoned, absorbed – tossed from wave to wave of language as we relapse into the wordsea. All serious readers of serious literature have had this experience: time, space, and all the workaday contingencies of their identity – sex, age, class, heritage – are forgotten; the mind cleaves to the page, matching it point-for-point; the mind is the text, and in the act of reading it is you who are revealed to the impersonal writer, quite as much as her imaginings and inventions are rendered unto you.[6]

Not everyone would agree here with Self's preliminary and reductive version of the reading experience as "searching out the nuggets of information", especially if this is related to reading literature, as opposed to service manuals for instance. However, in the spirit of provocation, Self also infectiously conveys the processes of deeper reading, how it draws the reader into imaginative and inventive revelations, particularly of the reader's self. He goes on in an even-handed (and yes, at the same time provocative) manner, pointing out that film and television have superseded the literary, at a time when the economic reigns:

> Since the abolition of the Net Book Agreement in the 1980s [in the UK], all the money in publishing has been funnelled into pipes that have a wider and a shorter bore; nowadays one big, thick pipeline carrying half the revenue from British retail book sales disappears deep into [CEO of Amazon] Jeff Bezos's pockets. The NBA itself was part of a government subsidy system that included preferential tax rates for newsprint, public libraries and even the grants awarded university students from poorer backgrounds – all of it was based on the assumption that the cultural value of reading and writing wasn't reducible to its economic worth. Nowadays all we can say about the production and

---

6 Will Self, "The Fate of Our Literary Culture Is Sealed", *Guardian*, 4 October 2014. http://tinyurl.com/WillSelf2014.

consumption of the written word is that it is subject to exactly the same iron laws of supply and demand as every other widget or pixel.[7]

There are indeed many global voices equating reading and writing merely to its economic worth, just as education is being reduced in the same way. These *are* the days in which we see "the written word . . . subject to exactly the same iron laws of supply and demand as every other widget or pixel". We might consider here the opening of *Eyrie*, which leaves us, fictionally, in no doubt that the moment of capitalism, of voracious forms of supply and demand, holds most people in the West in its iron grip.

Eyrie and Capitalism's Force Field

For Tom Keely, erstwhile environmentalist and lawyer, his life had been all about

> belching out soundbites like a spiv's PR flak. All the while trying to hold to the long view, the greater hopes he'd begun with. Like appealing to people's higher nature. And getting Nature itself a fair hearing. Which was, of course, in this state, at such a moment in history, like catching farts in a butterfly net.[8]

Such an ineluctable capitalist force field – media-driven, legally entrenched – characterises the Western Australian context in which Keely has tried "catching farts in a butterfly net". However, this does not mean that Will Self, or Tom Keely, or Tim Winton is *subscribing* to these as the *only* conditions in which reading and writing can be conducted. Winton's narrative in *Eyrie* scours and peels away the values of such a world. One question here is whether those who write and read *otherwise* – critically, imaginatively, with aesthetic and intellectual curiosity and depth, from passionate ideological beliefs – are merely the rearguard readers of old literary values, inevitably ground down into current modes of processing narrative, providing words for cash, "belching out soundbites". Self's final declaration in his essay is both pessimistic and possibly a call to arms:

> [W]hen it comes to the future of our literary culture – its fate is already sealed, and there is no going back. I began this provocation by describing what I think of deep reading – the kind of reading that serious books demand, and I promised that I would also discuss writing, the kind of writing that's intended to be read deeply. But really, there's no point in this, because such writing depends for its existence on deep readers, and in the near future such deep readers will be in very short supply.[9]

Is this all about the demise of the literary, or can we hear a challenge here to all those erstwhile *and* future deep readers, to survive and keep reading? Is such provocation merely Will Self seeking to be up-to-date or even avant-garde about the changes to the world of narrative in the digital era, while at the same time giving himself the space to lament the

---

7 Self, "The Fate of Our Literary Culture".
8 Tim Winton, *Eyrie* (Melbourne: Penguin, 2013), 8. All subsequent references are to this edition and appear in parentheses in the text.
9 Self, "The Fate of Our Literary Culture".

loss of deep reading and those literary values of questioning, thinking and wondering that otherwise hover somewhere on the margins – not simply the profit margins – of modern universities, reading groups, literary reviews and criticism? These places in which literature once regally held sway are in decline as nurturers of deep reading, according to Self, yet he is still a novelist, a writer of literary reviews and criticism. So, is deep reading still about? Are deep readers?

Quantitative Answers: Winton's Sales Figures

If we take just one segment of the sales figures for Winton's novels over the past ten years, looking at the bestsellers in Australia for 2004,[10] what do we see about his readers, at least quantitatively? In terms of readership Tim Winton is popular, but he's not a novelist who makes the very top of the bestseller lists. We might speculate whether this is because his fiction demands and rewards "deep reading" skills. The Nielsen BookScan data needs to be read and interpreted, but it does give us something to ponder in terms of readership size and possible impact.

The first thing to say is that sales figures do not simplistically equate to numbers of readers. Such figures can't include the reading done by book groups, students, and others borrowing volumes from libraries, or passing on used copies; and, on the other hand, they cannot include the fact that many purchased books go straight "under the bed". Further, e-book sales are not included in this data from the Nielsen BookScan, the most comprehensive international collector of sales data. However, the distinctions in sales numbers between authors in 2004 can tell us something about (1) what size audience constituted a "bestseller" in Australia in 2004; (2) the difficulty, or lack of interest of the book market (publishers, book distributors, Nielsen BookScan) in making any distinction between popular and literary books; and (3) the kinds of financial stakes we are dealing with. Consideration of the ongoing impact (beyond a year or two) of these books is a related but much larger question of course.

We can see from Figure 1 that Bryce Courtney's *Brother Fish* and Di Morrissey's *The Reef* led the pack in 2004, with Tim Winton's *The Turning* coming in third. All three were first published in 2004, so the figures are just for the previous year, whereas Winton's *Dirt Music*, which came in at number 8 in 2004, had been published in 2001. These figures are for hardback editions of *Brother Fish* and *The Turning*, with *The Reef* in paperback. The overall monetary values for each book are for an average of $20 each for paperbacks, and hardbacks around $45 to $50 each, although there are some variations. We can see clearly that Courtney's sales are three times larger than the two nearest authors, Morrissey and Winton, going on monetary value as well as on sales figures.

If we jump to 2008, the next year in which Winton published a literary fiction book, we will notice some similarities in trends (Figure 2). Bryce Courtney continues in 2008 to perform strongly in sales, with the bestseller for the year being *Fishing for Stars*; as does Di Morrissey with *The Islands*, Geraldine Brooks' *People of the Book* and Tim Winton's *Breath*, all published in 2008. It's interesting to note that Winton's and Courtney's sales are almost on a par, with both books published in hardback in 2008. Another strong performer in the

---

10 Nielsen BookScan Australian figures, for works in the "General and Literary Fiction" category, supplied 2016. All data in this chapter supplied by Nielsen BookScan.

Title	Author	Publisher	Sales	Value	RRP	ASP
Brother Fish	Bryce Courtenay	Penguin Books	183,450	$4,670,300	$49.95	$25.46
The Reef	Di Morrissey	Pan Macmillan	63,400	$1,236,500	$30.00	$19.50
The Turning	Tim Winton	Pan Macmillan	52,460	$1,765,400	$46.00	$33.65
Wild Lavender	Belinda Alexandra	HarperCollins Publishers	40,840	$860,700	$29.95	$21.07
Shiver: A Novel	Nikki Gemmell	Random House	34,270	$170,700	$3.85	$4.98
Angel Puss	Colleen McCullough	HarperCollins Publishers	32,450	$881,300	$49.95	$27.16
The Alphabet Sisters	Monica McInerney	Penguin Books	32,210	$734,000	$29.95	$22.79
Dirt Music	Tim Winton	Pan Macmillan	27,060	$551,000	$25.34	$19.04
The Naked Husband	Mark D'Arbanville	Transworld	24,950	$485,000	$23.12	$18.27
Pacific	Judy Nunn	Random House	24,390	$544,700	$20.90	$17.51

Figure 1: Australian Book Sales in the category "General and Literary Fiction", 2004. Top 10 bestsellers, listed in descending order by sales units. RRP: recommended retail price; ASP: average sale price.

bestseller lists across the period 2004–13 is Matthew Reilly, who is number 1 in 2009 and 2013, ahead of Courtney, Morrissey and Winton in these years.

In Figure 3, we can see that *Breath* is still selling strongly in its second year since release. One factor that stands out across this decade is that Courtney, Morrissey and Reilly produce a new fiction book every one to two years (not counting new editions of books previously published), and new volumes *often* appear in consecutive years. All are marketed as popular fiction. Winton's volumes do not appear so rapidly, although he has been highly productive, with a new book (adult or children's literature), plus short stories and plays, appearing every two to four years, but with a five-year hiatus in adult fiction between *Breath* in 2008 and *Eyrie* in 2013. What this level of productivity means for each of the authors in terms of their income is a closely guarded secret, but all these writers obviously live well and independently from their sales.

If sales figures and income are one set of indicators of the impact of literature in terms of readership size, another is the scope of scholarly debates generated around literature and percolating in university classrooms. In 2015, the American Modern Language Association, the biggest international gathering of literary scholars, took place. The convention was entitled "Literature and Its Publics: Past, Present and Future". Publications from this gathering reveal an undertow of self-analysis, if not self-doubt, about the future of literature in a digital world, a world in which, in Will Self's terms, "all cultural value [is] being colossally devalued in order to achieve parity with the pound".[11] Along with these

Title	Author	Publisher	Sales	Value	RRP	ASP
Fishing for Stars	Bryce Courtenay	Penguin Books	126,900	$3,456,000	$49.95	$27.23
Breath	Tim Winton	Penguin Books	125,560	$4,334,300	$45.00	$34.52
People of the Book	Geraldine Brooks	HarperCollins Publishers	94,580	$2,607,500	$32.99	$27.57
The Islands	Di Morrissey	Pan Macmillan	86,200	$1,816,700	$32.99	$21.08
The Book Thief	Markus Zusak	Pan Macmillan	62,030	$1,009,200	$19.95	$16.27
The Forgotten Garden	Kate Morton	Allen & Unwin	50,280	$1,281,000	$32.95	$25.48
The Spare Room	Helen Garner	Text	38,930	$1,052,400	$29.95	$27.04
Shantaram	Gregory David Roberts	Pan Macmillan	38,180	$1,238,200	$25.00	$32.43
The Persimmon Tree	Bryce Courtenay	Penguin Books	35,140	$803,100	$49.95	$22.85
The Six Sacred Stones	Matthew Reilly	Pan Macmillan	31,750	$768,300	$32.99	$24.20

Figure 2: Australian Book Sales in the category "General and Literary Fiction", 2008. Top 10 bestsellers, listed in descending order by sales units. RRP: recommended retail price; ASP: average sale price.

scholarly practitioners we need to ask: Who are the reading publics for literary narrative, and what impact does this literature have? The MLA's pluralising of "publics" is a reminder that many people in many different settings are reading diverse kinds of narratives – literary fiction, popular fiction, non-fiction (memoirs, essays, life-writing of various kinds, information books) and all the hybrids in between.

As the sales figures indicate, fiction such as Tim Winton's (literary, but with popular appeal) has a strong readership, particularly in Australia, but not as high as the clearly popular works of a Bryce Courtney or Di Morrissey; that he is read in the UK, the USA and China, but with relatively small figures in the UK and radically smaller ones in the USA.[12]

As we can see in Figure 4, the three most popular Winton novels in the UK are *Dirt Music*, *Breath* and *Cloudstreet*; the comparable US figures (not shown) are 15,105, 11,141 and 9620 respectively. While *Shallows*, Winton's second novel, won the 1984 Miles Franklin Literary Award in Australia, it sold only 1663 copies in the UK. This might be understandable, as Winton was just beginning his career. However, it is a little more surprising that *The Riders*, shortlisted for the UK-based Booker Prize in 1995, only sold

---

11   Self, "The Fate of Our Literary Culture".
12   Nielsen Book Scan figures, 2016.

Title	Author	Publisher	Sales	Value	RRP	ASP
The Five Greatest Warriors	Matthew Reilly	Pan Macmillan	143,930	$4,155,300	$49.99	$28.87
The Story of Danny Dunn	Bryce Courtenay	Penguin Books	132,390	$3,624,900	$49.95	$27.38
Breath	Tim Winton	Penguin Books	110,860	$2,514,600	$24.95	$22.68
The Slap	Christos Tsiolkas	Allen & Unwin	107,300	$3,280,600	$32.95	$30.57
The Silent Country	Di Morrissey	Pan Macmillan	81,560	$1,766,800	$32.99	$21.66
The Book Thief	Markus Zusak	Pan Macmillan	67,060	$1,126,600	$19.95	$16.80
Maralinga	Judy Nunn	Random House	45,570	$1,023,200	$32.95	$22.46
The Cattleman's Daughter	Rachael Treasure	Penguin Books	36,650	$867,400	$32.95	$23.66
Shantaram	Gregory David Roberts	Pan Macmillan	34,680	$1,161,600	$25.00	$33.49
Fishing for Stars	Bryce Courtenay	Penguin Books	26,750	$581,00	$49.95	$21.72

Figure 3: Australian Book Sales in the category "General and Literary Fiction", 2009. Top 10 bestsellers, listed in descending order by sales units. RRP: recommended retail price; ASP: average sale price.

8963 copies. It is evident from these figures that Winton's popularity is home-grown, and that while it does translate to a certain extent in the UK, his narratives seem to be an acquired taste for British readers. However, *Dirt Music* (nominated for the Booker in 2002) and *Breath* arguably have their own slow-burning popularity.

Still pursuing the question of impact, but arcing away from mere numbers, we need to note that Winton's works are regularly set on secondary and tertiary education syllabi in Australia. Many have been adapted for radio, stage, film or television, most notably *Cloudstreet*,[13] *The Riders*[14] and *The Turning*.[15] There are also numerous stage adaptations,

---

13   *Cloudstreet* was adapted for ABC Radio by David Britton and Paige Gibbs in 1996. It was adapted for the stage by Nick Enright and Justin Monjo and first performed by Black Swan Theatre Company, before touring internationally with Belvoir Street Theatre under the direction of Neil Armfield. *Cloudstreet* was also made into a television miniseries, written by Tim Winton and Ellen Fontana and screened in 2011 (Screentime Pty Ltd).
14   *The Riders* was adapted as an opera, with music by Iain Grandage and libretto by Alison Croggon. It was first performed in Melbourne by the Malthouse Theatre Company and Victorian Opera in September 2014, directed by the Malthouse Theatre's artistic director, Marion Potts.
15   *The Turning* was adapted for film, with a screenplay by Andrew Upton, Justin Monjo, Kris Mrksa, Circa Contemporary Circus and Marcel Dorney, and filmed as eighteen short films directed by eighteen different directors. Produced by Arenamedia and Screen Australia, it was first screened at the Melbourne International Film Festival in 2013.

8 Winton's Narratives: Market, Reading, Impact

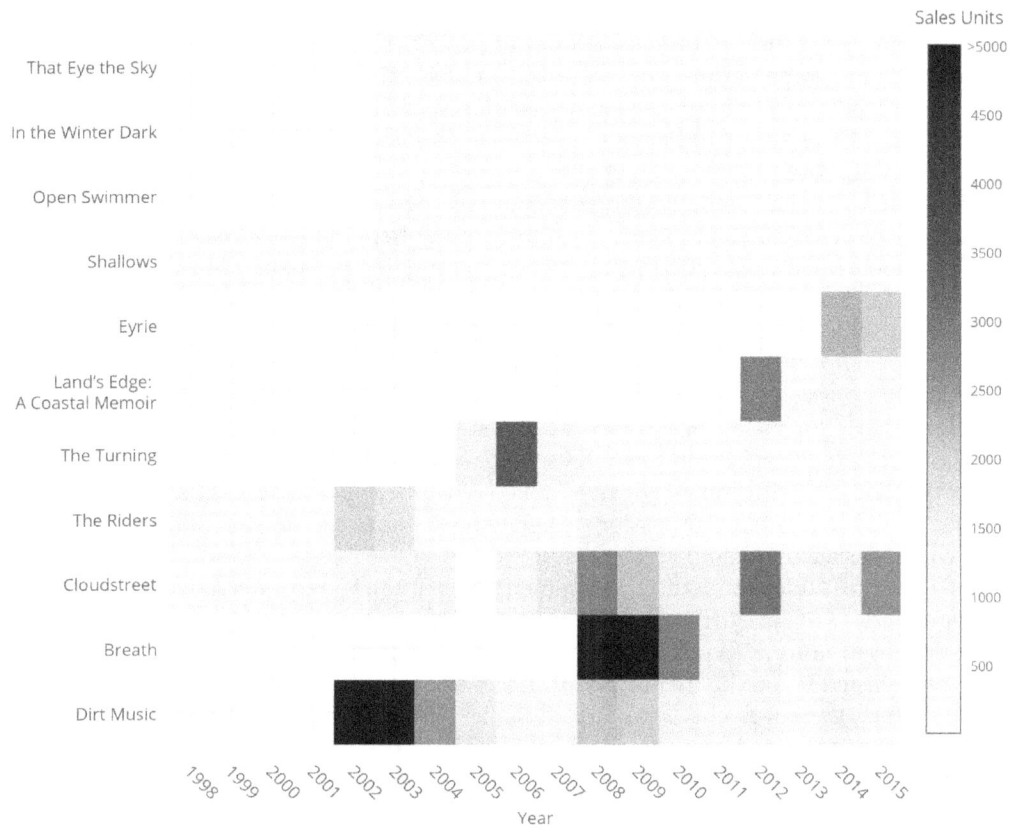

Figure 4. Heatmap of Winton's annual unit sales by title. UK TCM panel. Darker colours indicate greater sales in that year. For the full data set, see hdl.handle.net/2123/15592. Data for *Cloudstreet* was not available for 2004–5.

including puppet shows, of Winton's children's books such as *That Eye, the Sky* and the *Lockie Leonard* series, and film adaptations of *Shallows* and *Breath* are currently in production. Winton is also the writer of three stage plays, *Rising Water* (2011), *Signs of Life* (2012) and *Shrine* (2013).[16]

Winton's Preoccupations

Turning from this information about the size of Winton's literary/popular readership – information that needs careful scrutiny – and its contribution to debates about impact, we need to expand our understanding of the qualitative impact of his narratives through a consideration of the kinds and scope of narrative preoccupations evident in his works.

---

16   *Rising Water* (Sydney: Currency Press, 2011), *Signs of Life: A Play in One Act* (Melbourne: Penguin, 2013), and *Shrine* (Melbourne: Penguin, 2013).

How, for instance, are these preoccupations *evolving*, both formally and in their existential and thematic concerns? Winton is a storyteller who has developed a set of narrative techniques: characters who are recurrent across narratives; intimate and lyrical construction of place/setting; use of vernacular speech; direct speech without use of quotation marks or other indicators apart from indentation; realistic as well as magic realist forms of prose.

The fiction has had some core preoccupations. Across the three decades of Winton's writing, his narrators and characters constantly (and often fruitlessly) seek to belong. The novels are recurrently concerned with fallenness and redemption, childhood, masculinity, family, gender, land, place, imaginative encounters with the natural world, Australianness, class, white-settler and Indigenous identity, and with sacredness and meaning-making. But while many of these preoccupations have been recurrent throughout his writing life, Winton is in no way a static writer. His work has evolved and matured in some surprising directions. How, for instance, have Winton's religious and activist concerns, which have become increasingly public in the 2000s, impacted on his writing and evolved across his works? How do the nuanced, unsayable, restrained elements of his writing, their poignancy and lyrical sense of loss or melancholy or unbelonging, work in relation to his more comic, vernacular and magic realist writings?

In order to understand the development of Winton's many narrative strands, and their potential impact, the most important factors to consider include his writing professionalisation as a very young man, with seven volumes of prose (novels and short stories) published before he had turned thirty; his taking on of different forms, including the short story, the novel, children's and adolescent books, plays and memoirs, along with his interest in and contribution to adaptations of his work for film and television; his use of vernacular dialogue, with its class-based and local/national implications; and his own peculiar movement between vernacular, often comically deflationary prose, and highly lyrical, magic realist and stream of consciousness writing. The often rapid-fire movement between these kinds of prose techniques and existential positions produces an original, sometimes bamboozling mixture of effects, and sometimes bamboozled responses in readers, with the identity of the narrator sometimes purposely unclear. One prime, early example of this hybrid prose, and of a multiple narrator, can be found in *Cloudstreet*, as the damaged boy, Fish, stands down in the backyard talking with his pig, a scene we have earlier examined in a different context:

> Autumn comes and the long, cool twilights before winter hang over the rooftops of the city full of the sounds of roosting birds and quiet leaving. Down in the yard at Cloudstreet, down there in the halls and channels of time Fish and the pig exchange glances and dumbly feel the weather turning inward. The pig is battleworn, leathery beyond the threat of butchery and scarred like the trunk of an old tree. Fish handles him sweetly and without talk, just touches him on the moist snout and stands. What are you thinking, Fish? Do you feel that you're going, that you're close? Strange that you should be so hard to read these last stretching days. It should be rushing, like the whole planet is rushing down its narrow fixed course. But I can't read your face. I stare back at you in the puddles on the chilly ground, I'm waiting in your long monastic breath, I travel back to these moments to wonder at what you're feeling and come away with nothing but the knowledge of who it will be in the end. You're coming to me, Fish, and all that you might

have been ... No shadows, no ugliness, no hurtings, no falling down angry. Your turn is coming.[17]

Fish's pig has been a constant presence – "A blasted Pentecostal pig" (170), a bacon angel – and a source of delight for Fish, creating various effects in the novel. The pig is a touchstone, literally, for Fish, a living creature who understands and speaks to the boy's unspeakable needs: "What are you thinking, Fish?" So, the pig becomes momentarily an embodiment or alter ego of Fish. But the narrative voice in this passage is not a single entity. It slips between omniscient observer of seasons, time, death, and possible redemption, into being the voice of Fish. But it is Fish in another dimension, Fish speaking to his still human, boy self, beckoning him with news of a place and time beyond his present suffering: "You're coming to me, Fish, and all that you might have been". It is Fish talking to himself, who "stare[s] back ... in the puddles on the chilly ground". But it is also a god-like voice, one removed from time and suffering, able to promise, in the boy's forms of vernacular speech, a place of "no hurtings, no falling down angry". Winton's narrative here is at once comic, moving and multiple-voiced. This voice, in its god-like elements, assists the plot to move towards its conclusion, and Fish's departure, but it also enables a meditative and empathetic pausing, as readers of this scene contemplate the immensity of what has been lost for Fish, as well as for Quick, Oriel and Lester. In these ways Winton, again and again in *Cloudstreet* and many other works, plays with the identity of the narrative voice, working between realistic commentary and stream of consciousness, magic realist effects. As well as presenting us with a highly literary narrative multiplicity, *Cloudstreet* is also a very popular, well-loved novel.

Vision, but Not Naïvety

While readers might be touched by this depiction of a hurt and innocent boy, with its highly individualising representation of white, working-class families and their struggles to survive and build a future, a range of postcolonial commentators keep asking how to think about white identity within a wider set of cultural and historical contexts. Some of these critics, as we've seen in Chapter 7, feel uneasy with *Cloudstreet*'s individualistic and even sentimental treatment of such questions. As far back as 1989, *The Empire Writes Back* was concerned with white-settler futures in Australia, and with the ways literary writers attempt to "construct a future", "a hybridised and syncretic view of the modern world".[18] The authors of *The Empire Writes Back* champion, for example, Derek Walcott's vision of a "'historyless" world, where a fresh but not innocent "Adamic" naming of place provides the writer with inexhaustible material and "the potential of a new, but not naïve, vision".[19]

The authors of *The Empire Writes Back* call for vision, but not naïvety; history but with the hope of historylessness; the power to name in an originary way. Critics may argue that this is another mode of innocence regained, where lessons have been learnt, losses taken

---

17 Tim Winton, *Cloudstreet* (Melbourne: McPhee Gribble, 1991), 530. All subsequent references are to this edition and appear in parentheses in the text.
18 Bill Ashcroft, Gareth Griffiths and Helen Tiffin, *The Empire Writes Back: Theory and Practice in Post-colonial Literatures* (London and New York: Routledge, 1989), 37.
19 Ashcroft, Griffiths and Tiffin, *The Empire Writes Back*, 34–35.

stock of, and new beginnings enabled. Can we read the figure of Fish as some kind of innocent white presence, earning his place through the pain and sacrifice he and his family endure? New Zealand critic Linda Hardy writes, in an excellent essay on postcolonial poetics, of

> [t]he utopian or idealist moment that authenticates a European presence in Australasia... the epiphany which has always been the modernist subject's dubiously innocent mode of entry into a "new world", the "settler dream of an originary innocence".[20]

In aligning the utopian strand of postcolonialism with colonialist idealism, its very nemesis, Hardy is opening up the wilder debates in postcolonial studies. Such ongoing debates amongst postcolonial scholars, evident also in the fiction and poetry of many writers including Winton, are about how much history, with its violence and unrecuperability, can be borne; and how much history can be made and remade towards the future. Do the ghosts of the past, thematic or theoretical, prepare us for the possibility of transformation and renewal, or undermine any such possibility? In this debate, the tension is between a Romantic, idealistic, and even utopian impetus, and a less future-looking, freighted, much bleaker account of history.

We can see this ongoing set of arguments between history and fiction in the critical debates around Winton's *Cloudstreet*, with its sometimes bleak but finally optimistic representations of Indigenous Australians, often depicted as ghosts, and their quiet, even contented moving aside for white-settler Australia. For example, how do we read the scene in which Quick, as a policeman, has been hunting for the Nedlands Monster during "a night of endless lonely trudging, of holing up in ramshackle hollows and peering over back fences" (484)? At dawn, he goes to the river to clear his head:

> In the dawn the sky was clearing and summery steam rose off the jetty piles and out of the steam came the black man looking completely unsurprised.
> Geez, said Quick, recognising him fearfully. Haven't you got a home to go to?
> Not this side.
> Quick looked across the river. Through the steam he thought he saw moving figures, dark outlines on the far bank.
> Are you real?
> The blackfella laughed. Are you?
> Quick kicked the muddy grass before him.
> *You've* got a home to go to, Quick. Go there.
> Quick regarded the man. He was naked, naked enough to arrest.
> Go there.
> Orright, said PC Quick, already on his way. When he turned back, high on the hill, he saw more than one black man. He saw dozens of them beneath the trees, hundreds like a necklace at the throat of the city. (484)

---

20   Linda Hardy, "Natural Occupancy", in *Asian and Pacific Inscriptions: Identities, Ethnicities, Nationalities*, ed. Suvendi Perera (Melbourne: Meridian Books, 1995), 223.

This passage, and others like it in *Cloudstreet*, in which the Lambs and the Pickles encounter Indigenous characters in their house, or down by the river, or further from home, have led some critics to question Winton's mode of representing the past and Indigenous Australia in relation to the main characters and plot. Michael R. Griffiths asks of such scenes in *Cloudstreet*:

> Is this more corporeal spectrality of "the blackfella" a redemption of white-settler colonisation or a challenge to it? The two are perhaps not mutually exclusive but rather constitutive of an ongoing logic of dispossession, normalised and even (more problematically) exonerated as a naïve – if haunted – inheritance of stolen land?[21]

Griffiths is right to point out the ambivalence felt by many readers to Winton's representation of Indigeneity in *Cloudstreet*. Readers' ideological questions cannot but be informed by post-*Mabo* concerns about white colonisation of the land, and white settlers' role in perpetuating that colonisation. Dispossession of Aboriginal peoples from the land they had lived in for 200,000 years is uppermost in the minds of many Australians today, making it difficult to place the politics of this passage, and *Cloudstreet*'s broader attitude to white inheritance and the future. Griffiths acknowledges the hauntedness of Winton's representations, but also highlights the ambivalence of a dispossessed Aboriginal man, for the second time in the novel, prophetically directing Quick to go home: "*You've* got a home to go to, Quick. Go there". As discussed earlier, it is not back to England he is suggesting, but back to Cloudstreet and his family. The final image in this passage, of black men in their "hundreds like a necklace at the throat of the city", is equally ambivalent. This is Quick's perception, as he heads wearily home, and seems like a benediction *and* a threat, simultaneously. At this point it is important to return to the question of narrative impact, as well as to the postcolonial question raised above, asking, as *The Empire Writes Back* did, whether there is "the potential of a new, but not naïve, vision", as we relate this to Winton's text.

It is interesting that the word "naïve" appears in both the early theoretical text *The Empire Writes Back*, and in Michael Griffiths' suggestion that the novel depicts "a naïve – if haunted – inheritance". Just how naïve are white Australians in regard to the colonial history of the continent and their own search for belonging here? We need to remember that there are two different contexts to be considered: one in which the narrative of *Cloudstreet* was written, across four years, and the historically and politically different context in which the novel is read. Each is crucial, and distinct, in understanding how readers respond to Winton's representations of Indigenous and non-Indigenous Australia. Winton was writing *Cloudstreet* in the four years leading up to publication in 1991. This is the very same period in which the watershed High Court case on Indigenous land rights, the nationally, deeply significant *Mabo and Another v. The State of Queensland and Another* (1989)[22] was being assembled and heard. In 1992 the High Court delivered its decision. In the words of Justice Michael Kirby (who did not sit on this case):

---

21 Michael R. Griffiths, "Winton's Spectralities, or What Haunts *Cloudstreet*?" in *Tim Winton: Critical Essays*, ed. Lyn McCredden and Nathanael O'Reilly (Perth: UWA Publishing, 2014), 86.
22 *Mabo v. Queensland* (1988) HCA 69; (1989) 166 CLR 186 (8 December 1988). http://tinyurl.com/Mabo1988.

> The *Mabo* decision is legally significant in a number of respects. First, it recognised the entitlement of indigenous people of Australia to a form of native land title. This recognition required the overruling of the common law doctrine of *terra nullius* ... Second, the High Court offered guidance as to the circumstances in which an established common law doctrine may be overruled by a court.[23]

Debates about Indigenous rights, colonisation and *terra nullius*, focused on land rights specifically, had been escalating in Australia across the 1980s in cultural, legal and political contexts, culminating with the Australian Bicentenary in 1988. And here was Tim Winton, a young author of twenty-seven, attempting (and daring) to represent something of these issues in a book that focused on white Australian yearning for home and belonging. It might be considered naïve, or brave, to try to represent Indigenous Australia in fiction, especially in that period, and further, to do so from the perspective of white-settler Australia.

After the Bicentenary: *Cloudstreet* and *Master of the Ghost Dreaming*

The critical objections to *Cloudstreet*'s representation of Indigenous characters, many of which Michael R. Griffiths engages with, include: why are the Indigenous characters mostly absent, or represented as ghosts, magic realist clowns, or prophets, present in the novel for the white characters to define themselves against? Why are the Indigenous characters all victims, dispossessed of their home but able to offer forgiveness, even to exonerate white Australia, recreating a new form of *terra nullius*? Why don't the Indigenous characters have a future, whether hopeful or otherwise, unlike the white characters whose stories build towards the future? What becomes visible if we compare Winton's narrative, with its ghostly but generally forgiving Indigenous characters, to another novel that was published in the same year, *Master of the Ghost Dreaming*?[24] *Master of the Ghost Dreaming*, by the contentious Aboriginal author Mudrooroo, also from Western Australia, exhibits a number of similarities aesthetically, and some strong differences, to *Cloudstreet*.

Firstly, it is important to register that *Cloudstreet* is by a descendant of white-settler Australians, and *Master of the Ghost Dreaming* by an author who at that moment in history identified as a Nyoongah man.[25] This positioning of authorial identity, though never straightforward, takes into consideration the postcolonial question of who is speaking, and for whom. Second, we might note the fact that both narratives are concerned with Indigenous characters *in relation* to white settlers, in Mudrooroo's case the white missionary and overseer George Augustus Robinson. But it is the differences in the role of narrator and narrative perspective that are central in this current discussion. Mudrooroo's novel is embedded deeply in an Indigenous sensibility, with its omniscient, strongly Aboriginal-identified narrator able to measure both the diminishment of the Tasmanian

---

23 Michael Kirby, "In Defence of *Mabo*", *James Cook University Law Review* 3 (1994): 52.
24 Mudrooroo, *Master of the Ghost Dreaming* (Sydney: Angus & Robertson, 1991).
25 For critical debates about Mudrooroo's identity, see Adam Shoemaker, *Mudrooroo: A Critical Study* (Sydney: Angus & Robertson, 1993) and Maureen Clark, *Mudrooroo: A Likely Story – Identity and Belonging in Postcolonial Australia* (Amsterdam: Peter Lang, 2007).

Aboriginal peoples and their power, wit, comic abilities, and more. *Master of the Ghost Dreaming* is highly self-reflexive historically and in its techniques, not concerned with pyrrhic Aboriginal victories or defeats, but detailing the wealth of daily life and practices of the people in the context of overwhelming white colonisation.

Cloudstreet is written from a very different perspective. Its central concern is for white Australian futures. It is somewhat blind (or reticent?) about representing "the other", in ways that Mudrooroo's sharply parodic depiction of Mada and Fada, the white missionaries in *Master*, is not. The narrative of *Master* mimics the voices of these white figures, reveals their hypocrisies, and measures their blindness to a whole way of life conducted across millennia. *Cloudstreet*, in direct comparison, does not attempt to develop our understanding of Indigenous Australia. But nor was that its major focus. It is written by a white author interested in white, working-class, struggling characters two hundred years after European invasion of the continent. It is asking what traumas they suffer, what striving and failure constitute the inheritance of white Australia. But it does not (cannot) speak from Indigenous perspectives. In fact, it could be argued that it refuses to do so, or stops short of usurping Indigenous voices, simply gesturing to them as they circle "like a necklace at the throat of the city". This comparison in no way seeks to value one novel above the other, but to think about their different (necessarily different) narrative perspectives and voices. *Cloudstreet* is a novel by a young and emerging white author from Western Australia, written from the perspective of a non-Indigenous Australian looking back at Australia as it began to grapple with its postwar and 1960s European identity. It does have a consciousness that Indigenous Australians have something very important to say to white Australia, but it has not yet fully found a way of addressing or acknowledging what that is.

The Unredeemable Facts of History

Undoubtedly belonging to the bleaker school of postcolonial studies, in contrast to Bhabha and Ashcroft et al., is literary critic David Punter. His book *Postcolonial Imaginings: Fictions of a New World Order* deplores what he sees as the "triumphalist stance of the [post-colonial] theorist"[26] (and by implication, hope-filled novelists?). He argues that we need to

> break with the disavowal of pain and exclusion ... and to re-encounter again the melancholy, the ruin and the loss, the ineradicable fact of genocidal violence in the past and the equally ineradicable fact of its continuation in the present day.[27]

The wording "re-encounter again" is striking here, a double action to ensure that the need to encounter violence and loss is understood, relevant to both our reading of the past and in recognition of the present ramifications of such violence. Obviously, Punter does not like the kinds of postcolonial theorising that seem to forget the trauma of the past and lose sight of the melancholic repercussions of history. He sees a range of theorists

---

26 David Punter, *Postcolonial Imaginings: Fictions of a New World Order* (Edinburgh: Edinburgh University Press, 2000), 186.
27 Punter, *Postcolonial Imaginings*, 187

(a long list) as "succumbing to the utopian lure"[28] and advises the need to "continually remember to investigate the fictionality of . . . any 'new world order'".[29] Punter's larger argument privileges the fiction writer over the theorist, seeing them as truer postcolonial guides who can represent the loss he is talking about as overwhelming and unchanging reality, with, arguably, little sense of the future.

In one regard I would agree with Punter when he describes the need for a cultural rhetoric that is able to remember the loss and violence, the overwhelmingly unredeemable facts of history. How can we ever think of forgetting? Punter is justified in seeing a utopian pull in the works of many theorists, a pull that can sound as if it is seeking to forget, to move on. Such theorists, he argues, emphasise empowerment, emancipation, agency and futurity in the hybrid and transformational literatures of the colonised, but at the cost of adequately remembering the losses. Some critics, like Bill Ashcroft, elaborate the creative and intellectual processes of such emancipatory "post-colonial transformation";[30] others, like Homi Bhabha, working more from poststructural and psychoanalytic methodologies, emphasise the linguistic ambivalences of such transformations founded in the processes of cultural hybridisation, mimicry and identity formation.

What is still the most slippery ground in contemporary postcolonial writing – theoretical, fictional and political – is the ways in which this tension, this attempting both to acknowledge the defiles of history and to wing imaginatively towards a new future, is held. What might they look and sound like, these narratives which simultaneously seek to recognise history's horror, but also attempt to see how history might be converted into "newness" and futurity by the cultural productions of the colonised and oppressed? Is such a simultaneity, or further, such a redemptive narrative, ever possible, given poststructural and postmodern questioning of such resolutions? Do the optimistic textual and cultural semiotic approaches to narrative convince? Ashcroft writes of "the transformation of that material culture presented to it as 'dominant' or 'civilized' [as] a sign of a surprisingly potent and even gleeful capacity for self-fashioning in colonised societies".[31] In Gloria Anzaldua's narratives Ashcroft sees

> the conversion of the nightmare into the numinous . . . the essence of post-colonial transformation, the location of an experience and an identity that is always pushing beyond itself. Into the horizon.[32]

And what do we make of Homi Bhabha's more ambivalent version of transformation, which argues that "culture as a colonial space of intervention . . . can be transformed by the unpredictable and partial desire of hybridity"?[33] Hardly a resounding endorsement of reconciliatory forces.

Some critics, like Punter, argue that the explicitly fictional, narrative worlds of postcolonial writers is a more convincing site in which to develop a rhetoric capable of taking us into the future. After all, novelists, he argues, have at their fingertips permission

---

28 Punter, *Postcolonial Imaginings*, 189.
29 Punter, *Postcolonial Imaginings*, 189.
30 Bill Ashcroft, *Post-colonial Transformation* (London: Routledge, 2001).
31 Ashcroft, *Post-colonial Transformation*, 220.
32 Ashcroft, *Post-colonial Transformation*, 193.
33 Homi K. Bhabha, *The Location of Culture* (London: Routledge, 1994), 115.

to imagine, to fictionalise, to move identities and fates in desirable directions, to conclude history, or at least the novel's history, in the direction of fulfilment, newness, change, even redemption. Perhaps we should envy the novelists, as Punter suggests, who are able to let the imagination fly. We give them permission to be utopian, but we are suspicious of the theorist who does the same. Yet there is an answering sting in Bhabha's parodic quip, in his discussion of *Heart of Darkness*, that novels end because they cannot bear too much fictionality. In this clever reversal of T. S. Eliot's dictum, the tension between "reality" and "imagination", history and narrative is tightened. Can postcolonial cultures be genuinely new, based upon acknowledgement of, but also sufficient release from, the horrors and losses of history? What are the different impacts of theory and fiction in helping us to think through these issues?

In Winton's *Dirt Music*, the narrative voice is author-like, but it is focalised through the inner voice of the protagonist, Luther Fox, a white man suffering traumatic personal losses who heads off into the deserts and islands of the Australian far north, seeking release from the burdens of his life. As discussed in Chapter 4, in terms of narrative redemption he seems at the end of the novel's romance narrative to have achieved a form of salvation in the arms of his lover, Georgie Jutland. However, what is remarkable about this novel, beyond its romance narrative, is the ways in which it both acknowledges "power of place" in relation to the land as Aboriginal, but also turns back from any simplistic form of indigenisation of Fox. Arguably, Fox is, at novel's end, still a white man seeking meaning or revelation in the land, but also having to acknowledge his otherness from it. It is that balance in the narrative and in the main character that needs examination.

If we approach Winton's narratives in this way, as seeking new modes of understanding *white* habitation in what is predominantly Aboriginal country, are we conceding that Winton fails, or is blind to, or refuses to enter into, some of the most important dialogues about Indigenous Australian history? In other words, does *Dirt Music*, along with *Cloudstreet*, by taking on questions of white existence and the future, fail sufficiently to acknowledge "the ruin and the loss, the ineradicable fact of genocidal violence in the past and the equally ineradicable fact of its continuation in the present day",[34] reducing these issues to intimate, individual romance, the land to mere backdrop, and Indigenous presence once again to spectral absence?

Australia, Land of Orphans

These questions go to our consideration of the impact and significance of narrative, as linguistic and as ideological. Is *Dirt Music* finally only a white romance set in exoticised Aboriginal country? One way of responding to such questions is to look closely at how the writing constructs its position, not merely reiterating the aesthetic effects of a work but examining how the narrative carries the heavy freight of meaning in narrative voice and perception, asking whether it is ideologically positioned, and how. In what ways are the ethics of the narrative – conscious and unconscious – apparent? In Chapter 4 of *Dirt Music*, Luther Fox flees from home, seeking something beyond himself, seeking to escape, or to recapture his childhood links with his father through connection to place. At the beginning of his journey, Fox's meeting with Menzies and Axle takes place, and is,

---

34 Punter, *Postcolonial Imaginings*, 187.

arguably, a strange microcosm of the novel's narrative position towards Australian identity. Although the story is told in the third person, the writing nevertheless is focalised through Fox, whose journey it is. It's through his eyes that we see the country, source of beauty and fear, as he is flown along the northwest coast:

> Beneath the overcast they bear northeast into the interior and Fox sees how old and beaten-down the land is with it crone-skin patterns, its wens and scars and open wounds. The plains, with their sparse, grey tufts of mulga scrub, rise into the high skeletal disarray of the sandstone ranges where rivers run like green gashes toward the sea. All rigid geometry falls away; no roads, no fences, just a confusion of colour. Out at the horizon the jagged island-choked coast. (299)

The land is narrated through Fox's tired, anxious eyes. It is old and beaten down, crone-like, scarred and wounded. The plains are sparse and skeletal, pitted with gashes, edging a "jagged island-choked coast". Yet read carefully, the narrative reveals two perspectives at once. It registers Fox's fear, his outsider status, and it captures the intense and wild beauty, the "confusion of colour" beyond the colonised world of fences and roads. This is the northwestern limit of Australia depicted through the eyes of a white Australian who has an openness to the place, but does not belong there. In this way, Winton is asking questions of place from his own non-Indigenous perspective. Fox is neither a fool nor a hero, but is asked often where he is going and what he is doing, by the pilot who flies him north, and by Menzies, the parodically named character whom he accidentally meets as he begins his trek.

In what ways can this meeting of Fox, Menzies, and his erratic young friend, Axle, be described as microcosmic of the novel's position? In a land that is not hospitable for Fox, who clutches his inadequate map, he finds two characters who offer hospitality. One nominates himself as half-Aboriginal, half-Chinese, so he thinks, and the other is a rootless Aboriginal young man seeking his spirit people. Both are orphaned, having come from the nuns at New Norcia:

> How long you blokes been here?
>   All time, says Axle. Everywhen.
>   Couple seasons, says Menzies, crouching to stir up the fire. Come and go, you know. Is this—?
>   Our country? Menzies shrugs dramatically. Dunno. Orphan, I was. Well, thas what the nuns said. Ever bin down New Norcia way?
>   Fox can't help but smile as he nods.
>   All them kids. Noongars, Wongai People. But you look at me. Half-Chinese fulla. Think my mother from Bardi people maybe. Who knows. Them nuns and priest fullas didn't hardly talk no English. Didn't tell me nothing! he utters, looking more bemused than bitter.
>   Dis *my* country, says Axle.
>   Mebbe, says Menzies with a diplomatic shrug. (303)

From Fox's perspective (and Winton's?) Australia is not a simple, single place; nor is it exotic or seductive. It is hybrid, but certainly not utopian in Bhabha's sense of the word. It is a place of orphans (Fox among them); many of its peoples are in danger of losing their grip on heritage and identity, but nevertheless they yearn for these things: "But you look at me. Half-Chinese fulla. Think my mother from Bardi people maybe". Menzies' namesake is "Pig Iron Bob" Menzies, conservative prime minister of Australia from 1949 to 1966, who oversaw an Australia in which the White Australia policy (1901–73) was firmly in place, though it was slowly being dismantled. This is a quirky choice of name by Winton, suggesting even further the mixed, volatile and unsettled nature of "Australia". And then there is Axle, an Aboriginal who wants to find his people and place, but who is fighting history and loss of both memory and heritage. It is Axle who grabs Fox's maps from his hands and throws them in the campfire. Perhaps he does this to set Fox free, pushing him to read the country otherwise, giving him the gift of a boat in which he can move among the islands and find a spot to be.

Afterword

How significant is Tim Winton's fiction, at this moment and into the future? Both quantitative and qualitative measures need to be considered in addressing this question, but one fact we know: tens of thousands of Australian and international readers have encountered Winton's writings, whether as set texts on school or university curricula, or at book clubs, introduced by word of mouth or by the publicity about his prizes. A test in considering Winton's lasting impact as a writer, for this reader, has been to register how his novels and short stories travel with me into my everyday life, in my understandings of place and belonging, and in my thinking about the forces of sacredness and meaning-making in Australia. Equally, I have found the critical debates around Winton's work to be revealing of who "we" are, as Australians, as readers, as men and women, as members of particular classes.

And now, at the time this critical volume is being completed, *Cloudstreet* the opera has just appeared, making its debut with the State Opera of South Australia. It was described by the *Australian* newspaper's reviewer as "impressive from every angle"; as "a resounding triumph [which] thoroughly deserved the standing ovation it received on opening night".[1] It was developed by many hands: the writer of the score, George Palmer; the music director, Timothy Sexton; director Gale Edwards; actors; singers; and the State Opera. Echoing Winton's inimitable and hybrid style – eclectic, popular, lyrical, vernacular – the music for the opera was described by the reviewer as "a curious but highly effective fusion of traditional styles from late romantic Italian opera to Broadway".[2]

In this book I have argued that Tim Winton is one of Australia's most popular *and* literary authors. His fiction has garnered a reputation for probing explorations of becoming and belonging in Australia. These explorations take place, for author and reader – *imaginatively* and sometimes *literally* – in his representations of beaches and deserts, small country towns and the cities of this continent, and in far-off Europe; in his writing about dysfunctional and loving families; in his complex men and children and women; in vibrant vernacular language; and in profound ideological struggles about how meaning

---

1   Graham Strahle, "*Cloudstreet*: Opera a Resounding Triumph", *Australian*, 16 May 2016. http://tinyurl.com/Strahle2016.
2   Strahle, "*Cloudstreet*: Opera a Resounding Triumph".

might be made. Winton's stories continue to be explored in films, telemovies, stage plays and operas.

However, what is the most intriguing revelation about the fiction of Tim Winton, realised by this critic in the writing of this volume, is that every representation of desire to belong, to find or defend home, expressed by Winton's narrators, characters and plots, contends with a deep undertow of unbelonging. This is possibly the necessary inheritance of white Australia, and of working-class Australia. Just as *That Eye, the Sky*'s Ort Flack had to discover, along with *Cloudstreet*'s Quick Lamb, *The Rider*'s Scully and Billie, *Breath*'s Pikelet and Eva, and *Eyrie*'s Tom Keely: the idea of home is made and re-made, not given. It involves risk and choice, and, often, dire loss. Home – national, familial, personal – and the meanings it fosters or fails to foster is constantly reached for, and made, as it shimmers mirage-like on the horizon. It excludes, even as it embraces. Winton's home is not a comfortable, complacent or static reality. It is the place where belonging is negotiated and renegotiated. In his works, home is family, but also other; it is familiar, beloved land and ocean, and it is their threatened desecration.

Winton's narratives move, amuse, provoke and annoy readers. They reach out beyond themselves, beyond one place (even over East!), one kind of readership, and they don't always convince all readers. They certainly speak centrally from within non-Indigenous Australia and from "white" desires to belong in this place; but Winton has increasingly been coming to understand and honour the power of Indigenous place-making and history. Tim Winton continues (hopefully) to offer us – Indigenous and non-Indigenous Australians, men and women, children, non-Australians open to his stories – the shimmering gift of seeing and re-imagining ourselves. Through his eyes, and in his often radiantly lyrical, often boisterously playful words, we see ourselves mirrored: homely and transforming, vulnerable and precious, comic and brooding – fools often, but not monsters. In his words, and through the characters and places his readers have come to know so well, we witness the creative force and the elemental desire to make meaning of one ocean-loving, earthy, reverent man who is seeking both earthed and sacred understanding, for himself and for the many who read his fiction.

Works Cited

Abell, Stephen. "Australian Small-Town Life". Review of *Breath* by Tim Winton. *Telegraph*, 23 May 2008. http://tinyurl.com/Abell2008.
Anthias, Floya. "The Concept of 'Social Division' and Theorising Social Stratification: Looking at Ethnicity and Class". *Sociology* 35, no. 4 (2001): 835–54.
Ashcroft, Bill. *Post-colonial Transformation*. London: Routledge, 2001.
Ashcroft, Bill, Frances Devlin Glass and Lyn McCredden. *Intimate Horizons: The Post-Colonial Sacred in Australian Literature*. Adelaide: ATF Press, 2009.
Ashcroft, Bill, Gareth Griffiths and Helen Tiffin. *Key Concepts in Post-colonial Studies*. London and New York: Routledge, 1998.
Ashcroft, Bill, Gareth Griffiths and Helen Tiffin. *The Empire Writes Back: Theory and Practice in Post-colonial Literatures*. London and New York: Routledge, 1989.
Auden, W. H. *Collected Poems*. New York: Random House, 1976.
Baines Alarcos, M. Pilar. "She Lures, She Guides, She Quits: Female Characters in Tim Winton's The Riders". *Journal of English Studies* 8 (2010): 7–22.
Bakhtin, Mikhail M. "Discourse in the Novel". In *The Dialogical Imagination: Four Essays*, edited by Michael Holquist, translated by Caryl Emerson and Michael Holquist, 259–422. Austin: University of Texas Press, 1981.
Barthes, Roland. "Introduction to the Structural Analysis of Narratives". In *Image Music Text: Essays*, selected and translated by Stephen Heath, 79–124. London: Fontana Press, 1977.
Ben-Messahel, Salhia. *Mind the Country: Tim Winton's Fiction*. Crawley: University of Western Australia Publishing, 2006.
Bhabha, Homi K. *The Location of Culture*. London: Routledge, 1994.
Birns, Nicholas. "A Not Completely Pointless Beauty: *Breath*, Exceptionality, and Neoliberalism". In *Tim Winton: Critical Essays*, edited by Lyn McCredden and Nathanael O'Reilly, 263–82. Perth: UWA Publishing, 2014.
——. *Contemporary Australian Literature*. Sydney: Sydney University Press, 2015.
Blyth, Catherine. "Overextended and Underdeveloped: A Heartfelt Story of Disillusionment and Salvation Fails to Soar". Review of *Eyrie* by Tim Winton. *Telegraph* (UK), 18 June 2014. http://tinyurl.com/Blyth14.
Boer, Roland. *In the Vale of Tears: On Marxism and Theology*. Leiden, The Netherlands: Brill, 2014.
——. *Criticism of Earth: On Marx, Engels and Theology*. Leiden, The Netherlands: Brill, 2011.
——. *Criticism of Theology: On Marxism and Theology III*. Leiden, The Netherlands: Brill, 2010.
——. *Criticism of Religion: On Marxism and Theology II*. Leiden, The Netherlands: Brill, 2009.
——. *Criticism of Heaven: On Marxism and Theology*. Leiden, The Netherlands: Brill, 2007.

Works Cited

Bogle, Deborah. "Winton Uses Words as Way to Ponder Change". *Advertiser* (Adelaide), 21 October 2013, 15.

Burke, Edmund. "Of the Passion Caused by the Sublime". (1757) In *The Works of the Right Honourable Edmund Burke, Vol. 1 (of 12)*, part 2, sect. 1. Project Gutenberg, 2005. http://tinyurl.com/Burke2005.

———. *A Philosophical Enquiry into the Origin of Our Ideas of the Sublime and Beautiful.* (1757) Oxford and New York: Oxford University Press, 1990.

Butler, Judith. *Precarious Life: The Powers of Mourning and Violence.* New York and London: Verso, 2004.

Caldwell, Roger. Review of *Why Marx Was Right* by Terry Eagleton. *Philosophy Now* 96 (December 2015). http://tinyurl.com/Caldwell2015.

Caputo, J. D. *The Prayers and Tears of Jacques Derrida: Religion without Religion.* Bloomington: Indiana University Press, 1997.

Cattanach, Andrew. "10 Australian Books to Read Before You Die – *First Tuesday Book Club*". Booktopia Blog, 5 December 2012. http://tinyurl.com/Cattanach2012.

Clark, Maureen. *Mudrooroo: A Likely Story – Identity and Belonging in Postcolonial Australia.* Amsterdam: Peter Lang, 2007.

Connolly, Robert, creator. *The Turning* (film). Directed by ensemble. Produced by Arenamedia and Screen Australia, 2013.

Derrida, Jacques. "Structure, Sign, and Play in the Discourse of the Human Sciences". In *The Languages of Criticism and the Sciences of Man: The Structuralism Controversy*, edited by R. Macksey and E. Donato, 247–72. Baltimore: Johns Hopkins University Press, 1972.

DiCenso, James J. "Heidegger's Hermeneutic of Fallenness". *Journal of the American Academy of Religion* 56, no. 4 (1988): 667–79.

Dixon, Robert. "Tim Winton, *Cloudstreet* and the Field of Australian Literature". *Westerly* 50 (2005): 240–60.

Driscoll, Beth. *The New Literary Middlebrow: Tastemakers and Reading in the Twenty-First Century.* London: Palgrave Macmillan, 2014.

———. "On Culture, Cash and *Books Alive*". *Australian*, 26 July 2008. http://tinyurl.com/Driscoll2008.

Eagleton, Terry. *Why Marx Was Right.* New Haven, Conn: Yale University Press, 2011.

Erll, Astrid. "Cultural Studies Approaches to Narrative". In *The Routledge Encyclopedia of Narrative Theory*, edited by David Herman, Manfred Jahn and Marie-Laure Ryan, 88–93. Oxfordshire and New York: Routledge, 2005.

Flint, Nicolle. "Misogyny Lurks in Winton's World of Fiction". *Age*, 1 August 2013. http://tinyurl.com/flint2013.

Frow, John. "Is Elvis a God? Cult, Culture, Questions of Method". *International Journal of Cultural Studies* 1, no. 2 (1998): 197–210.

Goldsworthy, Kerryn. "Biblical World View Legitimised: Australian Feminist Icon Turns in Grave". *Still Life with Cat* (blog), 18 June 2009. http://tinyurl.com/Goldsworthy2009.

Gorski, Philip S. et al., eds. *The Post-Secular in Question: Religion in Contemporary Society.* New York and London: Social Science Research Council and New York University Press, 2012.

Greenwood, Susan. "The Wild Hunt: A Mythological Language of Magic". In *Handbook of Contemporary Paganism*, edited by James R. Lewis and Murphy Pizza, 195–222. Leiden, The Netherlands: Brill, 2008.

Grenville, Kate. *The Secret River.* Melbourne: Text Publishing, 2005.

Griffiths, Michael R. "Winton's Spectralities, or What Haunts *Cloudstreet*?" In *Tim Winton: Critical Essays*, edited by Lyn McCredden and Nathanael O'Reilly, 75–95. Perth: UWA Publishing, 2014.

Grogan, Bridget. "The Cycle of Love and Loss: Melancholic Masculinity in *The Turning*". In *Tim Winton: Critical Essays*, edited by Lyn McCredden and Nathanael O'Reilly, 199–220. Perth: UWA Publishing, 2014.

Hardy, Linda. "Natural Occupancy." In *Asian and Pacific Inscriptions: Identities, Ethnicities, Nationalities*, edited by Suvendi Perera, 213–27. Melbourne: Meridian Books, 1995.

Hart, Kevin. "Reading Theologically: Reduction and Reductio". In *Intersection in Christianity and Critical Theory,* edited by Cassandra Falke, 11–22. London and New York: Palgrave Macmillan, 2010.
——. *The Trespass of the Sign: Deconstruction, Theology and Philosophy*. New York: Fordham University Press, 1989.
Hecq, Dominique. "Writing the Unconscious: Psychoanalysis for the Creative Writer". *Text* 12, no. 2 (October 2008). http://www.textjournal.com.au/oct08/hecq.htm.
Heidegger, Martin. *Being and Time*. Translated by John Macquarrie and Edward Robinson. New York: Harper & Row, 1962.
Herman, David, Manfred Jahn and Marie-Laure Ryan (eds). *The Routledge Encyclopedia of Narrative Theory*. London and New York: Routledge, 2005.
Heydon, John Dyson. *Royal Commission into Trade Union Governance and Corruption*: Final Report. Barton, ACT: Commonwealth of Australia, 2015. https://www.tradeunionroyalcommission.gov.au.
Hirsch, Marianne. *The Generation of Postmemory*: Writing and Visual Culture After the Holocaust. New York: Columbia University Press, 2012.
Hitt, Christopher. "Toward an Ecological Sublime". *New Literary History* 30, no. 3, Ecocriticism (Summer 1999): 603–23.
Irigaray, Luce. *Key Writings*. London: Continuum, 2004.
Jones, Gail. *Sorry*. Sydney: Random House, 2007.
Katz, Wendy and Timothy Mahoney. *Regionalism and the Humanities*. Lincoln: University of Nebraska Press, 2008.
Kirby, Michael. "In Defence of *Mabo*". *James Cook University Law Review* 3 (1994), 51–77.
Kristeva, Julia. *The Powers of Horror: An Essay on Abjection*. Translated by Leon S. Roudiez. New York: Columbia University Press, 1982.
Lacan, Jacques. *Ecrits: A Selection*. Translated by Alan Sheridan. Hoboken and London: Taylor & Francis, 2001.
Lewis, Pericles. *Religious Experience and the Modernist Novel*. Cambridge: Cambridge University Press, 2010.
Mabo v Queensland. HCA 69; (1989) 166 CLR 186 (8 December 1988). http://tinyurl.com/Mabo1988.
Malouf, David. *Remembering Babylon*. Sydney: Random House, 1993.
Marx, Karl and Frederick Engels. *Selected Correspondence*. Moscow: Progress, 1975.
Matthews, Brian. "Burning Bright: Some Impressions of Tim Winton". *Meanjin* 45, no. 1 (March 1986): 83–93.
McCredden, Lyn and Nathanael O'Reilly, eds. *Tim Winton: Critical Essays*. Perth: UWA Publishing, 2014.
McCulloch, Alison. "Decline and Falling". Review of *Eyrie* by Tim Winton. *New York Times Sunday Book Review*, 25 July 2014. http://tinyurl.com/McCulloch2014.
McGahan, Andrew. *The White Earth*. Sydney: Allen & Unwin, 2004.
McGirr, Michael. "Great Leap of Faith". Review of *Eyrie* by Tim Winton. *Sydney Morning Herald*, 2 November 2013. http://tinyurl.com/McGirr2013.
McGloin, Colleen. "Reviving Eva in Tim Winton's *Breath*". *The Journal of Commonwealth Literature* 47, no. 1 (2012): 109–20.
Milton, John. *Paradise Lost*, book 1, lines 1–31. From *The Milton Reading Room*, edited by Thomas H. Luxon, http://www.dartmouth.edu/~milton.
Morrison, Fiona. "'Bursting with Voice and Doubleness': Vernacular Presence and Visions of Inclusiveness in Tim Winton's *Cloudstreet*". In *Tim Winton: Critical Essays*, edited by Lyn McCredden and Nathanael O'Reilly, 49–74. Perth: UWA Publishing, 2014.
——. "Figures of the Many and the One: Genre and Narrative Method in Tim Winton's *Cloudstreet*". *Sydney Studies in English* 25 (1999): 133–51.
Mudrooroo. *Master of the Ghost Dreaming*. Sydney: Angus & Robertson, 1991.
Neill, Rosemary. "Fully Formed: 30 Years of the Australian/Vogel Literary Award". *Australian*, 23 April 2011. http://tinyurl.com/Neill2011.

Works Cited

O'Reilly, Nathanael. "Postcolonial Issues in Australian Literature". In *Exploring Suburbia: The Suburbs in the Modern Australian Novel*. Amherst, NY: Teneo Press, 2012.

Ollman, Bertell. "The Utopian Vision of the Future (Then and Now): A Marxist Critique". *Monthly Review* 57, issue 3 (July–August 2005). http://tinyurl.com/Ollman2005.

Pardi, Philip. *Meditations on Rising and Falling*. Madison: University of Wisconsin Press, 2008.

Peede, Jon P. and Joanne H. McMullen, eds. *Inside the Church of Flannery O'Connor: Sacrament, Sacramental, and the Sacred in Her Fiction*. Macon, Georgia: Mercer University Press, 2008.

Plumwood, Val. "Nature in the Active Voice". *Australian Humanities Review, Ecological Humanities* 46 (May 2009). http://tinyurl.com/Plumwood2009.

Porter, Peter. "Rednecks of the Outback". Review of *Dirt Music* by Tim Winton. *Guardian*, 8 June 2002. http://tinyurl.com/Porter2002.

Potter, Emily. "The Anxiety of Place: Peter Read, *Haunted Earth*". *Colloquy: Text Theory Critique* 9 (2005): 124–29.

Punter, David. *Postcolonial Imaginings: Fictions of a New World Order*. Edinburgh: Edinburgh University Press, 2000.

Schürholz, Hannah. "'Over the Cliff and into the Water': Love, Death and Confession in Tim Winton's Fiction". In *Tim Winton: Critical Essays*, edited by Lyn McCredden and Nathanael O'Reilly, 96–121. Perth: UWA Publishing, 2014.

See, Carolyn. "Young Men and the Sea". Review of *Breath* by Tim Winton. *Washington Post*, 27 June 2008. http://tinyurl.com/See2008.

Self, Will. "The Fate of our Literary Culture is Sealed". *Guardian*, 4 October 2014. http://tinyurl.com/WillSelf2014.

Shoemaker, Adam. *Mudrooroo: A Critical Study*. Sydney: Angus & Robertson, 1993.

Steger, Jason. "The Truth of Publishing is Stranger than Fiction" *Age*, 13 June 2002. http://tinyurl.com/Steger2002.

Stow, Randolph. *To the Islands*. Sydney: Penguin, 1958.

Strahle, Graham. "*Cloudstreet*: Opera a resounding triumph". *Australian*, 16 May 2016. http://tinyurl.com/Strahle2016.

Stratton, Jon. *Writing Sites: a Genealogy of the Postmodern World*. London: Harvester Wheatsheaf, 1990.

Swirski, Peter. "Popular and Highbrow Literature: A Comparative View". *Comparative Literature and Culture* 1, issue 4 (1999). http://dx.doi.org/10.7771/1481-4374.1053.

Tacey, David. *Re-enchantment: The New Australian Spirituality*. Melbourne and Sydney: HarperCollins, 2000.

——. *The Edge of the Sacred: Transformation in Australia*. Melbourne and Sydney: Harper Collins, 1995.

Taussig, Michael. *What Colour Is the Sacred?* Chicago: Chicago University Press, 2009.

Taylor, Andrew. "Tim Winton's *The Riders*: A Construction of Difference". *Westerly* 59, no. 3 (Spring 1998): 99–112.

——. "An Interview with Tim Winton". *Australian Literary Studies* 17, no. 4 (1996): 373–77.

Taylor, Charles. *A Secular Age*. Cambridge, Mass.: Harvard University Press, 2007.

"The Wintoning Project". *The Worst of Perth* (blog), 30 April 2011. http://tinyurl.com/wintoning.

Turner, Graeme. *National Fictions: Literature, Film, and the Construction of Australian Narrative*. 2nd ed. St Leonards: Allen & Unwin, 1993.

White, Patrick. *The Eye of the Storm*. London: Jonathan Cape, 1973.

——. *The Vivisector*. London: Jonathan Cape, 1970.

——. *The Solid Mandala*. London: Eyre & Spottiswoode, 1966.

——. *Riders in the Chariot*. London: Eyre & Spottiswoode, 1961.

——. *Voss*. London: Eyre & Spottiswoode, 1957.

Williams, Linda. "Film Bodies: Gender, Genre and Excess". *Film Quarterly* 44, no. 4 (Summer 1991): 2–13.

Winton, Tim. *Island Home: A Landscape Memoir*. Melbourne: Penguin, 2015.

Works Cited

——. "Tim Winton's Palm Sunday Plea: Start the Soul-Searching Australia". *Age*, 29 March 2015. http://tinyurl.com/Winton2015.
——. *Eyrie*. Melbourne: Penguin, 2013.
——. *Shrine*. Melbourne: Penguin, 2013.
——. *Signs of Life: A Play in One Act*. Melbourne: Penguin, 2013.
——. "Some Thoughts About Class in Australia: The C Word". *Monthly*, December 2013. http://tinyurl.com/Winton2013.
——. *Rising Water*. Sydney: Currency Press, 2011.
——. *Breath*. Melbourne: Penguin, 2008.
——. *The Turning*. Sydney: Picador, 2004.
——. *Dirt Music*. Sydney: Picador, 2001.
——. *Lockie Leonard, Legend*. Sydney: Pan Macmillan, 1997.
——. *The Riders*. Sydney: Macmillan, 1994.
——. *Land's Edge: A Coastal Memoir*. Sydney: Pan Macmillan, 1993.
——. *Lockie Leonard, Scum Buster*. Sydney: Piper, 1993.
——. *The Bugalugs Bum Thief*. Melbourne: Puffin, 1991.
——. *Cloudstreet*. Melbourne: McPhee Gribble, 1991.
——. *Lockie Leonard, Human Torpedo*. Melbourne: McPhee Gribble, 1990.
——. *In the Winter Dark*. Melbourne: McPhee Gribble, 1988.
——. *Minimum of Two*. Melbourne, McPhee Gribble, 1987.
——. *That Eye, the Sky*. Melbourne: McPhee Gribble, 1986.
——. *Shallows*. Sydney: Allen & Unwin, 1984.
——. *An Open Swimmer*. Sydney: Allen & Unwin, 1982.
Wright, Judith. *Born of the Conquerors*. Canberra: Aboriginal Studies Press, 1991.
Wyld, Evie. "Tower Block Blues". Review of *Eyrie* by Tim Winton. *Guardian*, 30 May 2014. http://tinyurl.com/Wyld2014.
Žižek, Slavoj. *On Belief*. New York: Routledge, 2001.

Index

Abell, Stephen vii
abjection v
  and the 'fall' 50
  in *Eyrie* 29, 52
  in *Shallows* 21–22
  in *That Eye, the Sky* 25
  in *The Riders* 42
  in *The Turning* xiii
  into redemption 31–33
  through language 32
  within families 64
Aboriginal *see* Indigenous Australia, Indigenous characters
'aboriginalisation' 72
abortion 60
action heroes 101
Adam and Eve 36, 50
adaptations 130
  film 84, 99
  radio 130
  stage 104, 143
addiction 60, 61, 64, 85
  and fallenness 60
adolescence *see* childhood
Amazon 125
An Open Swimmer (1982) v, 35, 77
Anthias, Floya 89, 96
'Aquifer' (short story) xiii
Ashcroft, Bill 134–135, 138
astonishment, definition by Burke xii
Auden, W. H. 49
Australia vi, 93, 94, 139–141; *see also* Western Australia, regionalism
  secularism xvi, 73

Australian identity vii, 72, 85, 106, 108, 132; *see also* class
Australian vernacular i, ix, 24, 53, 56, 105
  and class 84
Australian/Vogel National Literary Award v
authenticity of self 57, 82
author 38, 136, 143
  'death of the' i
authorial judging 57, 60

Baines Alarcos, Pilar 38
Bakhtin, Mikhail 124
Barthes, Roland 123
beauty as antithesis to the fall 65
becoming 36, 45, 111, 143; *see also* identity
belief, substance of 101
belonging vi, 106, 135–136, 143, 143
  and 'non-belonging' vi, 109, 115, 132, 144
  and white narratives xiv, 72, 119
  Indigenous and non-Indigenous 109–110
  within 'place' vii, xii, 108–109, 112, 135
Ben-Messahel, Salhia x, 107
Bezos, Jeff 125
Bhabha, Homi 70–72, 137, 138, 140
biblical references 21, 23
'Big World' (short story) 40, 110
bildungsroman 103
'blockbuster' books 97–98, 128–130
Blyth, Catherine 99–100, 105
Bogle, Deborah 54
'Boner McPharlin's Moll' (short story) 82, 85
book industry *see* fiction market
Books Alive 97–98
Breath (2008) ii, iii, 44, 105, 110, 129
  and becoming 45, 120

Index

and desire 44
and gendered identity 44–45, 47; *see also* gender
and misogyny ii, 47
and the sacred v, 73
critical reception x
fall and redemption 69
Miles Franklin winner i
narrative iii, vi
Buck, Gemma (character) 30, 54, 56, 82, 90, 112
Bugalugs Bum Thief, The (1991) 99
Burke, Edmund xii–xiv, 80, 112
Butler, Judith 112, 120
   and becoming 45–46
   and self 36, 40, 43

Caldwell, Roger 88–89, 92
capitalism 88–89, 96
   and family 55
   and Fremantle
   and religion 73
   and risk-taking 80
   and Western Australia 32, 53, 88
change through writing 54
characters i, iii, vi, 69, 81–82, 92, 94, 144
   abject ii
   as 'ordinary' vi
   in *The Turning* 60
   non-belonging 110
childhood viii, xi, 83, 95, 132
   and language 78, 102
   in *That Eye, the Sky* 24, 26
   innocence xiii, 113
Christianity viii; *see also* religion, sacred
   and redemption 28, 61
   and Winton's identity i, vii, 74
   in *Breath* v
   in *That Eye, the Sky* 26–28
   in 'The Turning' 61
   the Christian God 52
class vi, x, xvi, 81–96, 132, 133, 137, 143
   class 'traitor' 83
   in Australia 81, 82
   in *The Turning* 84–87
   in Winton's works 84
   origins of Australian writers 82
classism vi, 60
climate change 68, 124; *see also* environmentalism
closure 72; *see also* redemption
Cloudstreet (1991) vi, viii, xiii, 91, 95, 112, 129, 130, 133, 135, 136
   adaptations 104, 130
   and childhood xi
   and 'the fall' 52
   closure and redemption xiv, 67–69, 68, 104, 110
   earthed 77
   narrative of belonging vi
   nostalgia 76, 103
   popularity 104
   the pig 103
   vernacular presence 19
Cockburn, Bruce xiii
'Cockleshell' (short story) 82
coincidence 32
'Commission', short story 63
   film adaptation 84
commonalities in Winton's works vi, 50
Connolly, Robert 84, 99
conservatism and Cloudstreet 76
Cookson, Cleve (character) 23, 32
Cookson, Queenie (character) 20–22, 23, 113
   childhood xi, 32
Coupar, Daniel (character) 23
Coupar, Nathaniel (character) 20
critical reception i, 99–101, 105

death xiv; *see also* abjection
   and 'the fall' 50
   'of the author' i
   presaging redemption 68, 69
'Defender, The', short story 87
Deo Gloria prize viii
Derrida, Jacques 19, 70, 75; *see also* logocentrism
desire iii, 41–45, 144
   and gender 39
   and risk-taking 78
   and the sacred xiv
'dialogic imagination' 124
dialogue, use of vii
DiCenso, James, 'Heidegger's Hermeneutics of Fallenness' 57
Dirt Music (2001)
   and 'aboriginalisation' 72
   and belonging 72, 108
   and ghosts 70
   and 'the fall' 52
   as 'dark fable' 99
   critical reception of vi, 37
   fall and redemption 69
   importance of 'place' xi
Dixon, Robert 76, 103
Driscoll, Beth 97
Dryden, John xiii

Index

Eagleton, Terry, *Why Marx was Right* 88
earthed 116
  and groundedness 26
  and the 'ordinary' 77
  and the sacred 80
  juxtaposition xiv
economics xi, 88, 90–91
Enlightenment, the xv
Enright, Nick 104
environment 88, 91
environmentalism 109, 118
  and Winton i, 73
  in *Eyrie* 53, 57
  in *Shallows* 21
Erll, Astrid 124
essentialism 36
ethics 40; *see also* morality
Eurocentrism xii, 115, 116; *see also* white narratives
Eva *see* Sanderson, Eva (character)
evangelism 26
Eve *see* Adam and Eve
everyday stories vi
Eyrie (2013) 28, 88–89, 99, 126–127
  abject setting 53, 100
  'ambiguity as constant' 32
  and belonging vi, 47, 54
  and capitalism 54, 118
  and class 82
  and 'the fall' 52
  as 'protest novel' 55
  critical reception 54, 99, 107
  endings (and non-endings) 33, 59
  genre of 30, 101, 101
  importance of place 53
  reader reception 105

fall, the ii, 52
  and class 85
  and death 50
  and human nature 51, 56
  and original sin 50
  and redemption 69, 85
  as narrative arc iii, 59
  causes of 57
  for other writers 50
  in *The Riders* 37
  physical representations 56, 59
'fallen women' 38, 63
families 25, 91–91
  alternative archetypes iii, 55, 121
  in *Eyrie* 30–30
  in Winton's works 54
  setting for fall and redemption 52, 64, 68
fatherhood 63
  in *Breath* 79, 120
  father–son relationships 84
femininity *see also* gender, women
  and identity 44–45
  and mothers 58
  and myths 36
  in *Cloudstreet* 37
  in *Dirt Music* 37
  in *The Riders* 38
  language of 20
feminism 36, 47, 63
  Australian context 39
  women's silence 38, 40
fiction market 97–98, 125
  statistics 98
film *see* adaptations
Fish *see* Lamb, Fish (character)
Flack, Morton 'Ort' (character) 24
  childhood 26
  narrative focus 27, 102
Flack, Sam (character) xiii
Flanagan, Richard 82
Flint, Nicolle 37, 39
forgiveness 85; *see also* redemption
  and Christianity v
Fox, Luther (character) 113
  death 71, 115
fragility *see* vulnerability
freedom 111
  and childhood xi
Fremantle, Western Australia i
  and fallenness 53
  'moral dystopia' 59
Frow, John xv

gender 35–38, 58, 89, 111
  and sexuality ii
  gender politics 63
  gendered identity 38, 39, 56
  spectrum of 38
genres 99; *see also* popular fiction
  binaries 36
  comic 91, 94, 109, 133
  detective 30, 90, 101
  thriller 90–91
ghosts 70
globalisation viii

Index

God *see* Christianity, sacred
Goldsworthy, Kerryn i–ii
Greenwood, Susan 42
grief 37, 41, 105
  as identity-forming 46, 117
Griffiths, Michael R. xiv, 109, 135, 136
Grogan, Bridget 111
  and identity through loss 40

Hardy, Linda 134
Hart, Kevin 73, 75
  on participant methodology xv–xvi
hauntedness 109
  and ghosts 70
Hecq, Dominique 32
Heidegger, Martin 57
Heydon, (John) Dyson 82
Hirsch, Marianne 81
Hitt, Christopher 118
'holy fool' 25
hope *see* redemption
horror xii, 22, 138; *see also* abjection
  presaged 42
human nature 23, 35
  and abjectness v, 29
  and original sin 50
  and risk-taking 77, 78
  contradictions of iv
  in the 'fall' 56
humour 19, 67, 73, 99, 111
  in *Eyrie* 52

idealism 59
identity 112; *see also* belonging, becoming, class
  and feminism 47
  and loss 40–41, 45, 47
  and trauma 43
  gendered 36, 36, 47
  in *Eyrie* 29
  in relation to others 46
  in *Shallows* 21, 23
  Indigenous and non-Indigenous 116, 117
  quest for iii, 112
In The Winter Dark (1998) xiii
Indigenous Australia 109
  and loss 73
  and the sacred 75
  pre-European settlement xii, 115
  Winton's concepts of xvii
Indigenous characters 109–110, 116, 136
  silence xiv, 104, 135, 136

vernacular 19
Indigenous 'country' xii, 116, 119
innocence *see* childhood
international audience viii, 105, 129
Ireland 41, 106
Island Home: A Landscape Memoir (2015) 68, 106, 107

James, Henry 28
Jasper, David xv
journey (narrative arc) xi; *see also* becoming, narrative arc
judgement v
juxtaposition 25, 99, 108, 116
  adult and child 30
  in fall and redemption 52
  in feminism 36

Katz, Wendy ix, x
Keely, Tom (character) 47, 112
  as abject 28–29, 52, 57, 105
  as fallen 52–54
  environmentalism 57, 100
  transformation 31
Keneally, Thomas 82
Kirby, Justice Michael 135
Kristeva, Julia 32
  on the abject 22, 29
  on 'the fall' 50

Lacan, Jacques 35
Lamb, Fish (character) 103–104, 113
land 72, 110; *see also* place
Land's Edge: A Coastal Memoir (1993) 68
Lang, Vic (character in *The Turning*) 63, 84, 105, 112
language 19, 95, 124; *see also* Australian vernacular
  and abjection 32
  and action 31, 32
  and marginalisation 19
  and meaning 24, 28, 32
  and structuralism 123
  as signifier 22
  meaning-making 20
  of nature 25
  of the sacred 80
  significance 139
  significance in *Eyrie* 30
  storytelling 132
  vernacular 19–20, 94–95, 102, 131–133

literary criticism 124
  and Indigenous religion 75
  and post-secularism 76
literary techniques 105
  self-reflexivity 137
  definition 97
literature 98, 125
  and capitalism 126
'literature of despair' 105
locatedness *see* regionalism; *see also* place
Lockie Leonard, series 131
  narrative of belonging vi
logocentrism 19
loneliness iii, iv, 115
  and isolation x, 114
  in *Shallows* 23
loss 109, 113
  and poststructuralism 70
  of self 57–58

Mabo, Eddie 135
magic realism 132, 133, 136
  in *Cloudstreet* 103
male violence 58, 62
Man Booker Prize viii, 105
market *see* fiction market
Marx, Karl 88–89, 92, 93
masculinity 35, 42
  and loss 37, 57
  and love 40
  and myths 36
  and risk-taking 79
  and the 'fall' 57–58
  and Winton's identity i
  in *Breath* 44, 47, 121
  in *Cloudstreet* 69
  in *The Riders* 39
  initiation 44
  stemming from religious beliefs 74
McCulloch, Alison 105
McGirr, Michael 32
McPharlin, Boner (character) 85
meaning *see also Eyrie* (2013), *That Eye, The Sky* (1986), *Shallows* (1984), language
  created in 'place' xii
  quest for v, 32
  through risk-taking 79
  through signs 23–24
Miles Franklin Literary Award i, 105, 129
Milton, John 51
  and the 'fall' 52, 56

Minimum of Two (1987) 110
miracles *see* sacred
misogyny 37–39, 74
  in *Breath* 47
  in *The Riders* 38–39, 42
modernism ix
morality ii, iii
  and *Breath* 44, 45
  in Winton's work iii–iv, xv
Morrison, Fiona 19, 94, 95
motherhood 58, 113
Mudrooroo 136
Murray, Les 73
mythopoesis xiii
myths vi, 36
  of the 'fall' 50
  of 'white settler' vi, 120

narrative 123
  commonalities x
  focalising iii
  narrator 136
  realist 132, 136
narrative arc *see also* fall, the
  in *Eyrie* 31, 58
  non-human forces xiii
  redemption and falling 24, 49–50, 69–72
  through tranquility and pathos 102
narrative tension 99
  in *Eyrie* 30
narrative voice 106, 111, 114, 133, 139
  in *Cloudstreet* 132
  in *Eyrie* 105
  in *That Eye, the Sky* 78
  in *The Riders* 38
  in *The Turning* 60, 61
natural world vii, 43, 79
  and childhood xi
  and harmony 43
  and regionalism x, 114
  and Winton xvii, 68, 118
  as numinous *see* numinous zones
  earthed 26
  'horrors' xiii–xiv, 113, 121
neoliberalism 79
Net Book Agreement (UK) 125
nostalgia 102, 103, 106
  and conservatism 76
numinous zones xii

objectivity in religion xv

Index

O'Connor, Flannery x, 74
Ollman, Bertell 93
'On Her Knees' (short story) 82
ontological themes xiii
ontology 77
  and belonging vii
  and gender 38
  and hope xiv
  and regionalism ix
  and the self 43, 79
opera *see* adaptations
O'Reilly, Nathanael 110
organised religion 26–27, 61; *see also* religious institutions
original sin 50; *see also* religion
Ort *see* Flack, Morton 'Ort' (character)

Palm Sunday speech (2015) vii
Pardi, Philip 49–50
parenthood *see also* families
  in *Eyrie* 55
parochialism *see* regionalism
participant observation xv
patriarchy 36; *see also* feminism
  and women's silence 38
perfection 69, 104
Pike, Bruce 'Pikelet' (character) 78–80, 112, 120–121
  as abject 45, 46
place xi–xii, 107, 119; *see also* regionalism
  and belonging 116–118
  and identity 114, 115
  informing redemption 68
Plumwood, Val 108
politics
  and redemption 67
  in *Eyrie* 32
popular fiction 98, 128
popular–literary fiction divide 100–106
Porter, Peter 108, 111
postcolonialism 72, 95, 112, 138
  and belonging 112–113
'postmemory' 81
post-secularism 75
poststructuralism 70–71
Potter, Emily 119, 122
poverty 60, 81
prophet 115, 136
Punter, David 137, 138

quest for meaning *see* meaning

Raelene (character in 'The Turning') 61–63
Read, Peter 119
readers xiv, 70, 85, 96, 125–127
  and judgement 57
  reception to Winton's works 39, 74, 105
  within the narrative 21, 30
realism vi, 95, 104
  'as convention' 28
redemption 50, 87, 116, 133; *see also* fall, the
  and class 85
  earthed and sacred 67–68, 69, 80, 104
  in *Cloudstreet* xiv
  in *Dirt Music* 37, 71
  in *Eyrie* 55, 58, 59
  in *Shallows* 23
  in *That Eye, the Sky* 26, 28
  through relationships iv, 52–53, 54, 72
  through risk-taking 79
refugees xv, 108, 124
regionalism vi, ix
  and mythology x
  of Mark Twain x
relationships ii
  depicting redemption 67
  in *Breath* 47
religion ii, 56; *see also* sacred
  and criticism 74, 75
  as antithetical to capitalism 73
  Christianity *see* Christianity
  in *The Turning* 61–63
  narrower than 'sacred' 77
  resurgence 76
religious beliefs 62, 74
  Australian compared to American 74
  of other writers 73
religious influence 73
  in other writers' works 52
religious institutions 61
  in *Cloudstreet* 78
repentance *see* redemption
resurrection 71; *see also* redemption
reviews *see* critical reception
Riders, The (1994)
  and desire 43
  and regionalism viii, 43
  and the 'fall' 53
  as 'dark fable' 99
  critical reception of 38
  social context 39
  stage adaptation 130
  the eponymous riders 42

Rising Water, stage play (2011) 131
risk-taking 77
   in *Breath* 73, 78–80, 121
Romanticism 77
Royal Commission into Trade Union Governance and Corruption 82

sacred i, v, viii, 75–78; *see also* religion
  and belief 63
  and place 116, 119
  as redemptive 68, 73
  beauty and terror 80
  definition xvi, 77
  in *Dirt Music* 113–114
  in *Shallows* 21, 32
  in *That Eye, the Sky* 26, 27
  informing Winton's works 69, 74
  juxtaposition xiv
  meaning-making 23, 76
  metaphysical xii, xiii, 25, 68, 77, 114
  possibilities of xiv, 78
  religious experience 62, 115; *see also* religion
  through vocabulary 32
sadness *see* grief; *see also* abjection
sales *see* fiction market
Sanderson, Eva (character) 45, 78, 112
  death 46
Scully, Fred (character) 37–39, 41
secularism i, 73
  and regionalism 76
See, Carolyn x
Self, Will 125–126, 126, 128
selfhood *see* identity
serendipity xiii
sex ii–ii, iii–iv, 44
  and risk-taking 78
  asphyxiation ii, 46, 46
sexism *see* feminism; *see also* Flint, Nicolle, gender
sexuality 44–44
Shallows (1984) 23–24, 77
  and childhood xi, 20–21
  and desire 35
  epigraphs xiii
Shrine, stage play (2013) 131
signs
  in *Eyrie* 29
  in *Shallows* 23
Signs of Life, stage play (2012) 131
sin 64
slang viii; *see also* Australian vernacular

'Small Mercies', short story 60, 82; *see also Turning, The* (2004)
'soul' vii
'spots in time' 77
Stalin, Josef 81
Steger, Jason 97
stereotypes 101
  evolution of 39
  of gender 37–39
storytelling 26
Stow, Randolph 74, 117
Stratton, Jon 20, 28
sublime, the xii, 112; *see also* sacred
  and the sacred 80
suburbia xi, 107
suffering 69, 133
surfing x, 121
  and risk-taking 78
Swirski, Paul 98, 100–101, 106

Taussig, Michael 77
Taylor, Andrew viii, 73, 74
terra nullius vi
That Eye, The Sky (1986) 102; *see also* Flack, Sam (character), Flack, Morton 'Ort' (character)
  abjection and joy 25
  and childhood xi
  and the sacred 78
  climax 27
  earthed 26
  metaphysical forces xiii
  narrative drive 102
  narrative focus 24, 103
  narrative of belonging vi
theology iv, 77; *see also* sacred
tragedy iv; *see also* death
transformation 28; *see also* redemption
transformative fiction 70
tropes 50; *see also* narrative arc
'true sentences' vii
Tsiolkas, Christos 82, 130
Turner, Graham ix
turning 62
Turning, The (2004) 61, 86, 105
  and childhood xi
  and the 'fall' 53, 60–61, 61
  narratives of belonging vi
  film adaptation 84, 99, 130
'Turning, The', short story 61, 82; *see also Turning, The* (2004)
Twain, Mark x, 103

Index

un-belonging *see* belonging
unionism 82

vernacular *see* Australian vernacular; *see also* language
violence 78; *see also* male violence, white violence
vulnerability xvii, 37

Walton, Heather xv
Warburton, Henry (character)
  as 'abject prophet' 26, 78
Weaving, Hugo 84
Webb, Frank 74
Wenham, David 84
Western Australia x–xi, 88, 89–89, 126, 137
  and capitalism 32
  as remote vi
  'frontier' x, 108
  Winton the 'poet laureate' of 107
white 'indigenisation' 116, 120
white narratives 104, 112
White, Patrick 74
  and secularism 73
  and social class 83
  Voss (1957) 115, 117
white violence 72, 112
'Wild Hunt', the 42
'Winton effect', the vi

Winton, Tim 55
  as popular and/or literary 99; *see also* popular–literary fiction divide
  early career v
  literary influences x–x, xi, 103, 115, 117
  oeuvre v, 99
  personal life 53, 54, 106, 107
  personal opinions 81–82, 124
  religious faith xv, 73
  working class origins 81–83
Wintoning Project, The viii, 74
Winton's works v, 99
  as autobiographical 52
  as fluidic xvii
  commonalities 51, 52
  comparisons 32
  critical reception xvi, 105
  narrative impact 124
  sales figures 127–130
women 63, 105; *see also* feminism
words *see* language
Wordsworth, William 77
Wyld, Evie 107

youth *see* childhood

Žižek, Slavoj 75

www.ingramcontent.com/pod-product-compliance
Lightning Source LLC
Chambersburg PA
CBHW081827230426
43668CB00017B/2396